Strengthening Asset-backed Pension Systems in a Post-COVID World

OECD

BETTER POLICIES FOR BETTER LIVES

Please cite this publication as:
OECD (2022), *Strengthening Asset-backed Pension Systems in a Post-COVID World*, OECD Publishing, Paris, https://doi.org/10.1787/288cb3cf-en.

ISBN 978-92-64-77369-1 (print)
ISBN 978-92-64-93543-3 (pdf)
ISBN 978-92-64-86644-7 (HTML)
ISBN 978-92-64-81490-5 (epub)

Photo credits: Cover © AnnetteHyllested/Getty Images.

Corrigenda to publications may be found on line at: www.oecd.org/about/publishing/corrigenda.htm.

Foreword

The outbreak of the COVID-19 pandemic provoked a global health, economic and financial crisis. These events, unprecedented in recent history, have had an impact on asset-backed pension systems, adding to the significant challenges many countries were already facing in this domain, challenges like population ageing.

This report first assesses the impact COVID-19 had on asset-backed pension systems in OECD and selected non-OECD member countries and describes the policy guidelines that the OECD issued to assist pension policy makers, regulators and supervisors in addressing those challenges. Secondly, it presents a non-exhaustive compilation of the main policy initiatives implemented by OECD member countries during the COVID-19 pandemic in 2020 and 2021. Thirdly, it assesses those policies to see whether they were in line with the main OECD policy messages.

The second part of this publication takes a forward-looking approach. It first analyses the short-term and long-term impacts of COVID-19 on mortality. It provides views on how to incorporate the impact that COVID-19 had on mortality in 2020-21 for the estimation of future mortality and life expectancy. It then discusses how assets earmarked for retirement can be used to support economic recovery and sustainable investments while investing in the best interests of members.

Finally, this publication presents the main policy considerations or lessons learnt to guide pension policy makers, regulators, and supervisors through future shocks to asset-backed pension systems.

This report is the work of staff from the Pensions Unit in the Consumer Finance, Insurance and Pensions Division of the OECD Directorate for Financial and Enterprise Affairs. It has benefited from contributions by national government delegates, particularly delegates to the Working Party on Private Pensions, as well as from Members of the International Organisation of Pension Supervisors (IOPS). The views expressed here do not necessarily correspond to those of the national authorities concerned.

The editorial team for this publication was led by Pablo Antolín. Chapter 1 was prepared by Pablo Antolín and Romain Despalins; Chapter 2 by Romain Despalins; Chapter 3 by Stéphanie Payet; Chapter 4 by Jessica Mosher; and Chapter 5 by Diana Hourani and Stéphanie Payet. The authors of Chapter 5 would also like to thank Iota Nassr and Joel Paula from the OECD Directorate for Financial and Enterprise Affairs, as well as Fiona Stewart from the World Bank Group. Editorial and communication support was provided by Pamela Duffin, Liv Gudmundson and Eva Abbott.

Table of contents

FIGURES

TABLES

Executive summary

The outbreak of the COVID-19 pandemic in 2020 provoked a global health crisis, soon followed by an economic and financial crisis. Retirement savings and old-age pension systems were one of the many components of our societies impacted by these events, which are unprecedented in recent history. The economic effects of the crisis have been accumulating for the past years as governments introduced successive health measures to try and curb the spread of the virus. The slowdown of economic activity across the globe resulted in soaring unemployment and falling stock prices in the first quarter of 2020 as financial markets reacted.

This publication examines the implications of COVID-19 for asset-backed pension arrangements and provides policy guidelines for confronting similar shocks in the future. It documents the initial set of policy guidelines put forward by the OECD and how policy makers tried to cushion the impact on workers, employers, retirees and pension providers. While all countries faced similar challenges, policy responses differed according to the country-specific circumstances. Nonetheless, policy makers can still learn and benefit from each other's experiences. This publication also explores the impact of COVID-19 on mortality and on future mortality and life expectancy improvements, as well as the potential role that savings earmarked for retirement can play in supporting the economy, while ensuring that pension providers invest these savings in the best interest of members.

COVID-19 has entailed many challenges to asset-backed pension arrangements, reducing the level of assets when financial markets fell, straining the solvency of plans offering a benefit promise, reducing the ability to contribute, and inducing individuals and policy makers to prioritise short-term needs over long-term interests. It has also created general operational disruptions, leading pension providers and members to favour digital tools but exposing them further to cyber risks.

Policy makers swiftly responded to these challenges, in line with the OECD recommendations. They introduced measures that subsidise contributions to retirement savings plans, limit the materialisation of short-term investment losses, and provide leeway with respect to regulatory requirements to allow pension providers to focus on pressing issues given operational challenges.

Some of the implemented measures provided short-term relief but may have a lasting impact on the retirement income adequacy of future retirees. These measures include those allowing to defer, reduce or stop pension contributions, as well as those granting early access to retirement savings.

Early access to retirement savings should be a measure of last resort and only under specific exceptional personal circumstances of hardship. Early access should be legislated, as well as the conditions under which it could happen, to avoid legislative changes in the middle of a crisis that can have long-lasting negative impacts on retirement income adequacy.

There is a related policy issue, currently under discussion in many jurisdictions, about the need for emergency savings or rainy-day funds to face shocks. Building emergency savings is a good idea to help people face future shocks. However, the savings in those emergency accounts may need to come from new savings to avoid lower retirement savings that may affect retirement income adequacy.

COVID-19 has led to an increase in mortality rates during the last three years, 2020-22. However, whether this will translate into changes in future improvements in mortality and life expectancy is far from straightforward. Current knowledge suggests that future improvements will return to levels observed before the COVID-19 pandemic. Nevertheless, policy makers, regulators and supervisors should step up monitoring developments in mortality rates.

Pension providers can play a role to support the economy after the COVID-19 crisis. They already invest significantly in businesses through equities and corporate bonds. Given their long-term horizon, pension providers can also invest in long-term illiquid assets, such as infrastructure investments, that can finance the economic recovery.

Several obstacles may impede greater involvement by pension providers in supporting the economy, such as the lack of investment opportunities, regulatory barriers and limited investor capability to handle complex investments. Some risks also emerge, as there may be calls on pension providers to invest savings earmarked for retirement in companies or projects that may generate poor returns. Pension providers may also deviate from their strategic asset allocation to seize investment opportunities.

Safeguards and appropriate investment structures need to be in place to ensure that pension providers continue acting in the best interest of members. Strong governance and well-defined investment and risk-management strategies are necessary to prioritise the interest of members when engaging in new investment opportunities.

Policy makers can also facilitate the mobilisation of private capital to long-term investment through public-private partnerships, financial incentives, or special vehicles for alternative assets.

1 Asset-backed pension systems in the time of COVID-19

This chapter provides a historical account of the initial assessment of the impact that COVID-19 had on asset-backed pension arrangements and presents the initial policy messages that the OECD put forward to guide policy makers in 2020.

The OECD provides policy guidelines to assist policy makers in dealing with different challenges. The OECD Working Party on Private Pensions (WPPP) focusses on the policy, design, regulation, and supervision of pension arrangements where contributions are invested to build assets to back retirement income (asset-backed pension arrangements).

The outbreak of COVID-19 and its associated economic shocks presented serious challenges to asset-backed pension arrangements. Since the onset of the COVID-19 pandemic the OECD and its WPPP have been examining the different policies implemented by OECD and non-OECD countries to distil good international practices to confront shocks like the one posed by COVID-19.

This chapter provides a historical account of the initial assessment of the challenges posed by COVID-19 and the main OECD policy guidelines put forward during the first year of the pandemic. The OECD policy guidelines built on the experience of the financial and economic crisis of 2008-11 (Antolín and Stewart, 2009[1]) and the specific nature of the COVID-19 shock, which led to an unprecedented stop in economic activity. In the wake of the 2008 financial crisis, the OECD already provided policy guidelines to pension policy makers, regulators, and supervisors, arguing for staying the course, avoiding the materialisation of losses and continuing savings for retirement. It also recommended to use flexible, proportionate, and risk-based supervision and counter-cyclical funding and solvency rules for defined benefit (DB) plans, among others. Those recommendations together with the lessons learnt were still valid to address the shock posed by the COVID-19 pandemic.

The OECD presented in June 2020 a set of policy guidelines to assist pension policy makers, regulators and supervisors in navigating the shock posed by COVID-19 (OECD, 2020[2]). During 2020, the OECD and its WPPP continued to examine the impact of COVID-19 on pensions and asset-backed pension arrangements. This led to updated guidelines that were published in the OECD Pensions Outlook (OECD, 2020[3]).

This chapter consists of four sections in which it documents the challenges posed by COVID-19 and the development of the initial policy guidelines. Section 1.1 presents the main policy challenges that COVID-19 posed to asset-backed pension arrangements. Section 1.2 provides the initial policy messages issued by the OECD in June 2020. Section 1.3 provides further policy considerations examined during the year 2020, and Section 1.4 summarises the main resulting policy guidelines.[1]

1.1. Challenges that COVID-19 posed to asset-backed pension arrangements

COVID-19, the associated lockdowns and the economic downturns that ensued had or were expected to have several different impacts on retirement savings, providers, regulators, and supervisors and which could potentially lead to future lower incomes in retirement and important dysfunctions in the market. The main impacts were:

- An initial sharp fall in the value of assets in asset-backed pension accounts from falling financial markets
- An increase in liabilities from falling interest rates in asset-backed pension arrangements with retirement income promises (e.g. defined benefit retirement plans and life annuity arrangements)
- A lower capacity for individuals to continue saving for retirement, as they saw their wages reduced or lost their jobs, and employers were suffering financial distress
- Operational disruptions as a result of working remotely
- Cyber-attacks, frauds and scams directed at individuals, regulators, supervisors and providers of asset-backed pension schemes (e.g. pension funds)
- A need to tap into savings, including retirement savings.

1.1.1. Decline in the value of assets in retirement portfolios

There was a large fall in the value of equities at the onset of COVID-19 in the first quarter of 2020. Major stock markets suffered setbacks between mid-February and end-March 2020 as governments were taking precautionary measures to limit the spread of the virus and shutting down parts of the economy.

As a result, the market value of asset-backed pension accounts suffered a large reduction in the first quarter of 2020. Losses on financial markets lowered the value of assets in pension plans. Forecasts suggested at the time that pension fund assets would have declined by 8% in the first quarter of 2020 in the OECD area, from USD 32.3 trillion at end-December 2019 to USD 29.8 trillion at end-March 2020 (OECD, 2020[4]).

The inclination may be to sell when the value of assets in a portfolio falls. However, this locks in the losses, and may be far from the best reaction. This issue can be particularly relevant in jurisdictions where members of asset-backed pension plans can switch to another (more conservative) investment strategy. Opportunities to recoup losses are more limited as the expected return is lower with investments that are more conservative. Members may also lose an opportunity to benefit from an upturn of capital markets if they withdraw their retirement savings when markets are low.

1.1.2. Additional pressure on the solvency of asset-backed pension plans offering a benefit promise

The shock to financial markets in the first quarter of 2020 was a blow for the solvency position of defined benefit (DB) plans and for their sponsors. The devaluation of assets following falling stock prices affected all asset-backed pension plans. However, DB plans embed a benefit promise that is not necessarily linked to the amount of assets accumulated but depends on other parameters (such as the length of employment of plan members). The drop in the value of assets in the first quarter of 2020 was therefore a source of potential mismatch between the assets and the liabilities of DB plans.

While the value of pension assets was falling in the first quarter of 2020, the value of liabilities of DB plans increased, creating another source of mismatch between assets and liabilities. When pension providers promise a future benefit level (such as providers of DB plans), they have to discount the value of future pension income payments to express it in today's terms and have an estimate of their liabilities. The lower the discount rate is, the higher is the valuation of liabilities. Some pension providers may use a risk-free rate as a discount rate, such as the long-term government bond yields (i.e. long-term rates). These long-term rates tend to follow the direction of short-term rates. The COVID-19 outbreak, and its economic consequences led some central banks to cut interest rates to support the economy in March 2020, such as the Bank of England and the Federal Reserve Bank in the United States.[2] These moves worsened the funding levels of pension providers promising a certain benefit level.

1.1.3. Reduced ability to save for retirement

People may face more difficulties in saving and accumulating assets for retirement when they lose their jobs or experience a reduction in hours worked because of shocks like COVID-19. Spells of full or partial unemployment could lead to contribution gaps if employees or employers stop contributing to asset-backed pension plans. Employers may also face more difficulties in paying wages and contributions to their employees' pension plans while they experience business downturns. Likewise on the employee side, a salary loss or cut may also reduce voluntary contributions, as people may be less likely to contribute voluntarily to asset-backed pension plans when they are under financial strain. Interruptions or reductions in pension contributions would slow the accrual of pension assets for retirement. Members may also miss the opportunity to benefit from the upturn in capital markets.

It was thought at the onset of COVID-19 that the impact on contributions of such shocks depends on many factors. Countries may introduce policies to defer, reduce or stop pension contributions, or alternatively may subsidise wages directly or indirectly to help people to continue contributing to their retirement savings pots (e.g. job-retention schemes, JRS). Moreover, this type of shocks may change consumption and savings behaviours. Dire and uncertain times may divert people from saving for retirement, however, confinement may lead some people to reduce consumption and save more.

1.1.4. General operational disruptions

COVID-19 also led to important operational disruptions. Governments introduced preventive measures (e.g. lockdowns) aiming at limiting physical meetings and encouraging people to stay at home in order to limit the spread of the virus. These measures created disruptions in all operations where plan members have to meet staff of their pension providers physically (e.g. to deliver or sign documents in person).

Preventative health measures also affected the internal operation of pension providers. Staff of pension providers had to work remotely to carry out their regular activities (such as collecting and remitting contributions to schemes or individual accounts, investing assets, paying pensions and other benefits). The pandemic made it, at least initially, more complicated to apply usual processes that involve in-person meetings (e.g. meeting of board members and/or subcommittees).

All these general operational issues led to delays in some operations. Providers had to put in place business continuity plans, adapt their processes and tackle the challenges from the COVID-19 outbreak, on top of their regular duties towards their members and their supervisors (e.g. reporting, actuarial valuation).

Pension supervisors also faced disruptions because of the COVID-19 outbreak. They too had to carry out operations remotely and favour digital tools to exchange with pension providers and plan members. Some of the activities of pension supervisors, such as on-site inspections, had to be initially suspended.

1.1.5. Cyber risks, fraud, and scams

COVID-19 has bolstered the use of digital tools but may have also exacerbated the threat of cyber-attacks, frauds and scams to pension supervisors, providers and plan members.

The sudden increase in the number of staff from pension supervisory authorities and pension providers working remotely created unprecedented data privacy and cybersecurity challenges. Scammers may have tried to take advantage of people teleworking or members using online platforms to conduct cyber-attacks.

Plan members also had to rely more on online platforms and call centres than on physical meetings with their pension providers to manage their plans, and may have been subject to fraudulent attacks. Scammers may have tried to steal and use their personal information.

Scammers may also have exploited fears from members while they faced financial distress in a context of volatile financial markets to take their money. They could offer ways to access their pension savings, ways to transfer their pension assets or rights to another plan, or investment opportunities too good to be true. In the United Kingdom, the National Reporting Centre for Fraud and Cybercrime (ActionFraud) recorded 2 866 victims of COVID-19 related financial scams (including pension scams) by early July 2020.[3] These attacks have deprived some members of some of their savings for retirement.

1.1.6. A reduction in savings and compound interest earned because of prioritising short-term relief measures

The loss of income because of shocks like COVID-19 can lead to a reduction in savings and compound interest earned because of measures intended to provide relief in the short term, which can have a large negative impact in the long term, especially on retirement income adequacy.

Governments may implement policies lowering, stopping or pausing contributions to pension plans (contribution holidays). A one-year pause in contributions could lead to a reduction in income at retirement of around 2-3%.[4] While people could recoup this reduction by voluntarily increasing contributions once the economy recovers, evidence from the previous crisis suggests that this generally does not happen as the short-term needs prevail over the long-term financial planning. Moreover, people may not have more resources to increase contributions in the future than they had before the crisis.

Governments can also allow universal early access to balances accumulated to finance retirement, which may be attractive to offset the loss of income, but can, even if partial, easily jeopardise the future adequacy of retirement income. Early withdrawals could lead to lower balances accumulated at retirement, which would translate into lower income at retirement. The impact of granting universal access to retirement pots on future retirement income is potentially significantly larger than the impact of stopping contributions. The reduction in retirement income resulting from allowing a 10% withdrawal over a year could vary from 2% to 9% depending on the length of the contribution horizon, with older people experiencing a larger impact because they may have accumulated larger balances to withdraw income from.[5]

In addition, granting universal access to balances may lead to materialising the market losses and to liquidity management concerns. Pension funds have cash and liquid assets in their portfolios to address liquidity demands from regular payments and income withdrawals arising from exceptional circumstances. They also count on contribution inflows to manage liquidity needs. However, contribution holidays can create a negative cash flow. Coupled with substantial calls for cash from retirement pots, due to policies granting universal access, this can force pension funds to act pro-cyclically by selling assets in falling markets and materialising value losses. Long-term strategies can also be jeopardised. All these actions are in sharp contrast with the recommendation of staying the course, maintaining long-term retirement investment portfolios and avoiding the materialisation of asset value losses.

1.2. Initial policy messages

The OECD issued the following policy messages at the onset of the COVID-19 pandemic.[6]

Policy makers should make sure that people saving for retirement and pension providers stay the course:

- Saving for retirement is for the long term. Maintain investments in retirement portfolios to avoid selling and materialising value losses when markets are low.
- Continue contributing to retirement plans. Governments may make the income of people full as part of the many programmes to assist the populations facing the economic fall from COVID-19, the lockdown and the associated economic downturn.

Policy makers, regulators and supervisors should:

- Allow for regulatory flexibility in recovery plans to address funding problems stemming from retirement promises (e.g. DB pension arrangements, and lifetime income products).
- Make sure that funding and solvency rules for DB plans are counter-cyclical. Introduce flexibility in meeting funding requirements, thereby avoiding 'pro-cyclical policies' and allowing pension funds to act as long-term investors and potentially stabilising forces within the global financial system.

- Provide proportionate, flexible and risk-based supervisory oversight coupled with adequate communication to reduce frauds, and facilitate efficient operations. Supervisory oversight should concentrate on prudential and market conduct regulation, including ensuring protection of members and beneficiaries against COVID-19 related scams, especially of the most vulnerable individuals. Supervisors should communicate to market participants and individuals on their prudential expectations and recommendations in time of the crisis and actions made to facilitate pension funds' operations and to ease administrative burden.
- Allow access to retirement savings as a measure of last resort and based on individual specific exceptional circumstances. Retirement pots are to finance retirement. Accessing retirement savings could lead to materialising temporary asset values losses, liquidity and investment management problems for pension funds, and, more importantly to retirement income adequacy shortfalls. Current regulatory frameworks already allow for tapping retirement savings in exceptional circumstances when substantial income losses occur, and should not be expanded further.
- Develop close co-operation with stakeholders, regulators and supervisors at the national and international levels, to share solutions and effective ways to deal with the current crisis.

1.3. Additional policy considerations examined during 2020

The OECD and its WPPP continued monitoring policy developments and examining the usefulness of their initial policy messages during 2020 with a view to improving them. Developments during 2020 confirmed that the initial policy messages were well-founded and needed just a few adjustments to reflect the new experiences. Moreover, calls to use assets earmarked for retirement to support the economy led the OECD to examine the grounds for this policy.

1.3.1. Stay the course

The response to the decline of asset values in retirement portfolios is to stay the course and avoid materialising value losses by selling. Saving for retirement is for the long haul. Fluctuations in asset values are inevitable during the life of a retirement portfolio. Over the long term, portfolio investment provides a return to people's savings for retirement. Experience shows that selling when markets go down and buying when they go up, is far from appropriate as 'timing the market' (i.e. attempting to predict future market movements) does not work. Selling assets when shocks occur risks materialising the reduction in value and precludes opportunities to recover those losses.

As long as people do not sell their assets, they do not materialise the losses and their portfolios eventually could recover and resume their long-term trend upwards. OECD data published at the end of 2021 (OECD, 2021[5]), referring to end 2020, indicated that the value of assets in retirement savings accounts recovered at the end of 2020 to above pre-COVID-19 levels, thanks to the recovery of financial markets. Indeed, capital markets recovered after the first quarter of 2020 in many countries, and so did assets in retirement savings plans. Actual data shows that at the end of 2020, thanks to those positive developments in capital markets, the value of retirement savings was higher than at the end of 2019 (Figure 1.1).

Figure 1.1. OECD pension fund assets at end 2019 and 2020

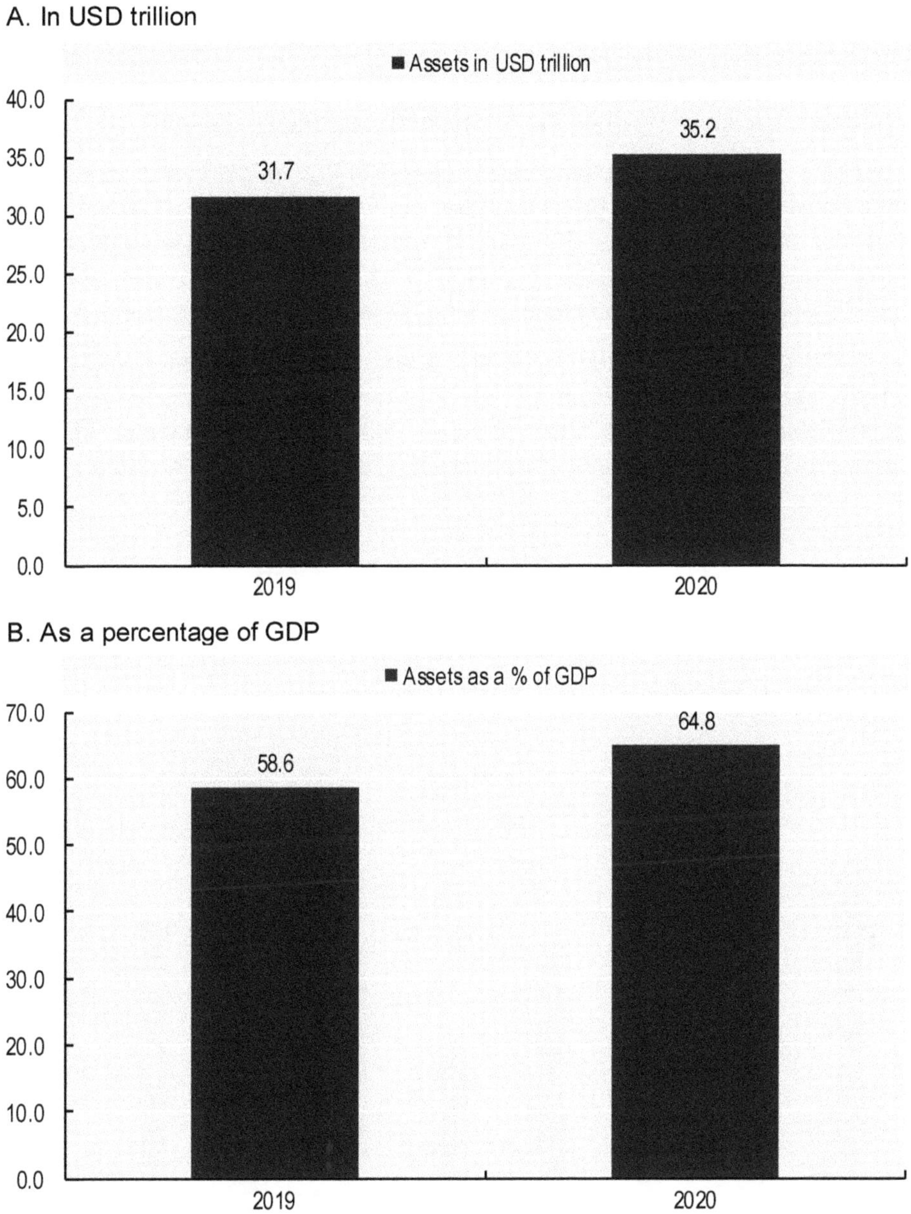

Note: Investments are used as a proxy of assets. Total pension fund assets as a percentage of GDP are calculated as the ratio between the sum of all pension fund assets and the sum of all the GDPs (in USD) of OECD countries.
Source: OECD Global Pension Statistics.

Pension providers should also stay the course and maintain their investment strategies. All pension providers should have an investment policy establishing clear investment objectives consistent with their retirement income objective and liabilities, and at arm's length from governments. It is important that pension providers act in accordance with these investment objectives to be able to deliver on their promises and keep trust in the system. In particular, pension providers should maintain diversified investments, both domestically and globally. They should also carefully assess new investment opportunities linked, for example, to the recovery post COVID-19, and not engage in those for which they lack the skills and expertise to appropriately assess the risks and rewards.

1.3.2. Regulatory and supervisory flexibility

It is important to allow for regulatory flexibility in recovery plans to address liability problems stemming from retirement promises. Regulatory rules, including mark-to-market valuation principles and recovery plans, remain essential for the long term but need to be flexible during exceptional circumstances. However, it is also important to reverse that flexibility once the exceptional circumstances fade.

Flexibility with respect to regulatory compliance and supervisory oversight in a proportionate, flexible and risk-based manner could help alleviate pressures that could lead to poor decisions or exacerbate the financial difficulties that the sponsor faces. Flexibility in regulation and supervisory oversight should focus on making sure that the increase in the liabilities of DB pension plans and insurance companies offering life annuities would not put further strain on those offering retirement income promises during difficult times.

The funding ratio of DB plans deteriorated in the first quarter of 2020 but improved thereafter. Funding ratios declined in the first quarter of 2020 in a number of countries, including Finland, the Netherlands, Switzerland and the United Kingdom (OECD, 2020[3]). However, the recovery of financial markets contributed to the improvement of the funding ratio of DB plans by the end of 2020 in several countries (Figure 1.2).

Figure 1.2. Funding ratio of defined benefit plans in selected OECD countries, at the end of 2019 and 2020

In percent

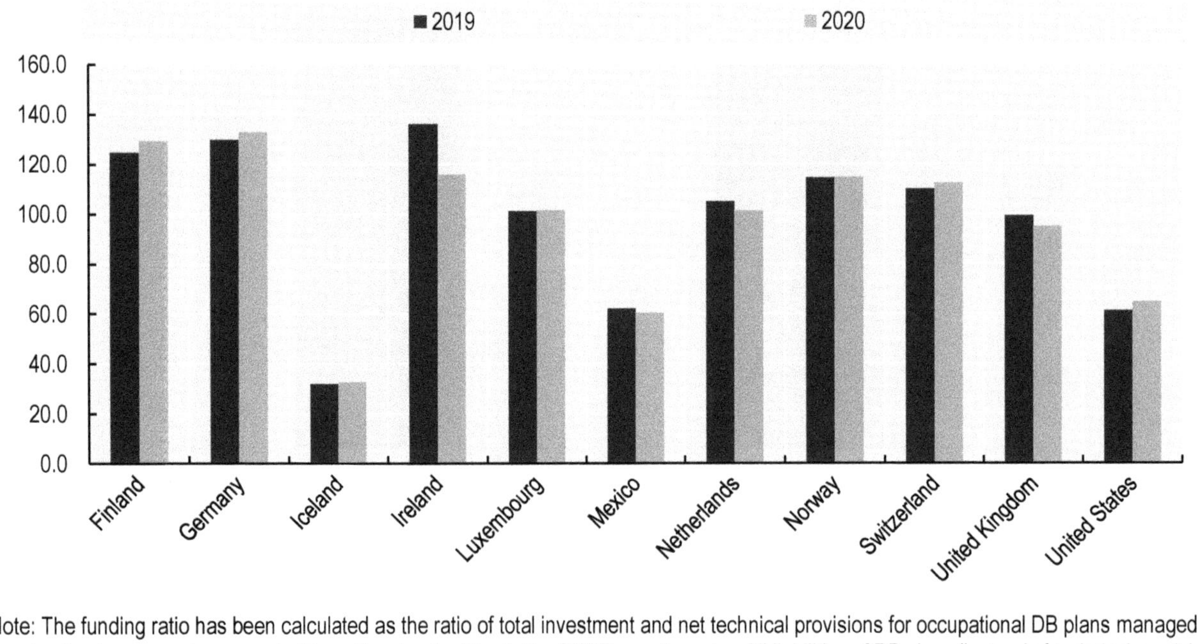

Note: The funding ratio has been calculated as the ratio of total investment and net technical provisions for occupational DB plans managed by pension funds using values reported by national authorities in the OECD questionnaire. All liabilities of DB plans (instead of technical provisions only) are considered for Ireland, Mexico (occupational DB plans in pension funds only) and the United States. Data for Finland refer to DB plans in pension funds only. Data for Luxembourg refer to DB traditional plans under the supervision of the CSSF. Data for the Netherlands and Switzerland include all types of pension funds. Data for the United Kingdom come from the Purple Book 2021 published by the Pension Protection Fund and show the ratio of assets and liabilities valued on an s179 basis (instead of net technical provisions).
Source: OECD Global Pension Statistics.

Additionally, funding and solvency rules for DB plans should be counter-cyclical. Introducing flexibility in meeting funding requirements would help to avoid 'pro-cyclical policies' and allow pension funds to act as long-term investors and potentially stabilising forces within the global financial system.

1.3.3. Scams and frauds

Disclosure of the type of scams and frauds on the websites of national authorities and pension providers could reduce frauds and scams. Advice to trustees and advisors to send regular and clear information to plan members could also help in that regard as scammers may exploit misunderstandings and people's fears.

1.3.4. Inclination to prioritise short-term relief measures

Early access to savings in asset-backed pension plans should be a measure of last resort. Notwithstanding this, there can be room for the need for flexibility in exceptional personal circumstances. Specific exceptional circumstances include hardship situations like unemployment accompanied by protracted and large losses of income, or terminal illnesses. These measures should be maintained for people in the greatest need. Governments may already have and could favour the use of aid programmes, such as unemployment or job-retention programmes, as an emergency mechanism to assist people with large temporary losses in income. Access to retirement savings should remain an exceptional measure based on individual specific circumstances and, where needed, as a temporary expansion of measures already in place for that purpose.

Countries with regulatory frameworks that allowed early access to retirement savings in exceptional situations of hardship had lower retirement savings withdrawals that countries that introduced the possibility of early withdrawals during 2020. In some countries, existing regulatory frameworks allowed plan members to access their retirement savings before retirement under certain exceptional conditions when unemployment or substantial income losses occur (OECD, 2019[6]). In New Zealand for example, individuals are eligible to withdraw their own and their employers' contributions from their KiwiSaver plan if they experience financial hardship (e.g. if they cannot meet their minimum living expenses or pay the mortgage on their home). In Mexico, plan members are allowed to withdraw a part of their pension assets if they have lost their (formal) job and have been unemployed for a minimum of 46 days, and if they have not already requested a similar withdrawal in the last five years. In both countries, members made use of this possibility for early access. In other countries (e.g. Chile, Peru) a regulatory framework did not exist and early access to retirement savings was legislated during the pandemic in 2020. Countries that allowed access during the pandemic had larger overall withdrawals during 2020 (Figure 1.3), especially when they allowed mostly unconditional early withdrawals such as in Chile and Peru.

Figure 1.3. Value of early withdrawals in selected countries, in 2020

As a percentage of total assets in retirement savings plans at end-2019

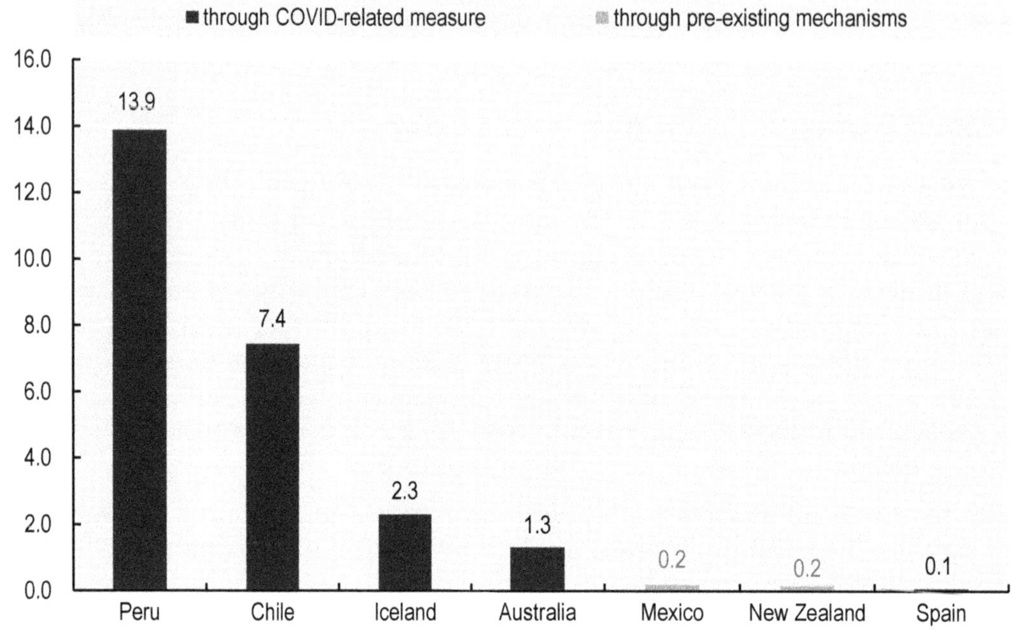

Note: Data refer to early withdrawals up to: end-July 2020 for Peru, end-September 2020 for Chile, October 2020 for Iceland, 8 November 2020 for Australia (as part of the Early Release Initiative only), end-June 2020 for Mexico (due to unemployment only), end-August 2020 for New Zealand (for financial hardship reasons only, and expressed as a percentage of assets in KiwiSaver schemes at end-March 2020), end-September 2020 for Spain.
Source: OECD (2020[7]), *Retirement savings and old-age pensions in the time of COVID-19*, https://doi.org/10.1787/b698aae4-en.

1.3.5. Assets earmarked for retirement

Policy makers should promote a favourable environment for pension providers to use assets earmarked for retirement to support the economy. During 2020, there were calls to use assets earmarked for retirement to assist economies in distress. The WPPP felt that was important to look at this issue. The analysis suggested that appropriate policies and regulations needed to be in place. In particular, policy makers could encourage long-term investment in alternative asset classes by considering structural solutions to develop the market for alternative investments, and making sure that such investments are available, transparent and financially attractive. They should better account for the desired risk-return profiles of pension providers when designing public-private partnerships to encourage their participation. Policy makers also need to make sure that appropriate investment vehicles are available to support programmes addressing the effects of the pandemic (e.g. COVID-19 bonds), to finance small and large businesses, and to contribute to the economic recovery. They may also have a role to play to help pension providers gain access to better quality data to assess investments and enhance pension providers' capabilities to invest in alternative asset classes through targeted educational initiatives. This could favour the loosening of some investment restrictions that limit investment in less liquid assets.

1.4. Policy guidelines at the time of the *OECD Pensions Outlook 2020*

The lessons learnt during 2020 led the OECD to publish at the end of that year an updated set of policy guidelines to assist policy makers, regulators and supervisors to confront the implications of COVID-19 on asset-backed pension arrangements (Box 1.1).

Box 1.1. OECD policy guidelines for asset-backed pension arrangements to confront COVID-19 presented at the time of the *OECD Pensions Outlook 2020*

Policy makers should make sure that people saving for retirement and pension providers stay the course:

- Saving for retirement is for the long term. Maintain investments in retirement portfolios to avoid selling and materialising value losses when markets are low.
- Continue contributing to retirement plans. Governments may make the income of people whole as part of the many programmes to assist the populations facing the economic fall from COVID-19, the lockdown and the associated economic downturn.
- Act in accordance with investment objectives. Pension providers should adhere to their investment objectives and carefully assess new investment opportunities. Their investment decisions should be at arms-length from governments.

Policy makers, regulators and supervisors should:

- Allow for regulatory flexibility in recovery plans to address funding problems stemming from retirement promises (e.g. DB pension arrangements, and lifetime income products). Make sure that once the emergency is over, measures providing flexibility are removed.
- Make sure that funding and solvency rules for DB plans are counter-cyclical. Introduce flexibility in meeting funding requirements, thereby avoiding 'pro-cyclical policies' and allowing pension funds to act as long-term investors and potentially stabilising forces within the global financial system.
- Provide proportionate, flexible and risk-based supervisory oversight coupled with adequate communication to reduce frauds, and facilitate efficient operations. Supervisory oversight should concentrate on prudential and market conduct regulation, including ensuring protection of members and beneficiaries against COVID-19 related scams, especially of the most vulnerable individuals. Supervisors should communicate to market participants and individuals on their prudential expectations and recommendations in time of the crisis and actions made to facilitate pension funds' operations and to ease administrative burden.
- Allow access to retirement savings as a measure of last resort and based on individual specific exceptional circumstances. Retirement pots are to finance retirement. Accessing retirement savings could lead to materialising temporary asset values losses, liquidity and investment management problems to pension funds, and, more importantly to retirement income adequacy shortfalls. Current regulatory frameworks already allow for tapping retirement savings in exceptional circumstances when substantial income losses occur, and may only be expanded further on a temporary and targeted manner, where needed, to address genuine financial hardship.
- Develop close co-operation with stakeholders, regulators and supervisors at the national and international levels, to share solutions and effective ways to deal with the current crisis.

Policy makers can promote the use of assets earmarked for retirement to support the economy while ensuring that these investments are in the best interest of members. They can enhance the quality of data to assess investments and pension providers' capabilities to invest in different asset classes; adjust investment regulations; promote a favourable environment for long-term investment and suitable investment vehicles; and ensure appropriate alternative investments are available and financially attractive.

The main additions with respect to those published in June 2020 were:

- Policy makers should make sure that people saving for retirement and pension providers stay the course and act in accordance with investment objectives. Pension providers should adhere to their investment objectives and carefully assess new investment opportunities. Their investment decisions should be at arms-length from governments.
- Policy makers, regulators and supervisors should make sure that measures providing regulatory flexibility in recovery plans to address funding problems stemming from retirement promises are removed once the emergency is over.
- Regulatory frameworks already allow for tapping retirement savings in exceptional circumstances when substantial income losses occur and may only be expanded further on a temporary and targeted manner, where needed, to address genuine financial hardship.
- Policy makers can promote the use of assets earmarked for retirement to support the economy while ensuring that these investments are in the best interest of members. They can enhance the quality of data to assess investments and pension providers' capabilities to invest in different asset classes; adjust investment regulations; promote a favourable environment for long-term investment and suitable investment vehicles; and ensure appropriate alternative investments are available and financially attractive.

The OECD continued monitoring policy developments and country experiences. What follows in this publication compiles the lessons learnt and it provides a set of policy guidelines to strengthen asset-backed pension systems in a post-COVID-19 world.

References

Antolín, P. and F. Stewart (2009), "Private Pensions and Policy Responses to the Financial and Economic Crisis", *OECD Working Papers on Insurance and Private Pensions*, No. 36, OECD Publishing, Paris, https://doi.org/10.1787/224386871887. [1]

OECD (2021), *Pension Markets in Focus 2021*, https://www.oecd.org/finance/private-pensions/pensionmarketsinfocus.htm. [5]

OECD (2020), *OECD Pensions Outlook 2020*, OECD Publishing, Paris, https://doi.org/10.1787/67ede41b-en. [3]

OECD (2020), *Pension Funds in Figures, June 2020*, https://www.oecd.org/finance/private-pensions/pensionmarketsinfocus.htm. [4]

OECD (2020), "Retirement savings and old-age pensions in the time of COVID-19", in *OECD Pensions Outlook 2020*, OECD Publishing, Paris, https://doi.org/10.1787/b698aae4-en. [7]

OECD (2020), *Retirement savings in the time of COVID-19*, https://doi.org/10.1787/b9740518-en. [2]

OECD (2019), "Are funded pensions well designed to adapt to non-standard forms of work?", in *OECD Pensions at a Glance 2019: OECD and G20 Indicators*, OECD Publishing, Paris, https://doi.org/10.1787/1231a36d-en. [6]

Notes

[1] Contained in the OECD Pensions Outlook (OECD, 2020[3]).

[2] See https://countryeconomy.com/key-rates/uk (for the United Kingdom) and https://countryeconomy.com/key-rates/usa (for the United States)

[3] https://www.actionfraud.police.uk/COVID-19

[4] These numbers are an approximation using a standard actuarial calculation for an individual contributing 10% of wages over a 40-year period, starting at age 25, with inflation at 2%, productivity growth at 1.5%, nominal returns at 4%, discount rate at 2%, life expectancy at age 65 of 18 years, and contributions to a retirement account stopping for a complete year for someone aged 30, 45 or 60.

[5] These numbers are an approximation using a standard actuarial calculation for an individual contributing 10% of wages over a 40-year period, starting at age 25, with inflation at 2%, productivity growth at 1.5%, nominal returns at 4%, discount rate at 2%, life expectancy at age 65 of 18 years, and withdrawing 10% of the assets accumulated at age 30, 45 or 60.

[6] https://www.oecd.org/coronavirus/policy-responses/retirement-savings-in-the-time-of-COVID-19-b9740518/

2 Policy and supervisory responses to the impact of COVID-19 on asset-backed pension arrangements

This chapter presents the main policy and supervisory responses that countries have implemented during 2020-21 to address the impact of COVID-19 on asset-backed pension arrangements. This compilation is based on publicly available information up to the end of 2021, complemented by inputs from delegates to the OECD Working Party on Private Pensions (pension and insurance regulators and supervisors).

2.1. Australia

2.1.1. Reduction of the superannuation minimum drawdown rates

March 2020: The Australian Government has temporarily reduced superannuation minimum drawdown requirements. People starting a superannuation pension or annuity on or after 1 July 2007 usually have to withdraw a minimum amount from their account each financial year.[1] This minimum amount is a percentage of the account balance at 1 July of each financial year and the percentage depends on the member's age.[2] Australia decided to halve the default minimum drawdown rates for all age groups for the financial years 2019-20 and 2020-21 as a result of the COVID-19 outbreak (Table 2.1).

Table 2.1. Reduction in minimum drawdown rates

Age	Default minimum drawdown rate (%)	Temporary minimum reduced rate for 2019-20 and 2020-21 (%)
Under 65	4	2
65-74	5	2.5
75-79	6	3
80-84	7	3.5
85-89	9	4.5
90-94	11	5.5
95 or more	14	7

Source: Australian Government.

May 2021: The temporary reduction in superannuation minimum drawdown rates was extended for another year to 30 June 2022.[3]

2.1.2. Adjustment and intensification of supervision

March 2020: Working closely with its peer regulatory agencies – the Australian Securities and Investments Commission (ASIC), the Australian Tax Office (ATO), the Australian Transaction Reports and Analysis Centre (AUSTRAC) and the Australian Treasury – the Australian Prudential Regulation Authority (APRA) recalibrated its supervision focus and intensified supervision of key risk areas brought about by the COVID-19 situation. In the superannuation space, supervision intensified across heightened risk areas – primarily:

- liquidity, brought on by member switching to cash, foreign exchange cash calls, lower levels of member contributions due to unemployment, some funds holding high levels of illiquid assets, and Early Release Initiatives
- investment-related matters, including market volatility, revaluation of unlisted assets, crystallising losses through selling assets in a move to hold higher liquidity and rebalancing to strategic asset allocations
- operational and processing matters (particularly given radical changes to workforce operating models)
- fund sustainability in a sustained period of volatility.

This intensified approach started with supervision conducting a preliminary COVID-19 impact assessment analysis (with funds responding to rounds of information requests from APRA) and continued through close engagement with all fund trustees, particularly those rated high-risk as a result of COVID-19 risk assessments. Supervisors were executing both centralised (thematic) and entity-tailored ongoing supervisory activities.

APRA's focus on maintaining financial resilience has been carefully balanced with responding to trustee requests for relief from certain requirements. APRA therefore suspended all substantive public consultations and actions to finalise revisions to the prudential framework that were underway or upcoming, including consultations on prudential and reporting standards.[4] APRA's core focus on delivery of strong outcomes to members by trustees remained central to this approach. APRA applied close scrutiny to trustee practices relating to matters of member equity, such as rebalancing fund and product asset allocations, to avoid material risk profile shifts, and also revaluation of unlisted assets, including infrastructure.

APRA also retained a focus on the smooth operating of the superannuation processing and payments system – particularly in view of member investment switching and early release withdrawal behaviours.

ASIC also re-prioritised its work to focus on COVID-19 issues.[5] This included monitoring and taking action in relation to scams, unlicensed advice and poor disclosure.

August 2020: APRA announced on 10 August 2020 that it would recommence public consultations on selected policy reforms.[6] Aligned with its policy agenda, APRA also restarted consultation on a limited number of its data collections, including the recommencement of its Superannuation Data Transformation project.

2.1.3. Suspension of the issuance of new licences

April 2020: APRA announced on 8 April 2020 that it would temporarily suspend its issuance of new licences for regulated entities, including superannuation funds.[7] This suspension was initially expected to last for six months, except where the granting of a licence would be necessary for APRA to carry out its mandate.

This decision intended to limit the risk of failure of new entrants that would otherwise face greater challenges than under normal economic conditions.

August 2020: APRA announced on 10 August 2020 that it would begin a phased resumption of the issuing of new licences.[8] This resumption occurred in two phases, with the first one starting in September 2020 and the second one in March 2021.

2.1.4. ASIC relief granted in relation to superannuation advice

April 2020: On 14 April 2020, ASIC announced three temporary relief measures to assist the industry in providing consumers with affordable and timely advice in relation to superannuation during the COVID-19 pandemic.[9] ASIC:

- issued a temporary no-action position for superannuation trustees to expand the scope of personal advice that may be provided by, or on behalf of, the superannuation trustee as 'intra-fund advice'. Intra-fund advice is provided free of charge to the recipient of the advice
- allowed advice providers not to give a statement of advice (SOA) to clients when providing advice about early access to superannuation
- permitted registered tax agents to give advice to existing clients about early access to superannuation without needing to hold an Australian financial services (AFS) licence.

The relief was temporary and subject to a series of conditions. The additional conditions were added to ensure consumer protection.

September 2020: ASIC announced on 23 September 2020 that it would extend two relief measures until 31 December 2020. These measures were ASIC's no-action position for superannuation trustees providing 'intra-fund advice', and financial advice relief related to the COVID-19 early release of superannuation scheme.[10]

Information and advice on early access to superannuation savings was also made available on ASIC's Moneysmart website.[11]

October 2021: ASIC further extended temporary financial advice relief measures designed to help the financial advice industry provide consumers with affordable and timely advice during the COVID-19 pandemic.[12]

The measure allowing financial advisers to provide a record of advice, rather than a statement of advice, to existing clients requiring financial advice due to the impact of the pandemic was extended. This temporary measure was automatically repealed on 15 April 2022.

ASIC also reintroduced the relief measure that allows financial advisers additional time to give their clients a statement of advice after time-critical advice has been provided. Under this measure financial advisers have up to 20 business days (instead of 5 business days). The original relief measure expired on 15 April 2021. This reintroduced measure was automatically repealed on 15 April 2022.

2.1.5. Raising awareness and communicating about scams and fraud

April 2020: APRA and ASIC released a joint letter to superannuation trustees to help them manage challenges associated with COVID-19.[13] This letter draws the attention of trustees to the heightened risk of scams that members may suffer from during the outbreak. Scammers could use the volatile market conditions and the potential misunderstanding about early access to retirement savings to target plan members.

Trustees were advised to remain vigilant and have a regular, clear and accurate communication with plan members.

This advice intended to protect plan members against misinformation and confusion, and enable them to make sound decisions in their best interest.

This joint APRA/ASIC letter can be accessed from the COVID-19 FAQ of ASIC. This FAQ is designed to help trustees with the various queries they may have.[14]

The ATO also warned individuals against scams on its website. The ATO was concerned that some people could pretend to be representatives from the ATO or a super fund to steal personal information, or to charge plan members for services that are free (such as gaining early access to superannuation savings).

August 2021: ASIC released its Corporate Plan in August 2021 which deals with the ongoing impacts of COVID-19.[15] It covers several areas, such as reducing risk of harm to consumers exposed to increased investment scam activity in a low-yield environment, and supporting enhanced cyber resilience and cyber security among ASIC's regulated population, in line with the whole-of-government commitment to mitigating cyber security risks.

2.1.6. Easier early access to pension savings

March 2020: Australia broadened the eligibility conditions for early access to savings in superannuation schemes as part of a coronavirus stimulus package. Eligible Australian and New Zealand citizens and permanent residents could withdraw up to AUD 10 000 between 20 April 2020 and 30 June 2020 (Tranche 1), and up to another AUD 10 000 from 1 July until 31 December 2020 (Tranche 2).

Eligible temporary visa holders could also apply for a single release of up to AUD 10 000 before 1 July 2020. However, temporary residents were not eligible to apply for COVID-19 early release of superannuation savings in the 2020-21 financial year.

Eligible Australian and New Zealand citizens and permanent residents had to satisfy one of the following requirements to benefit from this policy:

- being unemployed
- being eligible to receive a job seeker payment, youth allowance for job seekers, parenting payment (which includes the single and partnered payments), special benefit or farm household allowance
- on or after 1 January 2020: being made redundant or experiencing a 20% or more reduction in working hours. Sole traders were also eligible if their business was suspended or had suffered a decline in turnover by 20% or more.

The eligibility criteria for temporary visa holders depended on the type of temporary visa held and generally reflected the broader conditions for those visas.

Individuals could apply for early release of their savings with the ATO. For this purpose, they could use the myGov website: www.my.gov.au.

Early withdrawals under this temporary coronavirus measure were tax-free. This measure was expected (on 17 April 2020) to cost the government AUD 1.75 billion. This cost estimate was revised upwards to AUD 2.2 billion (on 23 July 2020). The government did not collect the taxes they usually receive for early withdrawals.[16]

The industry initially expressed concerns about the potential magnitude of early withdrawals by eligible members and the impact this would have on retirement outcomes of members and liquidity management of superannuation funds.[17] Concerns in relation to liquidity centred on the possibility that funds may have to sell assets to fund cash withdrawals at a time when markets are low.

The Australian Government originally estimated that AUD 29.5 billion would be released to members under the programme. This estimate represented less than 1% of the almost AUD 3 trillion in total assets managed by superannuation funds at the time. This estimation was surpassed, but superannuation funds were able to manage the liquidity impacts.

The combined figures (of both Tranche 1 and Tranche 2) for the programme are as follows.[18] The total value of benefits paid as part of the early release scheme amounted to AUD 36.4 billion as at 31 January 2021. There was a total of 3.5 million initial applications approved across the full period of the scheme, as well as 1.4 million repeat applications during the second tranche. The average amount withdrawn per member was AUD 7 638. Repeat applications were for an average amount of AUD 8 268 while initial applications were for an average amount of AUD 7 402.

The COVID-19 Early Release of Super programme closed on 31 December 2020. Payments for applications submitted by 31 December 2020 were completed throughout January 2021.

2.2. Austria

2.2.1. Advice to withhold dividend payments

April 2020: The Financial Market Authority (FMA) of Austria recommended insurance companies in April 2020 to withhold paying bonuses or dividends. It also advised them to refrain from share buy-backs.[19]

July 2020: The FMA reiterated its advice at the end of July 2020, urging insurance companies to continue refraining from dividend distributions and share buy-backs.[20] This recommendation is in line with the position of EIOPA.

July 2021: The FMA repealed the restrictions on distributions of dividends, share buybacks as well as variable remuneration.[21] However, the FMA continued to demand prudent and forward-looking capital planning on the part of financial service providers when considering dividend distributions, share buybacks and variable remuneration. In particular, financial service providers should give careful consideration to the sustainability of their business model and an increased credit risk that could arise from additional losses once government support measures cease to apply.

2.2.2. Adaptation of supervisory practices

March 2020: The FMA has been adapting its supervisory practices in line with the recommendations of European supervisory authorities.[22] The objective is to provide flexibility, allowing supervised entities to focus on maintaining their business operations.

The FMA temporarily suspended on-site presence as part of audits. Ongoing inspections continued and were completed off-site as far as possible based on the information and documents available. It also temporarily waived the requirement of the personal presence of the members at supervisory board committee meetings within the scope of its responsibility.

The FMA also extended reporting deadlines, in line with EIOPA's recommendations.[23]

2.2.3. Warning about fraudulent activities

April 2020: The FMA has warned its supervised entities about an increase in fraudulent activities related to the COVID-19 outbreak.[24] The FMA lists several types of fraud, including:

- CEO fraud: scammers deceive teleworking employees by sending them emails from their supervisors, and especially from top management
- Phishing: scammers attempt to get confidential information from customers via email or social media, and then use this information to carry out fraudulent transactions
- Pushing of penny stocks: scammers purchase worthless shares, push their prices up using fake news related to COVID-19, and then sell these shares to investors they target to deceive.

The FMA intends to keep its supervised entities and their customers informed about these risks.

2.3. Belgium

2.3.1. Flexibility in the supervision of IORPs

March 2020: The Financial Services and Markets Authority (FSMA), which is in charge of supervising institutions for occupational retirement provision (IORPs), provided more flexibility to IORPs to help them to cope with the business disruptions and effects of the outbreak.[25]

The FSMA published general guidance relating to COVID-19 on its website. This information has been regularly updated. Among others, this guidance relates to:

- the supervisory approach of the FSMA: postponement of deadlines, no launch of major supervisory actions, except monitoring the financial situation of the IORPs in the context of the COVID-19-crisis
- information regarding initiatives of EIOPA (reference to the EIOPA statement to mitigate the impact of COVID-19) and the national legislator regarding reporting deadlines and more flexible organisation of meetings
- a recommendation to communicate proactively and clearly with the sponsors, members and beneficiaries on the evolution of the financial situation and on possible adjustments to the operational functioning of the IORPs.

Given the impact of the outbreak on financial markets, the FSMA contacted directly IORPs with funding shortfalls for short-term liabilities, in order to discuss with them about a timeline for a recovery plan and related measures.

May 2020: Flexibility was provided by the law of 14 May 2020.[26] IORPs were allowed to postpone their ordinary general assembly until 30 August 2020. They could also organise their general assembly as a remote meeting. The governing bodies were also allowed to make unanimous decisions in written.

The same law modified reporting deadlines. The deadline for annual audited accounts and annual reports to the FSMA was postponed from 30 June to 31 August 2020, while the deadline for reporting to the National Bank of Belgium was postponed from 31 July to 30 September 2020.

The FSMA also published specific guidance in order to ensure that IORPs take appropriate steps to ensure continuity and regularity in the performance of their activities, including the development of contingency plans.[27]

2.3.2. Information on fraudulent activities

April 2020: The FSMA developed a webpage warning customers about fraudulent investment offers and scams on social media.[28] This webpage presents the methods of those tricking customers, and provides advice to prevent customers for falling in a trap. This webpage also informs customers on what they can do if they are victim of fraud.

2.3.3. Coverage continuity for temporary unemployed workers and deferral of premium payments

May 2020: Belgium introduced the possibility for employers to count periods of temporary unemployment due to COVID-19 as periods of employment for their temporary unemployed workers with respect to occupational pensions.[29] Before COVID-19, spells of temporary unemployment were usually not taken into account in the calculation of a pension for DB plans or could lead to a break in contributions into DC plans. Death coverage also stopped. Following the COVID-19 outbreak, the parliament allowed in May 2020 temporarily unemployed workers to continue to be covered by their occupational plans as if they were employed. Employers could refuse the application of this special COVID-19 measure, but the death cover was mandatory. The measure was effective until 30 September 2020 and allowed employers to postpone the payment of the premiums until that date.

December 2020: The measure was initially prolonged until 31 March 2021.

April 2021: The measure was further prolonged until 30 June 2021.

June 2021: The measure was further prolonged until 30 September 2021.

Pension providers (i.e. pension funds and insurers) were responsible for informing employers about the extension of the measure. Employers were first informed when these measures were introduced in May 2020. The legislator did not consider it necessary to provide for additional information obligations when this measure was extended, as employers had already received the information the first time and the extension of the measure aimed to maintain the existing situation.

If the employer or sector had refused the COVID-19 measure before 30 June 2021, this refusal was prolonged until 30 September 2021. By contrast, if the measures were applicable before 30 June 2021, they were automatically prolonged for all temporary unemployed workers until 30 September 2021.

Contribution payments had to continue for temporarily unemployed employees but employers could request to defer their contributions for these employees until 30 September 2021.

This initiative intended to ensure employees could continue to accumulate pension rights during their temporary unemployment. The employer had nevertheless an opt-out possibility for pension accrual during the period of temporary unemployment due to force majeure or economic reasons caused by the COVID-19 crisis. In that case, the rules of the pension plan were applicable. However, the government decided that the death coverage would still be maintained until 30 September 2021.

2.3.4. Information to consumers about the consequences of the COVID-19 crisis

April 2020: The FSMA published on its website several FAQs with an explanation of the consequences of the COVID-19 crisis on different situations or topics.[30] In addition, the FSMA set up a call centre where all consumers, including members and beneficiaries of a supplementary pension scheme, can ask questions related to the impact of COVID-19 on financial matters, including matters related to occupational pensions.[31]

2.4. Canada

2.4.1. Reduced minimum withdrawals for Registered Retirement Income Funds

May 2020: Canada reduced the required minimum withdrawals from Registered Retirement Income Funds (RRIFs) by 25% for 2020.[32] RRIFs are arrangements that individuals contract with an insurance company, a trust company or a bank. The selected provider is in charge of paying regular amounts to the subscribers based on assets transferred from a Registered Retirement Savings Plan (RRSP), a Pool Registered Pension Plan (PRPP), a Registered Pension Plan (RPP), a Specified Pension Plan (SPP) or another RRIF.

A similar measure applies to individuals who receive variable benefit payments from a defined contribution (DC) RPP or a PRPP. The minimum amount that individuals receive was also reduced by 25% in 2020.

2.4.2. Freeze on portability transfers and annuity purchases

March 2020: The Office of the Superintendent of Financial Institutions (OSFI) announced a freeze on portability transfers of rights and annuity purchases relating to federally regulated defined benefit (DB) plans on 27 March 2020. The OSFI only accepted a transfer or an annuity purchase on a case-by-case basis under exceptional circumstances.[33] This freeze did not affect the ongoing pension payments to retirees and other beneficiaries.

This measure was expected to protect the benefits of plan members and beneficiaries at a time when the funding status of DB plans was suffering from developments on financial markets.

August 2020: The OSFI lifted this portability freeze at the end of August 2020, following the improvement of solvency ratios of DB plans and the recovery from the market lows in March 2020.[34] From September 2020, portability transfers and buy-out annuity purchases have been subject to conditions mostly similar to those applying before 27 March 2020. As one of the new conditions for portability transfers, the amount of the initial transfer shall not exceed the transfer value, which is the commuted value of the pension benefit multiplied by the transfer ratio of the plan.

February 2021: The OSFI removed on 25 February 2021 the requirement to use a projected solvency ratio as of 31 March 2020 (or later) for portability transfers.[35]

2.4.3. Moratorium on solvency payments for sponsors of federally regulated defined benefit pension plans

May 2020: The Solvency Special Payments Relief Regulations of 2020 provided immediate temporary relief to sponsors of federally regulated DB plans by establishing a moratorium on solvency payment requirements for DB plans.[36] This moratorium applied to solvency special payments becoming due between 1 April 2020 and 30 December 2020.[37]

- The amounts of any solvency special payments that became due from 1 April 2020 to 26 May 2020 (i.e. the day before the coming-into-force date of the Relief Regulations, which is 27 May 2020), unless related to a plan year that ended before 27 April 2020, were reduced to zero and did not become due after 30 December 2020 once the moratorium was lifted.

- From 27 May 2020 until 30 December 2020, the amounts of any solvency special payments that became due were reduced to zero and did not become due after 30 December 2020 once the moratorium was lifted.
- The amounts of any solvency special payments that became due and are made from 1 April until 27 May may be deducted from the plan's required current service (or normal cost) contributions and/or going concern special payments in the period beginning on 27 May 2020 and ending on 30 December 2020.

The Solvency Special Payments Relief Regulations of 2020 did not set out a separate amortisation schedule for the solvency special payments that were foregone during the moratorium. Since the end of the moratorium, plans have been subject to the normal funding rules, which provide that any solvency deficiency is to be amortised at least through monthly instalments over a five year period.

2.4.4. Flexibility in the supervision of pension plans

March 2020: A three-month extension was granted for annual reporting on federally regulated private pension plans.[38] This deadline extension applied in particular to the filing of annual information returns, certified financial statements, actuarial reports and annual statements.

Pension regulators in several Canadian provinces also tried to provide support to pension plan administrators. Several provided deadlines extensions for required filings such as annual information returns, financial statements, member statements and member notices.[39] Regulators have also issued FAQs and website notifications to explain measures and address pension issues stemming from COVID-19.

February 2021: The OSFI cancelled on 25 February 2021 the extensions in place since April 2020 to file an annual information return, certified financial statement, auditor's report filing confirmation, actuarial report, actuarial information summary, and annual member statements.[40]

2.4.5. Waiver of 1% minimum employer contributions for DC plans

May 2020: The Canada Revenue Agency (CRA) announced on 5 May 2020 that it would waive the requirement for employers sponsoring DC plans to contribute at least 1% of the payroll on behalf of their employees until the end of 2020.[41] This waiver was conditional on the amendment of the plans to suspend all accruals for the year.

2.4.6. Relief for sponsors of registered pension plans

July 2020 / May 2021: In July 2020, the Department of Finance announced temporary amendments to the Income Tax Regulations applicable to RPPs and deferred salary leave plans (DSLPs).[42] In May 2021, the temporary relief was extended for another year (to 30 April 2022).[43] The amendments provided support to employers and employees who participate in RPPs and DSLPs:

- adding temporary "stop-the-clock" rules to DSLPs from 15 March 2020 to 30 April 2022, thus not requiring a DSLP to be terminated if an employee suspends a leave of absence in order to return to essential work or if an employee chooses to delay their paid leave of absence
- removing restrictions (until 30 April 2022) that prohibit RPP administrators from borrowing money
- permitting catch-up contributions to RPPs by 30 April 2022, towards remaining required contributions that otherwise had not been made in 2020 or 2021

- waiving the requirement that an employee needs at least 36 months of employment to qualify for an "eligible period of reduced pay" so that all employees, including new employees, may receive unreduced pension coverage
- in cases of wage rollback periods, allowing employer pension contributions to be based on 100% of wages prior to rollback.

2.5. Chile

2.5.1. Transfer of assets to an account during the process to start the pay-out phase

April 2020: Chile adopted a rule to transfer the pension assets of those about to receive pension payments to a separate account.[44] Before the new rule, the amount of assets in the pension plan could vary between the start of application for a pension payment and the actual moment when individuals received their benefits. This implied that members and beneficiaries were not sure about what their final balance would be at the time of calculating their pension. With the new rule, individuals who are about to retire can ask their Pension Fund Administrator (AFP) to transfer pension assets to a separate account at the beginning of the process, in order to maintain the level of pension assets unchanged during the process to get pension payments for retirement.

This measure intends to protect the pension savings of those who are retiring in times of volatile financial markets. This measure entered into force on 1 May 2020.

2.5.2. Adjustments in the operations and services

April 2020: Given the health measures to prevent the spread of COVID-19, the Superintendence of Pensions requested the public to use online service platforms and the call centre instead of going to premises for face-to-face meetings.[45] People could carry out procedures, enquiries or complaints and review the status of their applications on the website of the supervisor. People could also send some documents to the supervisor in a pdf format by email.

A temporary regulation was also issued in the context of COVID-19 to allow plan members to complete all pension procedures for retirement through the SCOMP platform completely remotely.[46]

These adjustments intended to guarantee the continuation of the operation of the supervisor and pension providers while protecting the health of the public.

2.5.3. Early access to retirement savings

July 2020: As a response to the COVID-19 crisis, Chile passed a law in July 2020 to allow plan members to withdraw up to 10% of accumulated assets in mandatory accounts, with a minimum of 35 *Unidad de Fomentos* (UFs) and a maximum of 150 UFs.[47] This withdrawal was voluntary and tax exempt. Plan members could submit their request to their AFP from 30 July 2020 to 30 July 2021. AFPs then had to distribute 50% of the withdrawal amount within 10 business days from the date of submission of plan members' request (unless the withdrawal amount was lower than 35 UFs).[48] Plan members received the remainder within 30 days of the first withdrawal payment.

More than 11 million people (more than 9 in 10 plan members) had withdrawn savings from their individual accounts as of 1 October 2021 for the first round of withdrawals. These withdrawals amounted to CLP 15 575 865 million (USD 19 184 million) overall.

November 2020: A second 10% early withdrawal was approved on 10 November 2020. Members could make this second withdrawal by 9 December 2020 and until the end of November 2021. The withdrawal was taxed for people earning more than 30 *Unidad Tributaria Anual* (around CLP18.3 million) annually.

Members could benefit from this even if they had not requested early access to their savings the first time through the possibility opened in July 2020. The first and second withdrawals were two independent procedures. Members could still make a request for the first withdrawal until the end of July 2021 if they wished so.

As of 1 October 2021, nearly 9 million people requested a withdrawal during the second round. The total amount of withdrawals reached CLP 12 660 640 million (USD 15 594 million).

April 2021: After these two laws, a third round of withdrawals of retirement savings was approved in April 2021. The law allows members to withdraw up to 10% of their savings for the third time. Pensioners receiving an annuity can also request an advance on the money they would get later. The application for the third withdrawals could start from early May 2021. Over 7.3 million Chileans had requested a third pay-out by 1 October 2021. These withdrawals amounted to CLP 10 516 467 million (USD 12 953 million).

2.5.4. Relaxation of investment rules to cope with requests for early withdrawals

July 2020: The Chilean Superintendence of Pensions announced at the end of July 2020 that some investment restrictions would be more flexible for six months.[49] For instance, the limit on investments in short-term deposits in foreign banks was increased from 2% to 4% of assets. These adjustments were an exceptional and transitory measure to facilitate the 10% withdrawal process and aimed at facilitating the payments from AFPs to plan members requesting an early withdrawal of their savings.

2.5.5. Government bonus paid to members who emptied their pension account

May 2021: The Law No. 21.339 introduced a state-funded CLP 200 000 bonus for members who had emptied their mandatory savings accounts due to the first two rounds of withdrawals between 30 July 2020 and 31 March 2021, and those with a balance of less than CLP 200 000 as of 31 March 2021.[50] For the latter, the bonus corresponded to a top up to reach a balance of CLP 200 000. Members had to be participating in the system since at least 1 January 2021 to be eligible for this bonus. The AFPs sent the list of people qualifying to get this bonus to Chile's Treasury. The Treasury then sent the money to the AFPs. The bonus was transferred to the individuals' accounts. Members could leave this bonus in their accounts if they wished so, they were not required to withdraw the money. As of 13 October 2021, 2.7 million members received a government bonus of CLP 188 214 on average.[51] The total cost amounted to CLP 510 785 million (USD 617.2 million).

2.5.6. Mitigation of volatility risks

July 2020: Following the entry into force of the rules that allowed the first withdrawal of up to 10% of pension assets, the Central Bank of Chile implemented a range of measures.[52] These measures addressed the fact that early access to pension savings represented a significant liquidation of assets by the administrators of these funds, and that the orderly liquidation of such assets was essential to preserve the financial stability and efficiency of the price formation process. The measures included:

- Establish a special programme of spot purchase operations carried out jointly and simultaneously with a forward sale, on the open market, of eligible instruments issued by banking companies (CC-VP Programme)
- Continue with the purchase window of Bank Bonds for the remainder of USD 4 100 million of the March programme, which was intended to contain volatility scenarios
- Add a term deposit purchase window for up to USD 8 billion, which was open to the same participants as the previous window, that is, to all SOMA participants.

The above programmes were initially in force for a period of six months.

December 2020: In the context of the second withdrawal, the Central Bank of Chile implemented the following measures, in force between 9 December 2020 and 15 February 2021:[53]

- Reopening of the special cash purchase and term sale (CC-VP) programme for the remainder of the first programme, equivalent to an amount of up to the equivalent of USD 8 500 million
- Reopening of the special programme for the purchase of Term Deposits for the remainder of the first programme, equivalent to an amount of up to the equivalent of USD 7 750 million.

May 2021: Following the enactment of the third round of early withdrawals, the Central Bank of Chile put measures in place to mitigate the volatility that this round of withdrawals could create in financial markets:[54]

- Reopening of the special cash purchase and term sale (CC-VP) programme, open to banking companies and other financial institutions, for the remainder of the programme, equivalent to an amount of up to USD 9 500 million and the renewal of the current amount, equivalent to an amount of USD 500 million. The CC-VP programme was in force from 3 May 2021 until the second week of July 2021
- The REPO window with banking companies was extended until August 2021 in operations of one month term.

AFPs also have market mechanisms at their disposal to provide liquidity and facilitate the adjustment of portfolios.

2.5.7. Laws maintaining working relationships and the continuity of pension contributions

April 2020: Chile introduced laws allowing the suspension of the contract of employees during the pandemic while ensuring their employers continued to pay monthly social security contributions during the time of the suspension.[55] Employees were getting monthly benefits from the unemployment insurance fund at a reduced wage replacement rate. The unemployment insurance fund has been paying the pension contributions, amounting to 10% of the unemployment benefits. There were a total of 964 568 beneficiaries accessing suspension contract benefits between April 2020 and October 2021.

2.6. Colombia

2.6.1. Transfer of the balances of retirees in programmed withdrawals from AFPs to the State Pension Fund

April 2020: Colombia introduced a decree transferring the duty to pay benefits to pensioners from private AFPs to the State Pension Fund (*Colpensiones*) under certain circumstances.[56] AFPs providing a lifetime programmed withdrawal usually have to ensure that the remaining accumulated capital is always enough to finance a life annuity at least equal to the minimum monthly wage.[57] If not, the AFP must purchase a life annuity equivalent to the minimum wage with an insurance company. Following the COVID-19 outbreak, AFPs were required to transfer the balance of pensioners in programmed withdrawals to *Colpensiones* if this balance was not enough to guarantee the lifetime payment of a monthly minimum wage according to the estimates of AFPs as of 31 March 2020. Pensioners in this situation received allowances equivalent to the monthly minimum wage from *Colpensiones*.

June 2020: Instead of requiring AFPs to transfer the balance of all eligible pensioners to *Colpensiones*, another decree made this a voluntary option.[58] AFPs who decided to make use of this mechanism had until 31 October 2020 to transfer the assets to *Colpensiones*.

July 2020: The court declared unconstitutional Legislative Decree 802 of 4 June 2020, which modified Legislative Decree 558 of 15 April 2020. In addition, it declared Legislative Decree 558 of 2020 unconstitutional and ordered the government, in the exercise of its powers, to adopt and implement a mechanism that, within a reasonable period of time, guarantees the reestablishment of the link to the AFPs of pensioners under the programmed withdrawal option who were transferred to *Colpensiones* in compliance with the provisions of Decree 558 of 2020.

2.6.2. Adjustment of processes and services

March 2020: The Financial Superintendence of Colombia (SFC) issued a series of instructions and general rules for compliance by the supervised entities, such as:

- External Circular 12 of 2020: the SFC instructed financial entities to promote the use of digital channels to carry out the greatest number of procedures and transactions for financial consumers, provided that the service expected by the consumer allowed for it.
- External Circular 09 of 2020: the SFC set forth transitory measures to help financial institutions in prioritising the continuity of service provision. For example, the SFC postponed the submission of the results of the stress tests until the last business day of July 2021.
- Circular Letter 19 of 2020: the SFC suspended the terms of the administrative actions carried out by the Superintendence for a period.
- External Circular 08 of 2020: the SFC issued guidelines for strengthening operational risk management of the supervised entities under the current state of financial markets and the health emergency situation.

April 2020: Colombia also introduced a decree to ensure that people over 70 could collect their pensions in a flexible and safe way during the sanitary emergency.[59] Those over 70 did not need to give a special power or authorisation before a notary or public official to let a relative or someone else close to them collect their pensions. Pensioners simply needed to give an original identity document and a written authorisation to let a third party collect their pensions on their behalf.

People over 80 (or over 70 if they were disabled) were entitled to receive their pensions at home from a transport company. The pension administrator was in charge of the logistics to ensure entitled retirees received their payments.

2.6.3. Reduction of the contribution rate to the General Pension System

April 2020: Decree 558 allowed for a reduction in mandatory contributions to the General Pension System for April and May 2020. Before this decree, employers and employees had to contribute 16% of gross earnings overall to cover pension insurance, disability and survivors' pensions and finance administrative costs. Contributions amounted to 12% of gross earnings for employers and 4% for employees. Decree 558 reduced mandatory contributions from 16% to 3%. Employers paid 75% of this 3% contribution and the employees paid the remaining 25%. The contributions paid in April and May 2020 still counted toward the minimum weeks of contributions that are needed to qualify for an old-age pension, despite the reduced contribution rates.[60]

July 2020: The court declared unconstitutional Legislative Decree 802 of 4 June 2020, which modified Legislative Decree 558 of 15 April 2020. In addition, it declared Legislative Decree 558 of 2020 unconstitutional and ordered the government, in the exercise of its powers, to adopt and implement a mechanism that, within a reasonable period of time, allows employers, employees and the self-employed to contribute the missing amounts of contributions to the General Pension System for April and May 2020, when payments were made partially under the provisions of Decree 558 of 2020.

April 2021: The Ministry of Labour issued a decree in April 2021 (Decree 376).[61] This decree stipulated that employees and employers who benefitted from the reduction of the contribution rate for April and May 2020 have 36 months from 1 June 2021 to pay the missing contributions. The payment form does not include the default interest (for late contributions) for April and May 2020. Employers can deduct the share of the contributions that employees must pay (i.e. 25%) from their salary without requesting their authorisation. If employees have stopped working for the company since May 2020, employers have to pay the 75% of the missing contributions and former employees have to pay their share (i.e. 25% of the missing contributions) within 36 months. If former employees make this payment after the 36-month period, they have to pay a penalty (default interests). In all the cases, default interests will apply for any payment of missing contributions (for April and May 2020) that is not made before 1 June 2024.

2.7. Costa Rica

2.7.1. Access to the Labour Capitalisation Fund

April 2020: Law 9 838 was published on 4 April 2020 to allow employees affected by the pandemic to withdraw funds from their individual account in the Labour Capitalisation Fund (FCL). This fund is financed by employers (1.5% of the employee's salary) and the individual account is managed by the pension administrator selected by the employee. This account is separated from the pension account. Initially, employees could only withdraw funds from the FCL under three conditions: i) the end of the employment relationship; ii) upon the death of the worker; iii) after having a continuous employment relationship with the employer for five years. Law 9 838 added the possibility to withdraw funds in the event of a temporary suspension of the employment relationship or of a reduction in the ordinary working day that implies a reduction in salary.[62] The amount that employees could withdraw corresponded to the balance available on the date on which the suspension of the employment relationship or the reduction of the working day began. The pension administrators had a maximum of 15 working days from the application date to make the payment.

2.7.2. Suspension of switches between pension operators

May 2020: The National Council for the Supervision of the Financial System (Conassif) approved on 25 May a temporary suspension of the transfer of members' resources between pension operators, for the entire duration of the declaration of emergency established by the Executive Branch in Executive Decree No. 42227-MP-S of 16 March 2020.[63]

The possibility to change pension operators resumed at the beginning of September 2020.

2.7.3. New pay-out options to accelerate benefit payments

October 2020: Law No. 9 906 accelerates the withdrawal of funds from the Mandatory Pension Regime (ROP) for people who have acquired the right to retire.[64] There are three different situations:

- Individuals who were retired and had not withdrawn all of their accumulated assets by 31 December 2020 could request the transfer of the funds in their individual accounts in three annual payments
- Individuals who acquired the right to retire under the ROP before 1 January 2021 can withdraw their funds in 30 months, either through monthly instalments until the accumulated balance is exhausted, or with the accelerated withdrawal option where the individual receives four instalments of 25% of the balance each, with the first withdrawal paid 60 days after the request
- Individuals who will retire from 1 January 2021 and until 18 February 2030 will be able to accelerate the withdrawal of their resources through the temporary income option for a period equal to the number of contributions paid.

2.8. Czech Republic

2.8.1. Suspension of dividend payments

April 2020: The Czech National Bank (CNB) called on pension management companies to withhold dividend payments and take any other steps that might jeopardise their capital resilience.[65]

2.8.2. Flexibility in the reporting for insurers, reinsurers and pension companies

April 2020: The CNB agreed to provide domestic supervised entities some flexibility in fulfilling their disclosure duty. The latter could submit and publish their 2019 annual report by 30 June 2020.[66]

2.9. Denmark

2.9.1. Coverage of pension contributions in the wage compensation scheme

March 2020: The wage compensation scheme became effective on 9 March 2020 for wage earners in the private sector. The government and the social partners reached a tripartite agreement to guarantee that firms who experienced a decrease in orders and consumers due to COVID-19 and thus could not afford their employees, received a partial refund for their incurred expenses, initially for three months until 9 June 2020. By applying for the wage compensation scheme, firms were obliged to refrain from laying off workers due to economic reasons, during the period they received compensation.[67]

The wage compensation scheme covered 75% of the monthly gross pay for waged employees and 90% of the monthly gross pay for non-waged workers. The maximum coverage was DKK 30 000.[68]

The salary taken into account to calculate the subsidy was the employee's total withholding income, including the company's and the employee's ATP contributions, as well as any contributions to the employer-sponsored pension scheme.

April 2020: On 18 April 2020, the government and the social partners reached an agreement prolonging the wage compensation scheme by one month, extending its effect until 8 July 2020.[69]

December 2020: On 10 December 2020, the government and social partners reached a tripartite agreement on the reintroduction of the wage compensation scheme.[70]

January 2021: On 14 January 2021, the government and social partners reached a tripartite agreement extending the wage compensation scheme until the tighter restrictions implemented following a surge in corona infection rates were lifted.

2.9.2. Flexibility in the reporting for insurers

March 2020: The Danish Financial Supervisory Authority (FSA) extended the deadline for reporting for insurers.[71] In this respect, the FSA followed the recommendations from the European Insurance and Occupational Pensions Authority (EIOPA). EIOPA itself extended its deadlines, providing more time to national insurance authorities to submit information on insurers.

Danish insurance companies wishing to report later than the usual deadlines only had to inform the FSA by email.

2.9.3. *Increased monitoring of the solvency of pension companies*

March 2020: The FSA requested Danish pension companies to report the solvency coverage and carry out a simplified stress test every week.[72] Pension companies were expected to calculate the solvency coverage on the day before the reporting deadline, and an estimate of what the solvency coverage would have been on that same accounting day in the worst-case scenario of a decline by 15% in equity prices and a 25 basis point change in interest rates. Pension companies had to submit this information each Wednesday between 18 March and 17 June 2020.

This request aimed at helping the FSA to monitor developments in the pension sector more closely.

2.9.4. *Suspension of dividend payments*

April 2020: EIOPA called on insurance and pension companies to temporarily suspend all dividend payments and share buybacks, as well as to restrain other variable remuneration. The FSA supported EIOPA's request and invited Danish insurance and pension companies to act in accordance with it. [73]

2.9.5. *Contribution breaks*

March 2020: Some pension companies provided consumers with the option to suspend their contributions. For example, Danica Pension allowed its self-employed members to suspend their pension contributions until the end of June 2020.[74] Self-employed workers only had to pay a small part of their insurance to be fully covered if they fell sick or were injured. The rest of the premium payment came from existing pension savings. Danica Pension also invited small and medium-sized companies to get in touch with their consumer advisor to reduce pension contributions if companies, employees and unions agreed.

2.10. Estonia

2.10.1. *Suspension of employer contributions to the second pension pillar*

September 2020: Estonia temporarily suspended the payment of employer contributions of 4% of salary to the second pension pillar, except for employees born between 1942 and 1960, for whom contributions continued as normal.[75] This suspension took place from 1 July 2020 until 31 August 2021. Employers continued to pay the 4% contribution (as part of their overall 33% social security contributions), but the 4% was retained in the public scheme instead of going to the second pension pillar.

Members, including those born between 1942 and 1960, had the option of stopping their contributions by applying for a suspension in October 2020. Employee contributions for those who applied were suspended between 1 December 2020 and 31 August 2021.

In 2023-24, the state budget will finance the missing 4% employer contributions for every month employees continued to make their 2% contributions between 1 July 2020 and 31 August 2021. This amount will be paid into second pillar pension plans. The state will also finance a return on these missing contributions. This return will correspond to the average return of second pillar pension plans between 1 July 2020 and 31 December 2022.[76]

In total, 9 575 people applied for a temporary suspension of contributions, of which 60% were women.[77] These people will not receive the 4% employer contribution back.

2.11. Finland

2.11.1. Adjustment of the solvency legislation of pension insurance institutions

March 2020: On 19 March 2020, the Ministry of Social Affairs and Health approved the amendment of the solvency rules for pension insurance institutions.[78] The amendment concerned the supplement factor. Under normal circumstances, old-age pension funds are supplemented annually by a supplementary factor determined on the basis of the average solvency of earnings-related pension insurers. The amendment allowed the non-payment of the supplement factor for a fixed period from 1 April 2020.

On 26 March 2020, the Finnish Government also gave the Financial Supervisory Authority the power to extend the deadline for the implementation of recovery plans for pension insurance institutions when their solvency capital falls below the required level. This policy shall remain in force until 26 March 2023. Under normal circumstances, the implementation of the recovery plan shall be one year, in certain exceptional cases two years.

2.11.2. Deferral of contributions into earnings-related pension plans

March 2020: Employers and the self-employed could agree with their pension provider to postpone the payment of pension contributions into earnings-related pension plans by three months.[79] They had to pay a 2% interest charge on these delayed contributions but were not subject to any penalty fee.

2.11.3. Reduction in employer contribution rates for earnings-related pension plans

March 2020: The Finnish Government approved the proposal of social partners to reduce contributions to earnings-related pension plans temporarily.[80] Employer contributions were lowered by 2.6 percentage points from 1 May 2020 and until the end of 2020. Pension providers could use buffer funds to offset this reduction in contributions and pay current pensions.[81] Employer contributions will increase again between 2022 and 2025 to make up for the missing contributions in 2020 and replenish buffer funds.

2.11.4. Facilitating premium loans

March 2020: The government facilitated employers' access to the contributions they paid into earnings-related pension plans through loans (premium loans). To get a loan, employers need a guarantee. The state-owned financing company, Finnvera, could provide guarantees for these loans.[82]

On 30 March 2020, the Ministry of Social Affairs and Health approved a possibility to restrict premium lending, to secure the liquidity of pension insurance institutions.

2.12. France

2.12.1. Suspension of dividend payments

April 2020: In early April 2020, the French Prudential Supervisory Authority (ACPR) called on insurers to refrain from paying dividends to shareholders at least until 1 October 2020.[83] COVID-19 has had multiple effects on the insurance sector, which could only be assessed in hindsight. One of the ACPR's essential missions is to prevent the failures of insurers, in the interest of consumers. The ACPR tried to ensure that the sector would remain solvent regardless of the severity of the crises it would face.

July 2020: Following the recommendations from the European Systemic Risk Board, the ACPR urged its supervised entities (including insurers) at the end of July 2020 to refrain from paying dividends until 1 January 2021.[84]

February 2021: In line with the recommendations from European authorities, the ACPR called on its supervised entities in mid-February 2021 to remain cautious with respect to dividend payments until 30 September 2021.[85] Supervised entities were invited to inform the ACPR before deciding to make dividend payments. Insurance companies had to provide 3-year projection of their own funds and solvency ratio, assessed under two scenarios: an intermediate scenario and another one with a deteriorating economic environment and very low interest rates.

2.12.2. Flexibility in the reporting for insurers

March 2020: Following EIOPA's recommendations, the ACPR decided at end-March 2020 to postpone the deadline for insurers to fulfil some of their reporting duties. The ACPR gave more time to insurers to submit their European prudential reporting, comply with national reporting requirements and return the other requested non-prudential information.[86]

2.12.3. Warning against frauds and scams

March 2020: The ACPR has issued a warning against frauds and scams on its webpage.[87] The ACPR and the French Financial Markets Regulator (AMF) called for vigilance as the risk of scams may be heightened during the COVID-19 outbreak and setbacks on financial markets. People may be offered false insurance policies with attractive features (such as high returns with low risk). The ACPR and the AMF provided advice for people to avoid being victim of frauds or scams.

June 2020: The ACPR was informed of a wave of fraudulent calls and emails by scammers impersonating ACPR staff in order to collect information on financial intermediaries (brokers or agents in banking, insurance or crowdfunding). The ACPR calls on the financial sector to be extremely vigilant and not to respond to these requests.

July 2020: In order to contribute to a successful deconfinement, the National Task Force for the Fight against Fraud and Scams proposed a guide to resume activities while protecting against scams. The COVID-19 outbreak was accompanied by an upsurge in fraud and scams, especially online. The ACPR has been active within the National Task Force for the Fight against Fraud and Scams involving government offices and supervisory authorities.

July 2021: The ACPR encouraged insurance companies to improve their cyber risk management, in a context of growing IT risk. The financial sector remains the sector most targeted by cyberattacks.

2.12.4. Option to defer payments of bonuses and profit-sharing to employees

March 2020: The French Government extended the deadline for companies to pay bonuses and profit-sharing to their employees from 1 June to 31 December 2020.[88] Employers only had to inform employee representative bodies if they wished to take advantage of this flexibility. Employees can decide to receive the money directly or to save it into a company savings plan, including an occupational pension plan (*plan d'épargne retraite collectif*).[89] Therefore, postponing the payment of bonuses and profits can have an impact on contributions to occupational pension plans.

2.12.5. Easier early access to retirement savings for the self-employed

July 2020: Following the COVID-19 outbreak, France allowed the self-employed to withdraw assets from their retirement savings plan (*Madelin* contracts, PER for individuals).[90] Self-employed workers could withdraw up to EUR 8 000 from their *Madelin* contract or their PER until the end of 2020, if they had opened it before 10 June 2020. Withdrawals were tax-exempt up to EUR 2 000.

2.13. Germany

2.13.1. Leniency regarding the investment ceiling in real estate for Pensionskassen

March 2020: To avoid the necessity of emergency sales under supervisory law in order to ensure compliance with the proportion of real estate and to safeguard the stability of the financial market, the Federal Financial Supervisory Authority (BaFin) announced that it would not raise any objections if Pensionskassen temporarily and passively exceeded the limit on investments in real estate under section 3 (5) of the German Regulation on the Investment of Guarantee Assets of Pensionskassen, Funeral Expenses Funds and Small Insurance Undertakings (Anlage des Sicherungsvermögens von Pensionskassen, Sterbekassen und kleinen Versicherungsunternehmen – AnlV). However, Pensionskassen were not allowed to make new investments in real estate if they exceed the 25% limit under section 3 (5) of the AnlV.

The flexibility for the investment in real estate for *Pensionskassen* remained until August 2021.

2.13.2. Extension of deadline to submit recovery plans for underfunded Pensionsfonds

April 2020: BaFin provided employers more time to address underfunding of *Pensionsfonds* as a result of the COVID-19 crisis. According to the German Insurance Supervision Act, employers usually have up to ten years to eliminate the funding shortfall when the guarantee assets of *Pensionfonds* are underfunded up to 10%. If the funding shortfall is larger than 10%, employers have to restore a 90% coverage without delay. In the case of an underfunding up to 10%, employers are normally required to submit a recovery plan within three months from the beginning of a funding shortfall, at the latest. Given the outbreak, BaFin accepted recovery plans to be submitted by 1 October 2020 at the latest. Additionally, employers did not have to make initial payments in 2020 and could start in 2021. Employers were also allowed to defer any other payments owed to limit the underfunding to 10% of technical provisions to 2021 if the employer declared to the *Pensionsfonds* that no capital-reducing measures in the form of profit distributions or share buy-backs would be taken. Underfunding exceeding 10% had to be reduced to 10% before the first instalment of a plan for re-establishing cover is paid.

2.13.3. Flexibility in supervisory requirements

March 2020 (updated in March 2021): BaFin provided flexibility with respect to the submission of the registers of guarantee assets that are requested under Section 126 of the Insurance Supervision Act (VAG). The deadline of 31 March 2020 was suspended. *Pensionsfonds* and *Pensionskassen* subject to VAG had to submit the registers in paper form by 30 June 2020.

The flexibility was also provided for 2021. *Pensionsfonds* and *Pensionskassen* had to submit the registers in paper form by 30 June 2021 (instead of 31 March 2021).

Some flexibility was also provided with respect to the reporting for EIOPA and the ECB.

2.13.4. Flexibility with respect to the declaration of principles of investment policy for IORPs

April 2020: IORPs must usually submit and publish the declaration of principles of their investment policy to the supervisory authority no later than four months after the end of a financial year. On 24 April 2020, BaFin published an interpretative decision to the declaration on the principles of the investment policy.[91] Due to the publication date of the interpretative decision and the pandemic, BaFin did not object if IORPs could not take the interpretation decision into account in their declaration on the principles of investment policy in 2020.

2.13.5. Advice to exercise caution when trading in shares

March 2020: BaFin advised investors on its website to carefully check whether the information on the COVID-19 pandemic contained in market letters and other promotional publications was accurate before trading in shares.[92]

2.14. Greece

2.14.1. Advice to insurers to withhold dividend payments

April 2020: The Bank of Greece advised insurance undertakings to withhold paying dividends to shareholders in line with the relevant statement from the European Insurance and Occupational Pensions Authority (EIOPA).

2.14.2. Recommendations to IORPs

May 2020: The Greek Competent Authorities issued general recommendations to IORPs on 20 May 2020 to mitigate the impact of COVID-19 on the occupational pensions sector.

2.14.3. Flexibility in the reporting for insurers

March 2020: The Bank of Greece exhibited flexibility regarding the reporting deadlines for insurance undertakings. In this respect, the Bank of Greece follows the recommendations from EIOPA that has extended the deadlines for insurance companies to comply with Solvency II reporting requirements.

2.14.4. Payment of contributions in Mandatory Occupational Insurance Funds

March 2020 onwards: A list of employers affected by the COVID-19 crisis were given the possibility to pay the contributions for February, March and April 2020 until 31 December 2021.

The contributions for the employees with mandatory suspension of employment contracts were covered by the state budget during 2020 and 2021.

The contributions for the employees, for the period of time when the employer joined the employment support scheme "SYN-ERGASIA" and the employee did not work due to the reduction of working hours, were paid by the state. The scheme SYN-ERGASIA was established in order to moderate the impact of COVID-19 on employment.

Intensification of supervision

April/May 2020: The national supervisory authorities intensified their monitoring through extra and special periodic reports in areas such as the status of collection of contributions, the liquidity of the occupational pension funds and the evolution of their assets value.

2.15. Hungary

2.15.1. Communication with supervised entities and plan members

March 2020: The Central Bank of Hungary (MNB) issued an Executive Circular (Executive Circular 8) that specified the risk mitigation measures pension funds were expected to take during the COVID-19 outbreak. This Executive Circular 8 was issued on 25 March 2020.[93] In particular, the MNB expected the funds to:

- monitor their processes on a daily basis, with a special focus on the development of the reserves for provisions, and in case it may happen, report any anomaly to the MNB via the fund's supervisor
- pay special attention to the assets in their portfolio, with a special respect to the exchange rates that had become more volatile as a result of the virus
- ensure daily business continuity and update their BCPs based on the current situation
- keep the fund members and service providers informed by providing them with the most up-to-date information about the significant changes in the running of business and communications
- take steps to ensure that services of the fund and communication can be available without keeping personal contact
- pay special attention to risk management
- take all reasonable measures to protect the employees.

In relation to the circular, the MNB sent a questionnaire containing 48 questions. Institutions were required to complete it on a daily or weekly basis, depending on the size of the fund. The questions aimed to assess the operational and liquidity situation of the institutions.

The MNB also proposed to remind pension fund members that it is not necessarily in their best interest to take their pension savings out of pension funds during the financial market downturn.

The MNB intended to pursue more intensive communication with its supervised entities within the framework of off-site supervision.

The MNB constantly assisted the institutions with legal interpretation and proposals to facilitate their operations.

The MNB also extended deadlines for meeting reporting requirements, in order to provide some flexibility to the entities it supervises. The deadlines were extended by one week for the information regarding the first quarter of 2020 and by four weeks for the information regarding annual reporting with reference to the year-end 2019.

The MNB also required extraordinary data in order to monitor the effects of COVID-19 on pension funds closely. The purpose of the extraordinary reporting was to monitor the payments to members (outflows) from pension funds continuously.

2.15.2. Adjustment of rules and practices

April 2020: The Hungarian Government issued regulations stipulating how to ensure the operating conditions of institutions in the situation caused by COVID-19 (Government Decree 102/2020 (IV.10)). These regulations contained rules applicable during the emergency situation, which apply, inter alia, to pension funds. Among other things, the provisions regulated the validity of mandates of members of the board of directors and the supervisory board and auditors; the way of holding general meetings, the possibilities of approving the annual report; and the borrowing conditions of funds within the monetary policy toolkit.

2.16. Iceland

2.16.1. Payment of pension contributions for workers in quarantine

March 2020: The Directorate of Labour paid the wages and the pension contributions of employees in quarantine under the Wages in Quarantine Act.[94] This Act applied from 1 February 2020 to 30 April 2020. Employers and employees could benefit from this measure only if employees could not perform their work while they were in quarantine. Employers were supposed to pay the salary of their employees and got reimbursed by the Directorate of Labour up to a certain amount. Wage payments could not exceed ISK 633 000 per month (or ISK 21 100 per day) per employee in quarantine. The Directorate of Labour paid both the mandatory 4% employee contributions and the 11.5% employer contributions to the pension fund the employee belongs to.

Second half of 2020: While this support for employees in quarantine was supposed to end initially during 2020, it was extended until 31 December 2021.[95] Applications for payments had to be submitted to the Directorate of Labour by 1 April 2022. Employers applying for the subsidy could get up to ISK 21 100 for each day an employee did not work (because s/he was in quarantine or had a child in quarantine).[96] The Directorate of Labour paid directly the part of the employers' contributions (i.e. 11.5% of the subsidy) to the appropriate pension fund. To cover the employee's share, 4% of the subsidies that was paid has to be transferred to the appropriate pension fund.

2.16.2. Payment of pension contributions for workers on reduced hours

March 2020: The Icelandic government also provided support to employees when their employers requested them to work fewer hours. Employees were initially entitled to payments from the Directorate of Labour when their working hours were reduced by 20% but were still over or equal to 25% of a full-time job. The Directorate of Labour validated the application from the day employees began to work reduced hours or from 15 March 2020 at the earliest.[97] The Directorate of Labour then paid partial unemployment benefits and an 11.5% matching pension contribution.[98] The combination of the wages from the employer and partial unemployment benefits could neither exceed ISK 700 000 per month nor 90% of the average total wages of the employee. Wages lower than ISK 400 000 per month (for a full-time job) were not reduced. This measure was temporary and was initially supposed to be in force until 1 June 2020.

Second half of 2020: The Icelandic government extended the support measure for employees working fewer hours until 31 December 2020, with some changes in the conditions. Employees had to be working at least 50% of a full-time job (instead of 25%) to be eligible from 1 July 2020. Partial unemployment benefits from the Directorate of Labour could not exceed ISK 342 303 per employee either.

First half of 2021: Partial (or full) unemployment benefits were further extended until 31 May 2021.[99] However, between 1 July 2020 and until 31 May 2021, employees had to have faced a minimum of 20% reduction in working hours while working at least 50% of a full-time job.[100] The amount of unemployment benefits could not exceed ISK 228 202 for people with a 50% reduction in working hours, ISK 114 050 for people with a 25% reduction, and ISK 91 280 for people with a 20% reduction. The combination of unemployment benefits and salary could not exceed 90% of the average income of the employee in the last three months, nor be greater than ISK 700 000, nor be higher than 100% of the average income in the last three months for a full time job with an average income of ISK 400 000 or less. An 11.5% top-up of this subsidy was sent to the appropriate pension fund.[101]

2.16.3. Change in investment regulations

March 2020: In consultation with the Central Bank of Iceland, pension funds stopped purchasing foreign currency from 17 March 2020 for three months.[102]

June 2020: The pause in pension funds' foreign currency purchases was extended for another three months until 17 September 2020.

May 2020: Icelandic authorities have also allowed pension funds to own up to 35% of the units or shares of venture capital funds (instead of 20% before) as long as these investments do not exceed 1% of pension fund assets. This authorisation is valid until 1 January 2025.[103]

This policy aims at supporting the Icelandic financial system and its stability, as well as the economy.

2.16.4. Advice to the pensions industry and flexibility on reporting requirements

April 2020: The Central Bank of Iceland issued a circular in April 2020 to give advice to the pensions industry.[104] The circular touches upon the continuity of operations of pension providers, operational risks, and liquidity among other things. The Central Bank of Iceland also provided some flexibility to its supervised entities on deadlines for submission of reports.[105]

2.16.5. Access to personal private pension savings

March 2020: The Icelandic government granted access to personal private pension savings as part of a response package to the COVID-19 crisis.[106] Plan members were allowed to withdraw up to ISK 12 million from their voluntary personal pension savings. If they wished to withdraw this maximum amount, they received it over a 15-month period. If they withdrew less, the pay-out period was shortened proportionally. Each monthly payment could go up to ISK 800 000 and was taxed as regular income. Pension providers directly withheld the income tax from the payments to plan members. Plan members who wanted to benefit from this measure had to submit an application to their pension provider and could apply until 1 January 2021.

Second half of 2020: Access to personal private savings was extended for 2021.[107]

May 2021: Members have been allowed to apply for access to personal private savings until 1 January 2022.

ISK 23 billion have been withdrawn during 2020.[108] According to data from the Central Bank of Iceland, as of September 2021, ISK 32.9 billion had been withdrawn.

If third-pillar pension savings withdrawals are large enough in scale that it becomes impossible to ensure equal treatment among pension fund members, custodians are authorised to delay the payments, provided that they satisfy certain conditions and obtain prior approval from FSA Iceland.[109]

2.17. Ireland

2.17.1. Flexibility regarding the compliance of pension trustees with their obligations

March 2020: The Pensions Authority does not have the power to waive obligations set out in pensions legislation, thus there has been no change in statutory obligations for supervised entities. However, in acknowledging the significant challenges faced by pension schemes, the Pensions Authority took into account the circumstances when assessing compliance with legislative requirements, including compliance with disclosure and member communication obligations.[110] In its public announcements, the Pensions Authority outlined its expectations that supervised entities would engage with relevant stakeholders, communicate major issues, get appropriate professional advice and be proactive and consumer focused. The Pensions Authority issued guidance on a number of issues raised by the industry, including communications with members, employers and service providers, investment decisions and, in particular, pension scheme contributions.

2.17.2. Guidance in relation to the possible temporary cessation of employer contributions to pension schemes

April 2020: The Pensions Authority advised trustees of both DB and DC schemes that the following matters should be considered by employers/trustees in consultation with their advisers:[111]

- scheme rules, in particular in relation to contribution cessation or reduction and notice periods
- provisions of employment contracts relating to pensions

- the obligation under section 58A of the Pensions Act to make any employer defined contribution payment due
- possible impact on death in service benefits
- possible impact on insured DC schemes if regular contributions cease
- engagement with/communications to affected employees.

In addition, the Pensions Authority outlined a number of matters that should be taken into account specifically by DB schemes, including:

- the effect of any suspension on the ability of the scheme to meet its benefit obligations
- the contributions required under a funding proposal
- whether ongoing contributions are necessary to meet current pension payments
- whether a suspension of contributions would unfairly affect a particular class of members.

2.17.3. Supervisory activity related to the COVID-19 pandemic

May 2020: The Pensions Authority started a programme of direct engagement with key regulated entities to discuss the impact of the current conditions on their ability to provide services to pension schemes.[112] This engagement aimed at focusing on areas such as:

- impact on core business and business continuity
- interaction with scheme stakeholders, i.e. trustees, employers, investment managers etc.
- queries and complaints from members
- receipt and investment of contributions
- notable trends amongst scheme members, e.g. fund switches, request for transfers etc.

2.18. Israel

2.18.1. Instructions to financial institutions and adjustment to supervisory practices and requirements

First half of 2020: The Ministry of Finance gave several instructions to financial institutions. Financial institutions were urged to focus and maintain their activities and provision of services to clients, in particular regular annuity payments, cash redemption and claim settlement. The Ministry of Finance also requested financial institutions to expand services that could be provided through digital tools.

The Ministry of Finance put resources in the close monitoring of the activities of institutional bodies and their ability to continue to work during times of crisis.

Supervisory requirements have been adjusted to take into account the COVID-19 context. For example, there was a temporary exemption from the requirement of a physical meeting of the Board of Directors and its committees once a quarter.

2.18.2. Change in investment regulations

First half of 2020: Israeli authorities amended some investment regulations applying to institutional investors in response to the COVID-19 outbreak. Institutional investors have been allowed to hold up to 49% of a single corporate bond series (instead of 25%). Institutional investors can also hold 7.5% of the means of control of other investors (instead of 5%).

2.18.3. Warnings to savers

March 2020: The Capital Market, Insurance and Savings Authority (CMISA) warned the public about misinformation on the selected default pension providers.[113] Rumours and statements pretended that these default providers lacked insurance coverage in case of pandemics. The CMISA clarified that this information was incorrect and that pandemics were not excluded from insurance coverage for these providers.

The CMISA also warned savers against attempts to provide false financial advice.[114] The CMISA identified attempts to impersonate and publish false financial advice to cause panic and persuade individuals to quickly withdraw funds and liquid their savings. The CMISA warned the public about imposters who provide general or individual advice regarding savings, including pension savings, that are not licensed and do not conduct the required examination of individuals' needs.

2.18.4. Easier access to retirement savings

October 2020: The Ministry of Finance allowed the self-employed to withdraw up to one-third of their savings from their mandatory pension plans.[115] It became mandatory for the self-employed to contribute to a pension plan in 2017. The 2017 law specified that two-thirds of the contributions would be set aside for retirement while one-third could be used in case of unemployment. However, in practice, the regulation that was supposed to let the self-employed actually withdraw a part of their savings because of unemployment had not been implemented yet. This changed as a result of the COVID-19 outbreak.

2.18.5. Loans against retirement savings

March 2020: Institutional bodies could provide loans to members against existing savings. The repayment could be spread in instalments over a longer period (15 years instead of 7). Individuals could also use their pension annuity as a collateral for a loan.

2.18.6. Cap on fees for members who stopped contributing due to COVID-19

September 2020: A directive stipulated that an institutional body would not be entitled to raise the rate of management fees for savers for which pension savings contributions stopped for a period of 12 months from the date of cessation of contribution, instead of six months in the existing directive. This applied to employees for whom the pension savings contributions were discontinued from 1 March 2020 until 31 October 2020.

March 2021: In order to safeguard the rights of savers when dealing with the consequences of the COVID-19 crisis, the supervisor of CMISA called on the institutional bodies to continue to act in solidarity with savers who stopped paying pension contributions and to set a management fee cap for these savers up to the average management fees charged by the body from all savers.[116] All institutional bodies, without exception, responded positively to the commissioner's request and replied that they would join the authority's initiative to maintain solidarity with savers in times of crisis.

2.19. Italy

2.19.1. Adjustment in supervisory activities and practices

March 2020: The Supervisory Commission of Italian Pension Funds (COVIP) extended several reporting deadlines of the institutions it supervises.[117] For example, COVIP postponed the submission of the 2019 financial statements of open pension funds from 31 March 2020 to 30 June 2020.[118]

COVIP also postponed the date it expected the usual payment of the supervisory commission from pension funds from 15 May to 15 September 2020.[119]

To ensure business continuity, COVIP also provided guidance to Italian pension funds for easing remote participation to Board meetings and the use of digital channels for exchanging information with financial managers, service providers and members.[120]

2.20. Japan

2.20.1. Flexibility with respect to the submission of reporting requirements

First half of 2020: The Ministry of Health, Labour and Welfare (MHLW) stated that it was ready to refrain from taking regulatory action if pension providers did not submit reporting requirements on time.

2.20.2. Adjustment of rules and practices

First half of 2020: The MHLW provided advice on how institutions could continue to operate in the context of the COVID-19 outbreak. For example, boards were allowed to hold meeting in other ways than physical meetings.

2.20.3. Flexibility regarding contributions to defined benefit plans

First half of 2021: The MHLW allowed some flexibility regarding contributions to defined benefit (DB) plans. DB funds could postpone raising their contributions for one year from April 2021 to March 2022 if the employer could not afford to pay the contribution rise following the actuarial valuation of the DB plans. This measure intended to provide some relief to employers during the COVID-19 pandemic.

2.21. Korea

2.21.1. Temporary easing of financial regulations

April 2020: The financial authorities announced on 17 April 2020 a set of temporary deregulatory measures on financial institutions' capital adequacy, liquidity and asset quality requirements to help boost their financing capacity amid the COVID-19 crisis.[121]

Financial regulators also provided exemptions from sanctions. For example, no penalties or administrative sanctions applied for failing to meet disclosure or business report deadlines.

August 2020: The Financial Services Commission (FSC) announced its decision to extend some of the interim deregulatory measures introduced on 17 April in order to continue to support the financial sector amid a protracted pandemic situation.[122]

September 2021: The FSC decided to extend the period on some of the pandemic response deregulatory measures.[123]

2.22. Latvia

2.22.1. Option for members of the state funded pension scheme to postpone the pay-out choice

April 2020: The Minister of Welfare provided members of the state funded pension scheme with the option of delaying their pension pay-out choice. At retirement, individuals usually have two options. They can either use the assets in their funded pension scheme to purchase a life annuity from a life insurance company, or add these assets to their notional DC account to get a public pension based on their notional and financial capital. As a response to the COVID-19 crisis, people who were reaching retirement were given the right to postpone their choice until 30 November 2021. If they did not make a choice, assets in their funded pension scheme will be transferred to their notional account from 1 January 2022 and they will receive a public pension.

2.22.2. Flexibility in the supervision of financial market participants

March 2020: The Financial and Capital Market Commission (FCMC) announced it would take a flexible and individual approach in its supervision of financial market participants.[124]

2.22.3. Call for caution with respect to dividend payments

December 2020: In line with the recommendations from European authorities, the FCMC called credit institutions and insurance companies to refrain paying dividend or be cautious when doing so until 30 September 2021.[125]

The objective of this recommendation is to ensure that institutions maintain a sufficient level of capital to be able to withstand potential losses in the future.

2.23. Lithuania

2.23.1. Adjustments in supervisory activities

April 2020: The Bank of Lithuania, which, among other financial market participants, supervises pension funds, adjusted some of its supervisory activities following the COVID-19 outbreak. For example, the Bank of Lithuania postponed the planned inspections of pension funds until the situation regarding the coronavirus became clearer.[126] It also informed the pension accumulation companies about the flexible approach it would take regarding compliance with the reporting deadlines. The Bank of Lithuania intensified communication with companies in order to find out possible threats and risks to pension fund participants.

2.23.2. Advice to plan members to keep calm

March 2020: The Bank of Lithuania recommended individuals with assets in pension funds to resist to the temptation to reduce investment risk and transfer their assets to lower-risk funds.[127] It provided a Q&A page for individuals to better understand why asset values vary and why it is important to keep paying contributions and not reduce investment risk when markets fall.

2.24. Luxembourg

2.24.1. Suspension of dividend payments

July 2020: The Insurance Commission of Luxembourg (CAA) advised insurance companies to withhold paying dividends and refrain from share buy-backs from 1 August 2020 until 1 January 2021.[128]

January 2021: The CAA published a Circular Letter in January 2021, extending the restrictions applicable to insurance companies on making dividend payments and other distributions until 30 September 2021.[129]

The CAA authorised the dividend payments and other distributions under exceptional circumstances. Companies had to take extreme care in the decision to make the payments, and these payments should not have led to a violation of the approved risk tolerance limits relating to the own risk and solvency assessment of the company. Insurance companies meeting these conditions had to notify the CAA, provide a description of the impact of the payments on the solvency and liquidity of the company, and update the stress tests.

If insurance companies wanted to make dividend and distribution payments even if they did not meet the conditions for exceptional payments, they had to request for a derogation to the CAA at least 30 days in advance and explain the rationale of these payments.

2.24.2. Flexibility with respect to reporting deadlines

March 2020: National authorities in Luxembourg provided pension providers with some flexibility to meet their reporting requirements. The Luxembourg Financial Supervisory Authority (CSSF) announced it would not use its enforcing powers over supervised entities that experienced a delay in meeting their reporting requirements if they duly explained the reasons for this delay.[130] Pension funds under the supervision of the CSSF could submit their quarterly reporting until 20 July 2020 (instead of 20 days after the end of the quarter) and their actuarial report until 30 September 2020 (instead of end-June).[131] They simply had to inform the CSSF by email if they needed this extra time to fulfil their reporting duties. Likewise, the CAA extended some of its reporting deadlines that pension funds under its supervision had to meet (e.g. quarterly IORP 2 reporting).[132]

2.24.3. Use of cloud-based tools and solutions

March 2020: As part of the adaptation of their working environment in response to the COVID-19 situation, supervised entities may opt for cloud-based tools and solutions (e.g. collaborative tools, virtual desktop infrastructure, etc.). To facilitate a rapid implementation of these solutions, prior authorisation by, or notification to, the CSSF is not required as long as this exceptional situation lasts. A simple communication by email to the CSSF's contact agent of the concerned entity is considered sufficient.[133] This is without prejudice to the entity's obligation to carry out appropriate due diligence and risk assessment of such cloud outsourcing.

2.24.4. Warning about scams

April 2020: The CAA issued warnings about scams on its website.[134] It published on its website the name of former insurance companies that scammers may be using to rip people off.

2.25. Mexico

2.25.1. Adjustments of practices

March 2020: The Mexican Pension Fund Supervisory Authority (CONSAR) announced several measures that pension fund administrators (AFOREs) had to follow.[135] CONSAR listed the operations that had to be maintained at all times, such as the receipt and remittance of contributions to individual accounts.

Some operations could be adjusted to take into account the COVID-19 context. For instance, the ordinary or extraordinary sessions of the Investment and Risk Committees of the Administrators could be held remotely.

CONSAR suspended on-site inspections.

2.25.2. Settlement of the procedure for partial unemployment withdrawals in a single appointment

March 2020: CONSAR requested the procedure of partial savings withdrawals from pension plans due to unemployment to be settled in a single appointment.[136] The Mexican pension system allows people to make partial withdrawals of their assets in individual accounts in the case of unemployment. People are entitled to these partial withdrawals when they have been unemployed for at least 46 days and have not already used this possibility within the last five years. Given the COVID-19 outbreak, CONSAR expected eligible individuals requesting access to their savings to receive the amount in a one-off payment.

This measure was put in place for precautionary health reasons. It intended to avoid people going multiple times in the same premises to request early withdrawals of their assets.

However, CONSAR encouraged people to keep assets in their plans and refrain from making early withdrawals during the outbreak to avoid materialising the investment losses on financial markets.[137]

2.25.3. Simplified reporting

March 2020: CONSAR allowed private pension fund administrators (AFORES) to send simplified reports instead of the regular ones if they requested so.[138] However, CONSAR expected the AFORES to submit their reports within the usual timeframe and deadlines through the Electronic Information System.

2.26. Netherlands

2.26.1. Payment of pension contributions by the state for workers of eligible companies

March 2020: The Dutch government announced that it would pay the salary and cover pension contributions for the workers of eligible companies during the outbreak for three months initially.[139] This policy response was part of the temporary emergency measure for the preservation of jobs (NOW) scheme. The government intended to pay the wages of employees between March and May 2020, up to 90% of the wage bill of the company depending on its loss of revenue. The government added a 30% top-up to this compensation amount to cover employer and employee pension contributions and other payroll charges.[140] The Employee Insurance Agency was in charge of making these payments to companies.

To be eligible for this help, companies needed to meet certain criteria. This help was available to companies expecting to lose 20% or more of their revenue compared to their quarterly average revenue in 2019. To be eligible for this help, companies could not fire any employee for economic reasons either.[141]

June 2020: This measure was extended a first time by four additional months (NOW 2).[142] The government top-up covering pension contributions and other payroll charges increased from 30% to 40% of the compensation amount for this new period (June-September 2020).

August 2020: The government extended this measure again by three more periods of three months, starting from 1 October 2020 (NOW 3).[143] The eligibility condition remained the same as before (at least 20% loss of revenue) for the period October-December 2020 (NOW 3.1). However, eligible employers only received up to 80% of their wage bill (instead of 90%). The government was planning to reduce the compensation amount to 70% of the wage bill for the period January-March 2021 (NOW 3.2), and to 60% for April-June 2021 (NOW 3.3). The subsidy was also supposed to be only available to companies experiencing a 30% loss of revenue at least from January 2021. The gradual reduction of the subsidy was expected to give time to employers to adapt to changing circumstances.[144]

December 2020: The government decided in December 2020 not to change the subsidy and conditions for the period January-March 2021.[145] The top-up to cover pension contributions and other payroll charges remained the same, at 40% of the compensation amount for the whole period (from October 2020 to June 2021).

January 2021: NOW grants, which enabled employers to continue paying their employees' salaries, were increased from 80% to 85% of the wage bill.[146] The amount by which the wage bill could be reduced without affecting the grant amount – the wage bill exemption – remained at 10%.[147] NOW grants for January, February and March 2021 could be applied for from 15 February 2021.

May 2021: The government extended the support package for jobs and the economy into the third quarter of 2021.[148] The government intended to discontinue the generic support measures, with effect from 1 October 2021.[149] However, due to rising COVID-19 cases and additional containment measures, the package continued through Q4 2021 and Q1 2022.[150]

2.26.2. Adjustments in supervisory activities

April 2020: The Dutch Central Bank (DNB), which supervises pension funds, adjusted and relaxed some of its supervisory rules.[151] The DNB postponed the deadlines of the annual reporting of pension funds by three months. Pension funds could submit their annual reports by 30 September 2020. The DNB was also ready to give more time to pension funds to submit their monthly and quarterly reports if they requested so.

The DNB allowed pension funds to deviate from their strategic investment policies temporarily. However, this deviation should be the result of a well-considered decision-making process.

The DNB also adapted its supervisory activities and turned its attention to ongoing specific risks for the pension sector, such as business continuity management, cyber risks, or the fall of the funding ratio resulting from developments in financial markets.

2.26.3. Extension of the cut in the minimum required funding ratio

September 2020: At the end of 2019, the Social Affairs Minister granted underfunded pension funds a temporary one-year reprieve from implementing cuts of pension rights and benefits, lowering the minimum required funding to 90% for 2020. In light of the macroeconomic situation, he extended this reprieve to 2021.[152]

2.27. New Zealand

2.27.1. Financial guidance service through a website

March 2020: The Commission for Financial Capabilities is providing financial guidance to people in New Zealand through its 'Sorted' website at: https://sorted.org.nz/. This website can help people manage their money and plan for retirement.

This website included a page advising people on how to manage assets in their KiwiSaver plans during the COVID-19 outbreak.[153] The page explains the consequences of withdrawing assets from the plans or changing investment strategies.

April 2020: The 'Sorted' website also included a page warning people about scams related to COVID-19.[154] The page gives the methods that scammers use, such as: phishing emails, offer of a coronavirus map app to download malicious softwares, investment offers in 'safe havens', phone calls. It gives tips to help people avoid traps.

August 2021: Additional guidance was provided on the 'Sorted' website to assist people to manage their money during the COVID-19 crisis.[155] In particular, this page recommends people to consider carefully before withdrawing funds from their KiwiSaver plan. The same warning was made on the website of the Financial Markets Authority.[156]

This website is a tool to provide clear and simple information. It intends to help plan members to make informed decisions on the management of their retirement savings and to avoid scams.

2.27.2. Employment subsidies

March 2020: Against the backdrop of the COVID-19 crisis, the Ministry of Social Development (MSD) provided subsidies for salaries and wages to eligible employers upon application, which also covered employee pension contributions. Employers who were entitled to a subsidy and received it had to pass it onto employees by paying them their regular wages. Employers had to deduct employee contributions to KiwiSaver accounts from wages and transfer these contributions to the Inland Revenue, in charge of channelling them to the pension provider of employees.

New Zealand designed and introduced two main types of subsidies that employers could be eligible to receive during the outbreak:

- a COVID-19 Wage Subsidy to support companies who faced laying off or reducing hours of their employees because of the outbreak[157]
- a COVID-19 Leave Support Scheme to help companies to pay employees who could not come to work because of social distancing measures and who could not work from home.[158]

Both subsidies have been paid at the same flat rate. The rate was initially NZD 585.80 for people working 20 hours or more per week (full-time rate), and NZD 350 for people working less than 20 hours (part-time rate). Since 24 August 2021, the rate is NZD 600 a week for each full-time worker and NZD 359 for part-time workers, for the COVID-19 Leave Support Scheme. The COVID-19 Wage Subsidy uses that rate since its August 2021 extension.

Employers have been expected to pay employees their usual wages – from which employee contributions are deducted – with the subsidy and satisfy all additional features of the employee's remuneration package, including employer contributions to their pension plan. However, the subsidy may be less than the usual wage of the employee. In that case, employers must undertake best endeavours to pay the employee at least 80% of their usual wage or at the very least the payment rate. If an employee's usual wage is less than the subsidy, they should be paid their usual wages, with the employer expected to use the difference for the wages of other affected staff. The subsidy is still subject to standard KiwiSaver contributions.[159]

Several changes were made to both subsidies, as explained below.

COVID-19 Wage Subsidy

March 2020: The 2020 COVID-19 Wage Subsidy was available to employers in New Zealand under certain conditions. To be eligible for this subsidy, the company initially needed to comply with all the following requirements: i) being registered and operating in New Zealand with employees legally working in New Zealand; ii) experiencing at least a 30% decline in actual or predicted revenue over a month from January 2020 compared to the same period in 2019; iii) taking active steps to mitigate the impact of COVID-19; and iv) retaining the employees for which a subsidy is requested for during the period of the subsidy. Employers could apply to this Wage Subsidy until 10 June 2020.

The Wage subsidy was paid for 12 weeks. An employer receiving this subsidy could not request it a second time for the same employee.

June 2020: A Wage Subsidy Extension was available from 10 June to 1 September 2020 to support employers (including the self-employed) who were still significantly impacted by COVID-19.[160] One of the eligibility criteria changed as employers had to experience (or expect) a minimum of 40% decline in revenue because of COVID-19 (instead of 30% before) over a period of 30 continuous days (after 10 May 2020 and in the 40 days before application to the subsidy) compared to the closest period in 2019.

The Wage Subsidy Extension helped employers to pay 8 weeks of wages for their employees.

August 2020: New Zealand then introduced a Resurgence Wage Subsidy, available between 21 August and 3 September 2020 for employers who were not getting a wage subsidy.[161] Employers had to experience (or expect) a revenue drop of at least 40% (due to COVID-19) for a 14-day period between 12 August and 10 September 2020, compared to a similar period in 2019.

The Resurgence Wage Subsidy was a 2-week payment.

March 2021: The Wage Subsidy March 2021 was intended to help employers keep their staff and protect jobs that were impacted by the changes in alert level on 28 February 2021.[162] This subsidy was a 2-week lump sum available from 4 March 2021 to 21 March 2021. Employers had to have or expect to have a 40% decline in revenue over 14 days in a row between 28 February and 21 March 2021 compared to a typical 14-day period between 4 January and 14 February 2021 to be eligible for the subsidy. Employers with highly seasonal revenue could compare their decline in revenue to the same 14-day period in 2019 or 2020. The decline of the revenue must also be related to the rise to the alert level on 28 February 2021. Employers also had to keep the employees for which they requested the subsidy, and pay at least 80% of their salary or the rate of the subsidy.

August 2021: The Wage Subsidy August 2021 was a payment to support employers, so they can continue to pay employees and protect jobs for businesses affected by the move to Alert Level 4 on 17 August 2021. The payment was a lump sum covering a 2-week period for employers who had or predicted to have a decline in revenue of at least 40% over the period between 17 August and 30 August 2021 compared to a typical 14-day consecutive period of revenue in the six weeks immediately before the move to Alert Level 4 on 17 August 2021. The Wage Subsidy Scheme will be available to all businesses while any part of the country is in Alert Levels 3 or 4.

COVID-19 Leave Support Scheme

March 2020: The government established the COVID-19 Essential Workers Leave Support Scheme, earmarked for workers in essential businesses.[163] The Health Act defines essential businesses as companies that are essential to the provision of the necessities of life, as well as companies that support the former. All these companies operate in the following sectors mainly: food, health care, energy, waste-removal, internet and financial support. Essential companies could request this type of subsidy for their employees who could not come to work and could not work from home.[164]

The Essential Worker Leave Support was for 4 weeks, but employers could apply to get this subsidy again for the same employee.

May 2020: The eligibility conditions to get a leave support changed. The Essential Worker Leave Support Scheme was extended to all employers (including the self-employed) from 1 May 2020 and was renamed the Leave Support Scheme. The requirement for a company to be financially impacted by COVID-19 was removed at 1 pm on 21 August 2020.

September 2020: The government introduced new changes in September, by expanding the eligibility to workers who were told to self-isolate by a doctor or health official and could not work from home.[165] Employers could also request this subsidy for parents and caregivers who could not go to work because they were taking care of a self-isolated dependent. This latest change was effective from midday 28 September 2020.

The Leave Support Scheme was paid as a lump sum and covered 4 weeks per employee before 28 September 2020, and 2 weeks afterwards. Employers can re-apply to the Leave Support Scheme for the same employee if the eligibility criteria are still met. This scheme is still running.

COVID-19 Short-Term Absence Payment

February 2021: New Zealand also has a COVID-19 Short-term Absence Payment for employers to pay their employees who cannot work from home while waiting for the result of their COVID-19 test.[166] The payment is a one-off lump sum of NZD 359 per eligible employee since 24 August 2021 (NZD 350 before).

COVID-19 Support Payment

February 2022: New Zealand introduced a new support payment for eligible businesses during the Omicron outbreak. Eligible businesses could receive payments of NZD 4 000 per business plus NZD 400 per full-time employee (FTE), capped at 50 FTEs or NZD 24 000.[167] Payments to employees would also include employee pension contributions.

2.27.3. Extension of the terms of KiwiSaver default providers

April 2020: New Zealand extended the terms of KiwiSaver default providers.[168] Individuals aged between 18 and 65 are randomly enrolled in a KiwiSaver default fund when they start working, unless they actively choose a fund or opt-out. The default providers are selected by the Minister of Finance and the Minister of Commerce and Consumer Affairs. The term of the nine default providers was originally supposed to expire on 30 June 2021, but was extended by five months to 30 November 2021.

The selection process of the default providers for a new term was delayed. The government released a request for proposals to appoint the next group of KiwiSaver default providers on 1 October 2020 (instead of during the first half of 2020 as initially planned). Since 1 December 2021, there are six default providers.

This deferral in the selection process of default providers aimed at allowing pension providers to focus their efforts on continuing to operate smoothly.

2.27.4. Easier KiwiSaver financial hardship applications in the context of lockdown

April 2020: KiwiSaver plan members wishing to access their savings under financial hardship circumstances have to complete a statutory declaration about their assets and liabilities in front of a witness authorised under the Oaths and Declarations Act 1957 and show that they have explored other options to get funding.

In light of the COVID-19 epidemic, a temporary law change was made to the requirements for witnessing declarations under the Oaths and Declarations Act. The change makes it clear that there is no requirement for a person witnessing a declaration to be in the physical presence of the person making it. The person witnessing the declaration is also not required to physically sign the same document as the person making it. Instead, oaths, affirmations or declarations can be administered using audio-visual or audio links, such over Skype, Zoom, Facetime, or over the phone.[169]

Taking into account this change, the Financial Markets Authority (FMA) of New Zealand has provided guidance to supervisors and pension providers for alternative steps to verify that plan members are entitled to financial hardship withdrawals.[170] In the lockdown context, the FMA recommends that lawyers witness the statutory declaration of the applicant by video. If this is not possible, the pension provider has to use the best alternative to verify the identity of the application in these exceptional circumstances. The applicant also has to provide evidence of his (or her) assets and liabilities to the provider and can as a last resort communicate this information over the phone if the provider agrees that there is no way to send this information by post or email.

However, the FMA has urged plan members to use hardship withdrawals as a last resort and try to use governmental assistance measures first.[171]

2.27.5. Flexibility in regulatory obligations

April 2020: The Financial Markets Authority (FMA) provided regulatory relief to market participants to give them an additional two months to comply with certain financial reporting and other obligations under the Financial Markets Conduct Act and Regulations, if their ability to produce financial statements was legitimately impacted by COVID-19.

The FMA also took a "no action" approach against a breach of a statutory or regulatory obligation.[172] This approach is aimed at allowing market participants to continue focusing on serving their customers' needs. The expectation remains that participants should be treating their customers fairly at all times and that where possible, breaches will be remediated at a later date, and as such the requirement to comply is being delayed rather than removed. Market participants are also expected to take steps to mitigate any risks resulting from the breach.

2.28. Norway

2.28.1. Possibility for temporary laid-off employees to remain members of occupational pension plans

April 2020: On 17 April 2020, it became possible for employers to decide whether temporarily laid-off employees could remain members of their pension plan.[173] This measure applied to employers whose pension arrangement did not already allow them to choose to keep temporary laid-off employees as members of their plan. Employers did not have to pay pension contributions, but employees retained insurance cover. Moreover, employers had to pay for the administration and management of the plan of their laid-off employees. This measure was initially planned to apply during six months.[174]

October 2020: This measure was extended on 9 October 2020 until 30 June 2021.[175]

June 2021: This measure was extended until 30 September 2021.[176]

September 2021: The government extended the duration of the temporary legislative changes that gave employers the opportunity to decide that laid-off employees could continue as members of the pension scheme until 31 October 2021.[177]

October 2021: This measure was further extended to 31 December 2021.[178]

2.28.2. Advice to withhold dividend payments

March 2020: The Norwegian Ministry of Finance recommended insurance companies to postpone decisions on dividend payments and other distributions of profits until the high uncertainty about the economic outlook was reduced.[179] The Ministry of Finance did not legislate on this aspect but expected insurance companies to follow the recommendation.

The Financial Supervisory Authority of Norway (Finanstilsynet) supported EIOPA's advice for a cautious and conservative approach to paying dividends. However, Finanstilsynet did not set a limit with respect to the proportion of dividends that could be distributed by insurance companies (unlike for Norwegian banks).[180] Profit distributions had to be assessed against the financial strength of the companies. Finanstilsynet had to be informed of the intention of insurance companies to pay dividends and could forbid it in case of insufficient financial strength.[181]

2.28.3. Postponement of reporting deadlines

March 2020: Finanstilsynet postponed the deadlines for the submission of annual reports.[182] The Financial Supervisory Authority has followed EIOPA's guidelines and extended deadlines for insurance companies to comply with Solvency II reporting requirements.[183]

2.29. Poland

2.29.1. Supervisory forbearance regarding investment restrictions

March 2020: The Polish Financial Supervision Authority (KNF) intended to take a case-by-case approach when pension companies exceeded investment limits. The KNF adapted its supervisory measures to the market situation.

2.29.2. Flexibility and adjustments in supervisory practices

March 2020: The KNF extended the reporting deadlines for open pension funds and employee pension funds. These pension funds had two more months than originally scheduled to return their annual financial reports.[184]

The KNF also postponed and adjusted some supervisory actions, such as on-site inspections, to allow supervised entities to focus on key processes and day-to-day operations. The KNF has been taking a pragmatic approach to some supervisory deadlines, such as the deadlines for the implementation of post-inspection recommendations, in relation to the initial deadlines.

The KNF adapted its communication process with its supervised entities in the context of the COVID-19 outbreak. It enables its supervised entities to use digital channels of communication only.

The KNF requested its supervised entities to follow suitable procedures to maintain business continuity during the COVID-19 outbreak.

2.29.3. Postponement of auto-enrolment in companies with 50+ employees

March 2020: Employers with 50 or more employees at the end of June 2019 were given six additional months to enrol automatically their employees into an Employee Capital Plan (PPK). These employers had until 27 October 2020 to sign a PPK management contract and until 10 November 2020 to sign a PPK operating contract.[185]

2.29.4. Pause in the payment of contributions to Employee Capital Plans during periods of economic downtime

In accordance with Article 25(4) of the PPK Act, employers fulfilling certain criteria can benefit from the exemption of contributions to a PPK.[186] According to this provision, which was particularly relevant during the COVID-19 crisis, employers may not finance PPK contributions in the following cases:

- introducing economic downtime or reduced working hours
- fulfilling the conditions for employer's insolvency
- during periods of temporary cessation or limitation of business activity as a result of flooding and lack of funds for the payment of salaries to employees.

The exemption from paying PPK contributions also applies to participants employed by these employers. However, they may continue paying their contributions by submitting a declaration to the employer.

2.29.5. Postponement of the pension reform

March 2021: A reform involving the transformation of open pension funds (OFE) into specialised open-end investment funds was postponed. Implementing the reform as originally scheduled (1 July 2020) could have been financially unfavourable for members of pension funds as well as for the state budget (due to stock exchange market turmoil). The new Act came into force on 1 June 2021. OFE participants had until 2 August 2021 to submit declarations regarding transferring their savings to the Social Insurance Institution (ZUS).[187] By default, their money was transferred to an Individual Retirement Pension Account (IKE).

2.30. Portugal

2.30.1. Financial consumer protection

April 2020: The Portuguese Insurance and Pension Funds Supervisory Authority (ASF) advised pension fund management entities to be flexible on the treatment of plan members and beneficiaries' needs, with a particular focus on the communication to members, beneficiaries and sponsors of pension funds.[188]

In this respect, when there was an intention to exercise the switching option (where applicable), pension fund management entities were expected to reinforce the need for prior contact with the sponsors or members, in order to promote their full understanding of the exceptional situation brought by COVID-19.

Pension fund management entities were also required to disclose their contingency plans on their websites, in order to inform members and beneficiaries of all the measures taken that could affect the contractual obligations that were established.

2.30.2. Advice to withhold dividend payments

April 2020: The ASF advised pension fund management entities, in its Circular Letter No 4/2020 of 2 April, to withhold dividend payments to their shareholders.[189]

August 2020: The ASF reiterated this advice in its Circular Letter No 10/2020 of 26 August.[190]

December 2020: The ASF issued a circular (Circular No 5/2020 of 23 December) providing guidance and recommendations to pension management companies with respect to dividend payments and other distributions.[191] Pension management companies should remain careful when distributing profits and strive to maintain or reinforce their capital. The ASF recommended pension providers to have a forward-looking approach when assessing their capital needs, based on scenarios on the evolution of the economy and financial markets. Pension management companies had to inform the ASF before distributing profits.

The ASF issued a similar recommendation for insurance companies (Circular No. 4/2020 of 21 December).[192]

2.30.3. Adjustment of supervisory practices

April 2020: In April 2020, the ASF suspended or cancelled scheduled supervisory on-site actions, in order to allow pension fund management entities to focus on their activities and to secure business continuity (Circular Letter No 4/2020 of 2 April).[193]

August 2020: The ASF announced in its Circular Letter No 10/2020 of 26 August 2020, that on-site inspections would resume from September.[194]

2.30.4. Extension of deadlines

April 2020: The ASF extended deadlines for reporting requirements. The ASF published a set of new deadlines (such as for accounting and financial information) in a Circular Letter to the industry in April 2020.[195]

August 2020: The ASF asked pension funds management entities on 26 August 2020 to comply again with the regular deadlines.[196]

2.30.5. Extraordinary monitoring and reporting

April 2020: The ASF expected pension fund management entities to report any serious disruption in their activities or with regard to the operation of the pension funds under management due to the outbreak. These disruptions could affect the financial and liquidity position of pension funds and, eventually, could also compromise the rules of proper functioning in the market conduct area, undermining the protection of members and beneficiaries. The ASF established an extraordinary reporting to collect information on the financial, liquidity and solvency position of pension funds and also an extraordinary reporting of some quantitative and qualitative indicators related to market conduct.[197]

The ASF also recommended pension fund management entities to monitor early withdrawals from PPR pension funds closely.[198] The ASF recalled the importance of explaining the impact of early withdrawals and the amount of loss to plan members.

This extraordinary monitoring provided a tool for pension fund management entities and the supervisor to detect problems due to the outbreak and take action as necessary to safeguard the interest of plan members.

2.30.6. Temporary extension of the legal conditions for early withdrawals in PPR

April 2020: The Law no. 7/2020, of 10 April 2020, temporarily extended the conditions for early withdrawals in PPR without tax penalties to certain situations.[199] Plan members could withdraw savings up to EUR 438.81 if they:

- were in prophylactic or illness isolation
- were providing assistance to children, grandchildren or another dependent
- had suffered a reduction of the normal working period or had their employment contract suspended, due to the economic crisis
- were registered unemployed
- were eligible for financial support to self-employed workers, or were workers from entities whose establishment, or activity, had been closed by legal or administrative imposition.

These broadened conditions were supposed to apply until 30 September 2020. For contracts opened up to 31 March 2020, the tax penalty for early withdrawal was not applicable.

July 2020: The promulgation of the Supplementary budget extended this measure until the end of 2020, and also added another circumstance under which members could benefit from this measure: tenants with difficulties in paying their rents who have been forced to apply to moratoriums and loan applications with the Housing and Urban Rehabilitation Institute (IHRU).

December 2020: The measure was further extended by Law No. 75-B/2020 approving the state budget for 2021 and establishing exceptional rules for people to access their retirement savings until 30 September 2021.[200]

Plan members could withdraw up to the monthly limit of the Social Support Index, currently at EUR 438.81, except if they needed their savings to pay their rent. The limit raised to EUR 658.22 in this last case. Members did not have to pay a tax penalty on this withdrawal if they had opened the plan by 31 March 2020.

Institutions offering retirement savings arrangements from which early withdrawals are possible were required to inform their clients about this option on their website and in the pension statement to their members.

2.31. Slovak Republic

2.31.1. Subsidising wages and supporting pension asset accumulation

March 2020: The state approved in March 2020 the "First Aid" package of economic measures to help employees, businesses and the self-employed. Direct support and aid for employers and the self-employed was managed through six measures:[201]

- Measure 1: Employers who were forced to shut down their operations based on the measures of the Slovak Public Health Authority and employers with furloughed workers could receive a compensation allowance of 80% of the employee's average salary, up to a maximum of EUR 1 100
- Measure 2: Self-employed workers with a drop in revenues of at least 20% (10% in March) could receive a flat-rate allowance of EUR 180 to EUR 540 (EUR 90 to EUR 270 in March), depending on the extent of revenue drop
- Measure 3A: Employers whose activity was affected by the economic slowdown could receive a compensation allowance of 80% of the employee's average salary, up to a maximum of EUR 880
- Measure 3B: Employers that recorded a drop in revenues of at least 20% (10% in March) could receive a flat-rate allowance of between EUR 180 and EUR 540 (EUR 90 to EUR 270 in March) per worker, depending on the extent of revenue drop, up to 80% of the average employee's wage
- Measure 4A: Self-employed workers could receive a flat contribution of EUR 210 (EUR 105 in March)
- Measure 4B: Single-member private limited liability companies could receive a flat contribution of EUR 210 (EUR 105 in March).

For the compensation allowances, the salary taken into account was the employee's monthly gross salary, i.e. before tax but including the employer's social security contributions.[202] This, therefore, includes contributions to second pillar pension funds for participating employees.

The period for which the measures were in force was extended several times in order to support the segments of the economy that continued being exposed to the decline in economic activity related to the

COVID-19 pandemic. As of 15 July 2020, the Government of the Slovak Republic had decreed that the measures would remain in force until 30 September 2020.

November 2020: The "First Aid Plus" scheme was launched in November 2020, extending the original scheme from October 2020 until the end of March 2021. The revamped scheme extended eligibility criteria to cover a broader range of affected employers, who were entitled to increased assistance. The different measures were amended as follows:[203]

- Measure 1 and measure 3A: The compensation allowance of 80% of the employee's average earnings increased to 80% of the total labour costs of the employee, up to a maximum of EUR 1 100
- Measure 2 and measure 3B: Depending on the decrease in revenues, the financial contribution for employers and self-employed individuals increased by 50%, ranging from EUR 270 to EUR 810
- Measure 4A and measure 4B: The flat-rate contribution increased to EUR 315.

February 2021: On 2 February 2021, the Government of the Slovak Republic approved the "First Aid ++" projects, which increased and expanded financial aid for employers and self-employed individuals to mitigate the impact of the COVID-19 pandemic.[204] The different measures changed as follows:

- Measure 1 and measure 3A: The compensation allowance increased to 100% of the total labour costs of the employee, up to a maximum of EUR 1 100. The sum of the aid granted as of February 2021 may not exceed the limit of EUR 1.8 million per undertaking. If the applicant exceeded the set limit, the compensation allowance was reduced to 80% of the total labour costs[205]
- Measure 2 and measure 3B: Depending on the decrease in revenues, the financial contribution for employers and self-employed individuals increased again, ranging from EUR 330 to EUR 870
- Measure 4A and measure 4B: The flat-rate contribution increased to EUR 360.

August 2021: Based on the adopted resolution of the Government of the Slovak Republic dated 10 August 2021, the Ministry of Labour, Social Affairs and Family of the Slovak Republic changes the conditions for the payment of "First Aid" contributions for eligible applicants from 1 September 2021 in connection with the adopted change of the COVID-19 automat, which defines the epidemiological situation in each district.[206] Depending on the epidemiological situation, rules from the "First Aid", "First Aid Plus" or "First Aid ++" apply.[207]

2.31.2. Adjustment of supervisory activities

April 2020: Pension fund management companies and supplementary pension management companies were requested to provide the regulator with new extraordinary reporting introduced during the pandemic at a high frequency. This request aimed at helping to monitor the situation with respect to supervisory board meetings and investment decisions, capital position, eligible own funds, observation of lapses and surrenders, funds return in guaranteed bond funds, performance and risk (potential loss/maximum loss).

The National Bank of the Slovak Republic (NBS) monitored the fulfilment of all obligations of the supervised entities to ensure the continuity of key operational activities and the protection of long-term interests of savers. Savers had to be provided with relevant and transparent information, including on their investment options/situation, to discourage potential short-term decisions in the current situation. The NBS monitored the investment decisions and asset allocation of pension funds to ensure savings of members were protected.

The NBS urged pension fund managers to communicate with savers at an increased pace, even in times of emergency, and to explain them that a decrease in asset value may, in some cases, lead to a possible impact on the amount of savings of pension savers, future retirement income or motivation of early withdrawal. Due to the COVID-19 outbreak, the possibility to physically meet a client was extremely limited, therefore the NBS recommended using digital communication tools and publishing information on the administrator's website.

Act No. 67/2020 Coll. also allowed the NBS to suspend sanctions and extend deadlines for acts or obligations arising from special regulations if circumstances related to the pandemic prevented them from being complied with.[208]

2021: The beginning of 2021 was marked by the tightening of anti-pandemic measures due to the worsening epidemic situation. This, however, did not have a significant impact on the activities of the supervision of pension savings. The second wave of the pandemic, along with the related closure of the economy and reduced mobility, redirected the activities of pension administrators to a secure online space, and the supervisory activities of the NBS focused on off-site supervision.

The priorities of supervision remained unchanged, as a regular monitoring of supervised entities focusing on the development of financial indicators, liquidity, operational capability, and communication with their clients continued. In the pension savings sector, the NBS focused primarily on the challenges that may have arisen in connection with possible scenarios for the development of COVID-19 in order to maintain business processes and ensure the protection of the rights of savers, participants and beneficiaries. In May 2021, the NBS, in agreement with the supervised entities, abolished the obligations to provide extraordinary information and data for supervisory purposes. The reason for the abolition of the monitoring obligation was the improving situation in the financial markets as well as the general situation associated with COVID-19.

However, the development of COVID-19 had a significant impact on the supervision planning. Due to the unpredictable development of the health situation, on-site inspections could only be planned and carried out during the period of relaxation of the quarantine measures. For this reason, supervision focused on proactive and intensive in-depth off-site supervision of all pension savings managers and the funds they manage.

The NBS continuously checked and evaluated the functioning of the supervised entities managing assets in the 2nd and 3rd pillars, including the compliance with capital requirements. The entities remained stable and were able to cope very well with the pandemic crisis by applying responsible policies and a prudent approach. The NBS also closely monitored the sensitivity of the pension sector to the fluctuations of the financial market.

Throughout the entire period, the NBS monitored the activities of asset managers in relation to the quality of care provided to savers, participants, and beneficiaries. In this sense, it can be stated that the pension administrators reacted very flexibly and responsibly during 2021, and the savers, participants and beneficiaries experienced no restrictions.

2.31.3. Suspension and deferral of pension contributions

April 2020: An employer or a self-employed person with mandatory pension insurance was not required to pay social insurance contributions, including mandatory contributions into the second pillar, for April 2020 if their business operation was closed due to a decision of the competent authority (Public Health Office of the Slovak Republic) for at least 15 days. The request had to submitted by 18 May 2020.

The due date of the social insurance contributions of employers and self-employed persons, including mandatory contributions into the second pillar, for March, May, June and July 2020 was postponed initially to 31 December 2020 if these persons suffered a drop in net turnover or income from business and other self-employment activity by 40% or more. The deferral only applied to social security contributions from employers and self-employed workers, but not to those from employees.

The government later on decided to further extend the deferral of the obligation to pay social security contributions. The revised due dates for the deferred contributions are as follows:[209]

- 30 September 2021 for contributions initially due in March 2020
- 31 March 2022 for contributions initially due in May 2020
- 30 June 2022 for contributions initially due in June 2020
- 30 September 2022 for contributions initially due in July 2020
- 31 December 2022 for contributions initially due in December 2020
- 31 March 2023 for contributions initially due in January 2021
- 30 June 2023 for contributions initially due in February 2021
- 30 September 2023 for contributions initially due in March 2021
- 31 December 2023 for contributions initially due in April 2021
- 31 March 2024 for contributions initially due in May 2021
- 30 June 2024 for contributions initially due in October 2021
- 30 September 2024 for contribution initially due in November 2021
- 31 December 2024 for contribution initially due in December 2021.

2.32. Slovenia

2.32.1. Advice to withhold dividend payments

April 2020: The Securities Market Agency (SMA) and the Insurance Supervision Agency (ISA) followed the recommendations of the Financial Stability Board and EIOPA and advised the financial entities they supervise to withhold paying dividends to shareholders.[210] The SMA supervises mutual pension funds while the ISA supervises pension and insurance companies.

August 2020: The ISA repeated this advice on 20 August 2020.[211]

February 2021: The Slovenian authorities provided advice with respect to dividend payments and other distributions in 2021. The SMA encouraged its supervised entities to be careful in their distribution of profits (until at least 30 September 2021) and ensure they have the appropriate capital level. Likewise, the ISA expected its supervised entities to withhold paying dividends until end-September 2021.[212]

2.32.2. Deadline extensions

March 2020: The SMA was allowed to extend deadlines for non-essential proceedings and relating to the performance of procedural acts by supervised entities.[213]

December 2020: The SMA could, by a decision issued at the request of a supervised entity, extend the time limit for fulfilling the obligation laid down by an individual administrative act if the party was unable to fulfil the obligation in good time for a legitimate reason.[214] This possibility was further granted in March and November 2021.

2.32.3. Warning about ill-intentioned financial advice

March 2020: The SMA issued a warning on ill-intentioned financial advice.[215] Scammers may advertise investments promising high returns. These investments are risky and the promised returns may not reflect the actual realised ones.

2.33. Spain

2.33.1. Advice to withhold dividend payments

April 2020: The General Directorate of Insurance and Pension Funds (DGSFP in Spanish) urged insurance companies to withhold paying dividends to their shareholders. This recommendation was line with that of EIOPA.

January 2021: The DGSFP reiterated its call upon insurance companies to withhold dividend distributions, in line with EIOPA's recommendations.[216]

2.33.2. Easier access to private pension savings

March 2020: Spain facilitated the early access to private pension savings as a result of the COVID-19 crisis (Royal Decree 11/2020).[217] Members of pension plans were able to withdraw assets from their pension plans with no penalty under certain conditions for a period of six months from the entry in force of the Royal Decree 463/2020 on 14 March 2020. This option was available to members of insured pension plans, company benefit schemes and mutual provident funds.

Members had to meet one of the following conditions to be allowed to withdraw assets from their pension plans:

- temporarily unemployed because of the COVID-19 outbreak
- unable to work as employers are obliged to close to the public because of the lockdown
- self-employed registered in the social security and unable to continue their activities.

The amount of assets that could be withdrawn was capped. It could not exceed the wages (respectively net income) that the temporarily laid-off employees (respectively self-employed) would have received if they had been able to continue working.

The tax treatment of these early withdrawals was the same as benefit payments. Benefits are usually taxed as labour income at the marginal tax rate of the individual (except for contributions made before 2007).[218]

As of 30 September 2020, close to 61 000 withdrawal requests had been processed, for a total of EUR 114 million.[219]

2.34. Sweden

2.34.1. Support of wages and pension contributions

March 2020: The Swedish government introduced a short-time work allowance programme to further subsidise wage payments (including public pension contributions) when employers reduced their staff's number of working hours. This programme initially lasted throughout 2020.[220]

The proportion of salary that the state and employers paid and that employees kept depended on the reduction in the number of hours. The short-time work allowance from the state was available for different levels of reduction in working hours: 20%, 40% and 60% (as well as 80% for May, June and July 2020). Employer staff costs were reduced by 19%, 36% and 53% (72% for an 80% reduction in working hours for May, June and July 2020) respectively under the short-time work allowance programme. However, employees still received over 90% of their salary for a 60% reduction in their working hours.

Employers had to meet some conditions to benefit from this allowance. The possibility for a reduction in the number of working hours had to exist in the collective bargaining agreement. If it was not the case, employers had to sign an agreement with at least 70% of the employees in the operating unit. Employers should also have tried to reduce their labour costs, such as by dismissing non-permanent employees who were not critical for their operations.

Employers could benefit from this allowance for a period of six months, which could be extended by three more months. This financial support could start from 16 March 2020.

This measure intended to provide support to both employers and employees in a context of economic and financial difficulties due to COVID-19. It reduced the staff costs for employers while allowing workers to get almost their full salary on which contributions to the pension premium system (PPM) are taken. This measure could limit the effects of COVID-19 and its economic and financial consequences on pension contributions.

February 2021: The Swedish government continued to provide financial support in the case of a reduction in working hours in 2021, with some adjustments compared to 2020. The new scheme (Short-Time Work Allowance 2021) covered a 7-month period, from 1 December 2020 to 30 June 2021.[221] Employers were eligible to this support if they had suffered temporary and serious financial difficulties due to circumstances beyond their control. They should not be bankrupt, nor subject to prepare a balance sheet for liquidation purposes, nor undergoing restructuring at the time of the application to get the financial support. They also had to have entered into an agreement of short-time work with their employees. The reduction in working hours should be 20%, 40%, 60% (or 80% between January and June 2021).

The Swedish government covered 75% of the employers' costs after the reduced working hours.[222] The calculation was based on the employees' salary, excluding the 31.42% social insurance contributions of the employers.[223] Taking into account employers' social security contributions, the share of support of the government was 98.565% (i.e. 75% of 1.3142).

Support could be granted for a maximum period of six consecutive months.

Second half of 2021: The Swedish government extended the short-time work allowance for the period July-September 2021.[224] Employers could apply to get financial support for the months of July, August and September retroactively between 3 and 30 November 2021.

2.34.2. Invitation for flexibility with respect to internal buffer requirements

March 2020: The Swedish Financial Supervisory Agency encouraged occupational pension funds to use the internal buffers they had built up on top of their risk-capital requirements under more favourable circumstances.[225] It also encouraged occupational pension funds to refrain from selling assets to meet internal buffer requirements.

This invitation aimed at limiting further negative effects on asset prices when they were already falling.

The Swedish Financial Supervisory Agency was also ready to discuss with companies whose capital fell below risk-based capital requirements.

2.34.3. Temporary measures to enable general meetings in companies to be held using digital communications and mail

April 2020: The Swedish government introduced the temporary possibility of conducting annual general meetings in companies and associations without the need for the concerned parties to meet physically.[226] Meetings could take place and the concerned parties exercise their rights at the meeting using digital communications and mail or just via mail.

This measure intended to limit the spread of the COVID-19 and was aimed at insurance companies as well as other businesses.

2.34.4. *Flexibility in the conversion process of pension funds into occupational pension companies*

June 2020: Following the plea of the Financial Supervisory Authority, the Swedish Finance Ministry agreed to provide leeway to pension funds in their conversion process into occupational pension companies under Sweden's domestic implementation of the IORP II Directive.[227] The Finance Ministry proposed a bill on 26 June 2020 allowing pension funds to go ahead and proceed with their conversion even if they failed to meet the solvency criteria. The proposed bill came into force on 15 December 2020.[228]

This legislation intended to avoid denying permission to pension funds to operate as occupational pension companies because of financial instability resulting from COVID-19 and affecting their solvency position.

2.34.5. *Warning about scams*

April 2020: The Swedish Financial Supervisory Agency has been warning customers about scams on its website.[229] It reports the cases of several customers who received a call from scammers pretending they were calling on behalf of the Swedish Financial Supervisory Authority. Scammers were pretending to assist customers to recoup lost money that was invested.

2.34.6. *Call to withhold paying dividends*

December 2020: The Swedish Financial Supervisory Agency expected financial companies to refrain from dividend payments and share buybacks until 30 September 2021.[230] Dividends and share buybacks shall not exceed 25% of the net profit of banks for the two financial years 2019 and 2020.

2.35. Switzerland

2.35.1. *Possibility for employers to use contribution reserves to finance contributions*

March 2020: Switzerland decided on 25 March 2020 to allow employers to temporarily tap into their contribution reserve to pay their contributions to occupational pension plans. This measure was initially in force for six months. Employers using this option had to inform their pension fund in writing.

November 2020: The Swiss Parliament authorised the Federal Council on 25 September 2020 to extend this measure. The Federal Council decided on 11 November 2020 to allow employers again to use their contribution reserve until 31 December 2021.[231]

This measure aimed at helping employers facing liquidity issues. It did not affect employees. Employee contributions continued to be withdrawn from employees' salary and transferred to their occupational pension plans. Their plans received all the expected contributions.

2.35.2. *Possibility for some laid-off workers to remain in the pension plan of their former employer*

September 2020: The Swiss Parliament allowed people aged 58 or above becoming unemployed after 31 July 2020 to request from 1 January 2021 to remain in the occupational pension plan of their former employer.[232] Before this temporary change in the legislation, people aged 58 or above who were losing their jobs had to leave the occupational plan of their employer and transfer their assets to a vested benefits account. The change in legislation allowed these people to remain in the plan of their former employer and have the same rights as other plan members.

2.35.3. Advice to withhold dividend payments

March 2020: The Swiss Financial Market Supervisory Authority (FINMA) recommended the entities it supervises to withhold paying dividends to their shareholders.[233] FINMA is the supervisor of insurance companies with which individuals can set up voluntary private pension arrangements.

2.35.4. Postponement of the reporting deadlines of insurers

April 2020: FINMA extended the reporting deadlines of insurers.[234] Insurance companies could submit a number of reports on their capital and financial situation until 31 May 2020 instead of 30 April 2020. Insurance companies wishing to benefit from this deadline extension had to let FINMA know by 30 April 2020.

2.36. Türkiye

2.36.1. Delay in the disclosure of financial reports of pension funds

March 2020: The Capital Market Board announced that the disclosure of quarterly financial reports for the first quarter of 2020 could be delayed until 30 April 2020.

The announcement dates and reporting periods of some transactions regarding pension mutual funds were extended.

2.36.2. Protecting pension providers against liquidity risk

The Notification on Principles Regarding Investment Funds authorises the Capital Markets Board of Türkiye to halt the calculations of unit fund values of the pension mutual funds, and to suspend trading these funds in extraordinary situations.

Trading the funds may be halted, if deemed necessary, to eliminate the liquidity risk that may arise from a large number of possible demands from participants to leave the system to meet their financial needs due to the pandemic.

2.36.3. Adjustments of practices

The Turkish authorities reported the introduction of a regulation enabling participants to terminate pension contracts via secure electronic communication tools. Before this measure was taken, signed documents were required to terminate contracts.

2.37. United Kingdom

2.37.1. Flexibility with respect to the disclosure and payment of transfer values of DB plans

March 2020: The Pensions Regulator (TPR) announced that it would not take legal action during three months if trustees suspended their cash equivalent transfer value (CETV) quotations and payments. The CETV is the cash value placed on pension benefits. It corresponds to the amount that plan members can transfer to another plan in exchange of giving up their rights in their current plan. Trustees are usually required to disclose this value upon the CETV terms and process.

This measure could help to protect the liquidity of the DB plan provider by limiting transfers between plans. It could also protect the interest of plan members in a context of volatile financial markets as the CETV may be fluctuating significantly. This measure also intended to help trustees to focus on other administrative activities (such as pension payroll) rather than assessing CETV.

TPR specified that it expected trustees to report any breach of their transfer obligations from 1 July 2020. TPR was ready to continue to take a pragmatic approach if a breach was related to COVID-19.

2.37.2. Flexibility with respect to the submission of recovery plans for DB schemes

March 2020: TPR announced that it was ready to refrain from taking regulatory action if trustees of DB plans did not submit recovery plans of underfunded DB plans on time.[235] TPR suggested that the submission of the recovery plan could be delayed by up to three months.

June 2020: TPR stated that it would continue to take a pragmatic approach to late submission because of COVID-19 issues.

This flexibility aimed at providing more time for trustees to consider the situation of the plan and of the employer for the recovery plan. TPR did not expect trustees who were about to calculate the funding of the plan to change their valuation assumptions. However, TPR suggested that trustees could consider the affordability of deficit repair contributions from the employers when agreeing the recovery plan.

2.37.3. Flexibility with respect to the payments of pension contributions to DB plans

March 2020: TPR announced in March 2020 that it would be ready to refrain from taking regulatory actions if employers failed to make deficit repair contributions (DRC) during three months according to the recovery plans. TPR advised trustees to be open to requests from employers to reduce or suspend DRC. This reduction or suspension should be for a period of time as limited as possible below three months.

June 2020: TPR repeated that DRC suspensions or reductions could still be appropriate. However, TPR did not expect trustees to extend suspensions or reductions on a three-month rolling basis unquestioningly.

TPR also made it possible for trustees to grant the same leeway for future contributions of employers (and members) to DB plans as for the reduction or suspension of DRC.

TPR expected trustees to check the actual financial conditions of the employers before allowing contribution breaks and ensure that dividend payments from employers to shareholders were suspended.

2.37.4. Continued guidance to trustees and pragmatic supervision

March 2020: TPR continuously provided guidance to trustees during the COVID-19 situation.[236] For instance, TPR acknowledged that deferring or reducing deficit repair contributions (DRC) could be appropriate. However, TPR expected trustees to undertake due diligence on the financial position of the employer before agreeing a new DRC suspension or reduction for three months.

TPR intended to regulate and monitor pragmatically. TPR expected trustees to report breaches of any legislative requirement, though. Trustees should comply with their reporting requirements from 1 July 2020.

TPR has also been providing guidance for DC trustees and its stances on some matters.[237] For instance, TPR agreed not to take action against employers failing to consult members for the full 60-day period on the reduction of employer contributions, subject to certain conditions. This flexibility could happen when the employer was only proposing a reduction of employer contributions for furloughed staff for instance to align with the job retention scheme.

2.37.5. Extension of deadline to pay the levy to the Pension Protection Fund

July 2020: The Pension Protection Fund announced that it would waive the interest charge on late payment of its levy over a 90-day period for defined benefit schemes struggling because of COVID-19.[238] In the past, pension schemes had 28 days to pay the levy. Schemes could apply for an interest-free deadline extension after receiving the levy invoice for 2020/21. The Pension Protection Fund requires evidence proving financial hardship from applicants.

September 2021: For a second year, the Pension Protection Fund offered a 90-day levy payment window, interest free, for schemes impacted by COVID-19. Schemes could apply for a payment extension of the 2021/22 levy bill.[239]

2.37.6. Coverage of wages and pension contributions to furloughed employees

March 2020: The United Kingdom introduced a Coronavirus Job Retention Scheme (CJRS) paying a grant to eligible employers for employees on temporary leave (furlough) due to COVID-19.[240] This scheme was in force from 1 March 2020, originally for three months.

May 2020: The Chancellor Rishi Sunak announced that this scheme would continue until end-October 2020 but would be gradually phased out from August 2020.[241]

October 2020: The CJRS was further extended from November 2020 to 31 March 2021.

March 2021: The CJRS was further extended until 30 September 2021.

The grant available under this Scheme initially covered 80% of the usual monthly wage of the furloughed employee, up to GBP 2 500 a month, plus the associated employer national insurance contributions and the minimum mandatory pension contributions. Pension contributions were financed up to the level of the minimum automatic enrolment employer contribution (i.e. 3% of qualifying earnings). Employers could not claim for pension contributions they made above the mandatory employer contributions. From August 2020, employers were required to pay the national insurance contributions and the minimum 3% pension contributions. The government reduced its salary payment down to 70% (up to GBP 2 187.5) in September 2020, and further down to 60% (up to GBP 1 875) in October 2020. Employers were requested to make up the difference (10% in September 2020, 20% in October 2020). The government increased again its salary payment up to 80% of the usual salary (up to GBP 2 500 a month) from 1 November 2020. It reduced it again to 70% of the wages (up to GBP 2 187.50) in July 2021, and 60% of the wages (up to GBP 1 875) in August and September 2021.[242]

Employers could claim the grant if they had created and started a pay-as-you-earn (PAYE) payroll scheme. They had to have enrolled for PAYE online and have a UK bank account.

Employers could initially claim the grant for furloughed employees who were on the PAYE payroll on or before 28 February 2020.[243] Employees had to be furloughed for a minimum period of three consecutive weeks. The grant was available regardless of the initial employment contract (e.g. full-time, part-time, flexible). Employers could not get a grant from the CJRS (before 1 July 2020) if employees were still working, even on reduced hours or for reduced pay. From 1 July 2020, employers could ask furloughed employees to come back to work for any amount of time and could be entitled to the extended version of the CJRS for the hours not worked.

The reference salary of the employee on which the calculation of the grant was based excluded non-monetary benefits provided to employees and benefits provided through salary sacrifice schemes (such as pension contributions). These benefits that reduced the taxable pay of the employee were not included in the calculation of the grant.

To continue to support companies facing lower demand due to COVID-19 after the CJRS (supposed to end at end-October 2020), the government was planning to introduce a Job Support Scheme from

1 November 2020 for six months. However, as the CJRS was extended from 1 November 2020, this Job Support Scheme has been postponed.[244]

The HMRC published in 2021 the list of companies who made furlough claims under the CJRS to provide transparency and to deter furlough fraud.[245]

Employers were able to claim up to the minimum automatic enrolment employer pension contributions to be included in the subsidy at the early stage of this scheme, but this top-up ended on 1 August 2020.[246]

2.37.7. Provision for COVID-19 in the conditions to exit salary sacrifice schemes

April 2020: Her Majesty's Revenue and Customs (HMRC) allowed individuals to exit salary sacrifice schemes in case of changes to circumstances directly resulting from COVID-19.[247] A salary sacrifice arrangement is an agreement to reduce an employee's entitlement to cash pay, usually in return for a non-cash benefit. HMRC usually lets individuals switch out from salary sacrifice schemes only in the case of a life event. HMRC agreed to consider COVID-19 as a life event that could justify a change to salary sacrifice arrangements. The related employment contract needed to be updated accordingly.

2.37.8. Relief at Source (RAS) repayment claims – wet signature easement

March 2020: Her Majesty's Revenue and Customs (HMRC) implemented process changes to ease burdens with the RAS process whilst many customers were working from home. This enabled scheme administrators who were ordinarily required to obtain wet signatures on interim repayment claims, to instead provide interim claims without a signature where submitted by the authorised signatory or signed by someone else, provided separate authority was emailed by the authorised signatory.

September 2021: This easement was extended pending wider work on pension tax administration.

2.37.9. Provision for COVID-19 in the conditions for protected pension age

March 2020: Some individuals who were members of pension schemes before 6 April 2006, including some police, firefighters and uniformed service personnel, have protected pension ages in respect of those schemes. This means they are able to receive pension benefits at an age below the current normal minimum pension age. Legislation was introduced in March 2020 to ensure that those who had retired but returned to employment to support the COVID-19 response did not lose their protected pension age.

2.37.10. Provision to pay tax-free lump sum payments from National Health and Social Care Coronavirus schemes

March 2020: In recognition of the increased risks frontline National health Service (NHS) and social care staff face in carrying out their duties during COVID-19, NHS England and NHS Wales were to pay a lump sum of GBP 60 000 in respect of the death of NHS and social care staff. Legislation was introduced to wholly exempt the lump sum paid.

September 2020: Northern Ireland and Scotland introduced similar schemes for frontline health and social care workers. Legislation was extended to exempt the lump sum payments made to the estates of eligible individuals who died from COVID-19 that was contracted during their frontline work.

2.37.11. Extension of deadlines to comply with the new rules of the Financial Conduct Authority

March 2020: Rules that were finalised by the Financial Conduct Authority (FCA) in January 2019 were due to come into effect on 6 April 2020. These rules changed the information that firms must give consumers entering pension drawdown or taking an income for the first time (including uncrystallised fund pension lump sum) and the annual information given to these customers.[248] In March 2020, when pension providers were expected to be in the final phases of implementation, the FCA acknowledged that some firms may face a short delay to implementation owing to pandemic-related operational challenges. The FCA emphasised its expectation that pension providers implement as soon as reasonably practicable and required the provider to make a formal notification if implementation would be later than 31 May 2020.

April 2020: The FCA Board made new rules that extended by six months the implementation deadline of the final suite of Retirement Outcomes Review remedies (Investment Pathways, active decision to invest in cash and actual charges disclosure rules).[249] This extended implementation period recognised the operational challenges of implementing new rules at a time when firms needed to reprioritise resources to focus on critical functions through which consumer harm is prevented.

2.37.12. Protection against pension scams

The FCA has an ongoing campaign (ScamSmart) to help consumers avoid investment and pension scams. ScamSmart has a specific webpage that TPR recommends to visit as necessary: https://www.fca.org.uk/scamsmart. This webpage identifies several types of pension scams. Scammers may offer one of the following opportunities: free pension review, taking money from a plan, pension transfer to another plan. ScamSmart lists the channels that scammers may use, such as emails, social media, or phone calls. ScamSmart provides assistance and explains to pension savers how they should deal with these scams.

March 2020: The FCA published alert on how consumers can avoid COVID-19 pension scams. This highlighted the tactics commonly used by scammers. The FCA also provided practical measures on how consumers can protect themselves.

April 2020: TPR reminds trustees and employers that there is a risk of scams from which members need protection.[250] Scammers may lure savers willing to transfer their pension, prompted by the volatility of financial markets or the risk of bankruptcy of the employer. TPR raised warning and asked trustees and employers to be vigilant if members asked about transferring their pension.

April 2020: The FCA published guidance on what firms can and should do to support customers who seek to access to their pension savings during the pandemic.[251] This identified scams as a key risk factor and set out what firms should ask their customers and what information firms should provide to help them protect themselves against pension scams.

May 2020: UK pension bodies published a consolidated guide for consumers on COVID-19 and their pension.[252] This guide brought together information from each of the bodies on issues that could affect consumers during the COVID-19 crisis. It set out responsibilities by organisation, answers to frequently asked questions, and contact information where appropriate.

November 2021: New measures came into force on 30 November 2021, giving trustees and scheme managers new powers to intervene and halt suspicious transfers.[253]

2.38. United States

2.38.1. Suspension of minimum distribution requirements from DC plans

March 2020: The United States enacted into law the Coronavirus Aid, Relief, and Economic Security (CARES) Act that includes provisions suspending the required minimum distribution (RMD) from DC plans for 2020.[254] Generally, individuals must take their first RMD by 1 April of the year following the year in which they turn age 72 (or age 70.5 for those who turned 70.5 before 1 January 2020).[255] Absent exception, failure to take a RMD when required results in a tax penalty of a 50% of the amount that should have been distributed. Individuals who had already withdrawn assets in 2020 before the CARES Act passed could, within 60 days of the distribution, roll over the withdrawn amount into individual retirement accounts (IRAs) or qualified retirement plans.

June 2020: The Treasury Department and the Internal Revenue Service (IRS) extended the rollover period for IRA distributions (within 60 days of distribution initially) to 31 August 2020.[256]

July 2020: The IRS reminded old-age people and retirees that there were not required to take money out of their IRAs and workplace DC pension plans during the whole year 2020.[257]

2.38.2. Deferral of employer contributions to DB plans

March 2020: The CARES Act allowed employers to defer their required minimum contributions into single-employer DB plans in 2020 until 1 January 2021.[258] Contributions were treated as timely if they had been made no later than 4 January 2021 (which is the first business day after 1 January 2021).[259] Delayed contributions are to be increased with interest accruing between the original due date and the date of payment at the effective interest rate for the plan for the plan year including the payment date.

2.38.3. Possibility to use the 2019 adjusted funding target attainment percentage for DB plans

March 2020: When determining whether benefit restrictions apply for underfunded DB plans with respect to any plan year that includes a portion of the 2020 calendar year, the CARES Act lets sponsors choose to use the adjusted funding target attainment percentage (AFTAP) for the plan year ending in 2019.[260] This could help employers avoid freezing benefits and continue offering lump sums and other accelerated payment forms in 2020, even if the plan's funded status significantly declined due to COVID-19.

2.38.4. Early access to pension savings without penalty

March 2020: The CARES Act allowed participants and beneficiaries to access savings in their DC plans up to USD 100 000 without penalty, providing certain COVID-19 related criteria were met. Before this Act, individuals withdrawing their savings before the age of 59 and a half had to pay a 10% tax penalty. The COVID-19 related withdrawal was also exempt from the normal 20% federal tax withholding on such distributions.

Additionally, under the CARES Act, if the qualified individual is unable to repay the withdrawal within three years, the income tax payment on these early withdrawals may be spread over three years and the qualified individual will not owe the 10% penalty. Thus, individuals did not have to pay the full amount of taxes in the year of withdrawal.

Under the CARES Act, qualified individuals are also allowed to put some or all of their withdrawals back into their plan within three years without having the amount recognised as income for tax purposes. Repayment is not counted towards the annual contribution limits.

Under the CARES Act, until 31 December 2020 for purposes related to COVID-19, an individual qualified for this tax relief if:

- a test that is approved by the Centers for Disease Control and Prevention (CDC) revealed they are diagnosed with COVID-19
- their spouse or one of their dependents was diagnosed with COVID-19 according to a CDC-approved test
- they experienced adverse financial consequences of COVID-19.[261]

December 2020: The Consolidated Appropriations Act (CAA) that was signed into law at end-2020 amended the CARES Act to allow in-service (i.e. early) withdrawal of savings in money purchase pension plans with no penalty like other plans eligible under the CARES Act.[262] Money purchase pension plans are pension plans into which employers contribute a percentage of the salary of the participating employees every year. Employees cannot contribute to the plan but can choose how to invest the assets based on the options that the employers offer.[263] The CAA allowed early withdrawals from these plans to qualify as COVID-19 related distributions, applying retroactively from 27 March 2020 until 30 December 2020.

2.38.5. Loans from DC plans

March 2020: The CARES Act permitted plans to lift the ceiling on the amount that individuals could borrow from their DC plans. The loan could amount to the full balance of the plan (instead of 50%) up to USD 100 000 (instead of USD 50 000). Individuals could also delay the repayment of their outstanding loan from their DC plan by one year. However, interest continued to accrue on delayed payments.

Individuals could benefit from this measure within 180 days of the enactment of the Act.

2.38.6. Special financial assistance for multiemployers DB plans

March 2021: As part of its response to the economic fallout of COVID-19, the United Sates passed a USD 1.9 trillion expenditure bill under the American Rescue Plan Act of 2021 (the ARPA) that also includes a number of provisions affecting pension plans.[264] The ARPA creates and funds a special financial assistance programme to extend the solvency of severely underfunded multiemployer DB plans. This government support represents an approximately USD 90 billion aid package for participants of a few hundred employer-union pension plans.[265] These plans are negotiated between unions and employers. The financial assistance is in the form of grants instead of a loan.[266]

July 2021: The Pension Benefit Guaranty Corporation (PBGC) issued an interim final rule outlining some of the aspects of the special financial assistance, such as the amount of this assistance, the application process and the way this assistance shall be invested.[267]

This programme provides one-off payments to allow the plan to continue paying all benefits through 2051. This in turn should allow the PBGC to avoid insolvency. The PBGC interim final rule provides that the amount of the special financial assistance would be the difference between the obligations of the plan and its resources. The obligations of the plan refer to the sum of benefits, including reinstated benefits, and expected reasonable administrative expenses until 2051. The resources of the plan are the fair market value of plan assets, the present value of future anticipated contributions, withdrawal liability payments and other payments to the plan (excluding the special financial assistance).

Multiemployer plans have to meet one of the following criteria to be eligible for this financial assistance:

- the plan must be in critical and declining status in any plan year beginning between 2020 and 2022
- the plan has a benefit suspension in accordance with the Multiemployer Pension Reform Act of 2014
- the plan is in critical status in any plan year beginning between 2020 and 2022, has a "modified funding percentage" (as defined by the law) below 40% and has a ratio of active to inactive participations below two-thirds
- the plan became insolvent after 16 December 2014, remained insolvent and has not been terminated as of 11 March 2021.

Eligible plans can submit their initial application for special financial assistance to the PBGC by 31 December 2025, and submit revised applications until 31 December 2026. The ARPA allows the PBGC to give priority consideration to certain plans by forbidding to file an application for a plan for up to two years unless the plan demonstrates a significant funding deficit or short-term insolvency risk.

After their application is approved, plans receive within one year a one-time special financial assistance payment from the PBGC, subject to certain restrictions. The payment is equal to the amount necessary to ensure that the plan can pay all benefits due until 2051. This financial assistance must be segregated from the other assets of the plan and must be invested in investment-grade bonds or other investments approved by the PBGC. Plans receiving such assistance will be considered in critical status until 2051. The ARPA does not require to cut the earned benefits of members.[268] Plans that suspended or cut their benefit payments and received this financial assistance must resume their benefit payments and provide retroactive adjustments.[269]

Plans will have to comply with certain conditions in exchange for the financial assistance. They will have to provide comprehensive reports to the PBGC regularly.

This programme intends to prevent the insolvency of significantly underfunded plans and prevent participant benefit reductions to the PBGC guaranteed benefit level in the event of a plan's insolvency (which would be expected to occur prior to 2051 in the absence of special financial assistance).

2.38.7. Repeal of benefit suspensions for severely underfunded multiemployer DB plans receiving special financial assistance

March 2021: No plan receiving special financial assistance is allowed any longer to suspend benefits (previously possible under the Multiemployer Pension Reform Act).

2.38.8. Temporary delay for designating the funding zone status

March 2021: The ARPA also allows multiemployer pension plans to keep the status of the year before the plan year starting between 1 March 2020 and 28 February 2021.[270] This will provide plans with flexibility and alleviate administrative burden.

2.38.9. Relaxation of funding requirements for DB plans

March 2021: The ARPA also allows multiemployer plans that are endangered or in critical status for a plan year beginning in 2020 or 2021 to extend their funding improvement or rehabilitation period by five years.[271] This intends to provide more time to improve contribution rates, limit benefit accruals and maintain the funding of the plan.

Multiemployer plans can also amortise losses they occurred in the first two plan years ending after 29 February 2020 over 30 years (instead of 15 years).[272] These losses could be investment losses or other COVID-19 related losses due to reduced contributions for example. Plans that choose to amortise losses over 30 years are not allowed to increase benefits in that time and the two years afterwards unless they are funded by additional contributions.

Multiemployer plans can also smooth actuarial investment losses over ten years (instead of five) for the first two years ending after 29 February 2020. Plans using this flexibility are also subject to limitations on benefit increases.

In the case of single-employer plans, starting for plan years beginning after 31 December 2019, new and future shortfalls can be amortised over a 15-year period, instead of seven. This relief is expected to lower the annual minimum required contributions. This extended amortisation period can apply retrospectively and the shortfall amortisation calculations of the previous year can be reset to zero.[273]

2.38.10. Extension and adjustment of the interest rate stabilisation

March 2021: The ARPA is maintaining the interest rate corridor that the Congress enacted in 2012 and that was supposed to be phased out in 2021. This interest rate corridor sets a floor and a ceiling on the interest rate to use in the calculation of pension liabilities of single-employer pension plans. Interest rates that are used to value pension liabilities had to be within 10% of the 25-year interest rate averages.[274] This 10% corridor was supposed to increase from 2021 by 5 percentage points until it reaches 30% of the 25-year averages. This widening of the corridor was expected to reduce its effects on the valuation of liabilities. However, the ARPA delayed the increase of the corridor and even reduced it at 5%, effective from 2020 to 2025. The phase-out of the corridor is postponed to 2026. From 2026, the 5% corridor will increase by 5 percentage points annually, until it reaches 30% in 2030. The ARPA sets an interest rate floor of 5% on the 25-year interest rate averages.

The floor would aim at protecting the funding of plans from extreme interest rate movements and ensure liabilities are stable and predictable over the long term.

2.38.11. Issuance of cybersecurity best practices

April 2021: The Department of Labour issued on 14 April 2021 a guidance for plan sponsors, plan fiduciaries, record keepers and plan participants on best practices for maintaining cybersecurity, including tips on how to protect the retirement benefits of America's workers.[275] This guidance stresses the obligation of plan fiduciaries to ensure proper mitigation of cybersecurity risks, which includes provisions on ensuring that electronic record-keeping systems have reasonable controls, adequate records management practices are in place, and that electronic disclosure systems include measures calculated to protect Personally Identifiable Information. This guidance may not be specifically in response to COVID-19 but is especially relevant in the time of COVID-19.

Notes

[1] Minimum annual payments for super income streams | Australian Taxation Office (ato.gov.au)

[2] For those drawing down their assets for the first year, the required minimum amount is calculated proportionately from the starting day to the end of the financial year.

[3] Supporting retirees with extension of the temporary reduction in superannuation minimum drawdown rates | Treasury Ministers

[4] APRA adapts 2020 agenda to prioritise COVID-19 response | APRA

[5] 20-086MR Details of changes to ASIC regulatory work and priorities in light of COVID-19 | ASIC - Australian Securities and Investments Commission

[6] APRA to recommence prudential policy programme and issuing of new licences | APRA

[7] COVID-19: APRA's approach to licensing | APRA

[8] APRA to recommence prudential policy programme and issuing of new licences | APRA

[9] 20-085MR ASIC grants relief to industry to provide affordable and timely financial advice during the COVID-19 pandemic | ASIC - Australian Securities and Investments Commission

[10] 20-220MR ASIC extends COVID-19 relief for certain capital raisings and financial advice | ASIC - Australian Securities and Investments Commission

[11] Getting your super - Moneysmart.gov.au

[12] 21-269MR ASIC further extends temporary financial advice relief measures in COVID-19 instrument | ASIC - Australian Securities and Investments Commission

[13] APRA and ASIC release joint letter to superannuation trustees on COVID-19 | APRA

[14] COVID-19 - Information for superannuation trustees | ASIC - Australian Securities and Investments Commission

[15] COVID-19 regulatory information | ASIC - Australian Securities and Investments Commission

[16] Tax treatment of the withdrawals from superannuation schemes for the financial year 2018-19: Financial-Incentives-for-Funded-Pension-Plans-in-OECD-Countries-2019.pdf

[17] Industry super funds ask for government help amid fears of mass COVID-19 withdrawals | Superannuation | The Guardian

[18] COVID-19 Early Release Scheme - Issue 36 | APRA

[19] EIOPA and FMA urgently recommend insurance undertakings to refrain from the distribution of dividends as well as share buy-backs - FMA Österreich

[20] FMA and European supervisory institutions recommend banks and insurance undertakings to refrain from dividend distributions and share buy backs this year as well as to pursue a conservative remuneration policy - FMA Österreich

[21] Repealing of the recommendation to financial service providers to refrain from paying dividends in light of the economic challenges caused by COVID-19. - FMA Österreich

[22] https://www.fma.gv.at/download.php?d=4339 (in German)

[23] https://www.fma.gv.at/download.php?d=4403 (in German)

[24] FMA warns about a strong increase in fraudulent activities in the financial markets in conjunction with the Corona pandemic - FMA Österreich

[25] COVID-19: information pour les institutions de retraite professionnelle | FSMA (in French)

[26] COVID-19: information pour les institutions de retraite professionnelle | FSMA (in French)

[27] https://www.fsma.be/sites/default/files/public/content/FR/Pension/COVID-19_irp_orientationscontinuite.pdf (in French)

[28] COVID-19: Beware of fraudulent investment offers and scams that are circulating on social media! | FSMA

[29] Conséquences en cas de chômage temporaire dû à la crise du coronavirus | FSMA (in French)

[30] COVID-19: Informations destinées aux consommateurs | FSMA (in French)

[31] Call centre | FSMA (in French)

[32] Registered Retirement Income Funds (RRIFs) minimum withdrawal reduced: CRA and COVID-19 - Canada.ca

[33] OSFI Actions to Address Issues Stemming from COVID-19 (osfi-bsif.gc.ca)

[34] Update on Temporary Portability Freeze (osfi-bsif.gc.ca)

[35] Directives of the Superintendent - FAQs (osfi-bsif.gc.ca)

[36] Canada Gazette, Part 2, Volume 154, Number 12: Solvency Special Payments Relief Regulations, 2020

[37] https://www.osfi-bsif.gc.ca/Eng/Pages/COVID-19.aspx

[38] OSFI announces regulatory flexibility to support COVID-19 efforts (osfi-bsif.gc.ca)

[39] https://www.bennettjones.com/Blogs-Section/What-Pension-Plan-Administrators-Need-to-Know-Amidst-the-COVID-19-Pandemic

[40] Directives of the Superintendent - FAQs (osfi-bsif.gc.ca)

[41] COVID-19 Measures Taken by Pension Regulators Across Canada Bulletin (lawsonlundell.com)

[42] Relief measures for Registered Pension Plans and Deferred Salary Leave Plans - Canada.ca

[43] Government extends relief for Registered Pension Plans and deferred salary leave plans - Canada.ca

[44] Superintendencia de Pensiones emite norma para que quienes inician trámite de pensión transfieran sus fondos a una cuenta corriente y eviten una disminución en sus ahorros - SP. Superintendencia de Pensiones - Gobierno de Chile (spensiones.cl) (in Spanish)

[45] https://www.spensiones.cl/portal/institucional/594/w3-channel.html

[46] Regulation 0262, available at: https://www.spensiones.cl/apps/normativaSP/getNormativa.php?id=ncgsp

[47] The minimum was lower for those with account balances under 35 UFs. Individuals with assets lower than 35 UF were allowed to withdraw all their savings.

[48] Withdrawals lower than 35 UFs were delivered in a single payment.

[49] Superintendencia de Pensiones flexibiliza normas de inversiones de los fondos de pensiones para facilitar proceso de liquidación de activos financieros - SP. Superintendencia de Pensiones - Gobierno de Chile (spensiones.cl) (in Spanish)

[50] Superintendencia de Pensiones instruye a las AFP procedimiento y plazos para implementar entrega de bono de hasta USD200.000 - SP. Superintendencia de Pensiones - Gobierno de Chile (spensiones.cl) (in Spanish)

[51] Bono de hasta USD200.000: sistema ha cursado más de 2.7 millones de pagos y el 93.7% de las solicitudes está al día - SP. Superintendencia de Pensiones - Gobierno de Chile (spensiones.cl) (in Spanish)

[52] Comunicado del Banco Central de Chile - Banco Central de Chile (bcentral.cl) (in Spanish)

[53] Banco Central dispone medidas ante nuevo retiro de fondos previsionales - Banco Central de Chile (bcentral.cl) (in Spanish)

[54] https://www.bcentral.cl/contenido/-/detalle/banco-central-dispone-medidas-ante-nuevo-retiro-de-fondos-previsionales (in Spanish)

[55] Law 21.227 empowers access to unemployment insurance benefits of Law 19.728 in exceptional circumstances (in place between 6 April 2020 and 6 October 2021, the measures related to contract suspension; reduction of working hours till December 2021): https://www.bcn.cl/leychile/navegar?idNorma=1144080. Law 21.247 establishes benefits for fathers, mothers and caregivers of children under certain conditions (in place between 27 July 2020 and 6 October 2021): https://www.bcn.cl/leychile/navegar?idNorma=1147763. Law 21.263 temporarily relaxes the access requirements and increases the amount of unemployment insurance benefits of Law 19.728, due to COVID-19, and improves the benefits of Law 21.227 (in place between 4 September 2020 and 6 October 2021): https://www.bcn.cl/leychile/navegar?idNorma=1149144

[56] DECRETO 558 DEL 15 DE ABRIL DE 2020.pdf (presidencia.gov.co) (in Spanish)

[57] Colombia-pension-market-2016.pdf (oecd.org)

[58] DECRETO 802 DEL 4 DE JUNIO DE 2020.pdf (presidencia.gov.co) (in Spanish)

[59] DECRETO 582 DEL 16 DE ABRIL DE 2020.pdf (presidencia.gov.co) (in Spanish)

[60] DECRETO 558 DEL 15 DE ABRIL DE 2020.pdf (presidencia.gov.co) (in Spanish)

[61] DECRETO 376 DEL 9 DE ABRIL DE 2021.pdf (presidencia.gov.co) (in Spanish)

[62] Sistema Costarricense de Información Jurídica (pgrweb.go.cr) (in Spanish)

[63] SUPEN implementa mejoras en favor de los afiliados - Buscar - SUPEN (in Spanish)

[64] President signs law for withdrawal of rop - Presidency of the Republic of CostaRica (presidencia.go.cr) (in Spanish)

[65] Overview of all CNB measures related to the coronavirus crisis in one place - the Czech National Bank

[66] Overview of all CNB measures related to the coronavirus crisis in one place - the Czech National Bank

[67] Tripartite Agreements in 2020 and 2021 (star.dk)

[68] The Danish Wage Compensation Scheme helping companies and employees through the COVID-19 pandemic

[69] Tripartite Agreements in 2020 and 2021 (star.dk)

[70] Tripartite Agreements in 2020 and 2021 (star.dk)

[71] Fleksibilitet i forhold til indberetninger mv. for forsikringsselskaber i lyset af COVID-19 (finanstilsynet.dk) (in Danish)

[72] Løbende opfølgning på solvensdækning i pensionsselskaber (finanstilsynet.dk) (in Danish)

[73] EIOPA-erklæring om udbytte og variabel aflønningspolitik i forbindelse med COVID-19 (finanstilsynet.dk) (in Danish)

[74] Danica Pension er klar med en hjælpende hånd til økonomisk pressede kunder (in Danish)

[75] Temporary suspension of II pillar contributions - Pensionikeskus

[76] https://www.rahandusministeerium.ee/sites/default/files/teise_samba_maksete_ajutine_peatamine.pdf (in Estonian)

[77] Sissemaksed peatas ajutiselt 9575 inimest - Pensionikeskus (in Estonian)

[78] Koronatilanne - TELA (in Finnish)

[79] Koronatilanne - TELA (in Finnish)

[80] Suomen hallitus hyväksyi työmarkkinajärjestöjen ehdotuksen eläkemaksujen tilapäisestä alentamisesta - Eläketurvakeskus (etk.fi) (in Finnish)

[81] These buffer funds are cash buffers in the balance sheet of pension providers. They are also called equalisation liability.

[82] Governmental grants and financial assistance available for Finnish companies in distress due to COVID-19 (twobirds.com)

[83] https://acpr.banque-france.fr/sites/default/files/medias/documents/20200403_communique_presse_dividendes_assurances.pdf and Les incertitudes sur l'ampleur des impacts de la crise imposent une gestion prudente des fonds propres des assureurs | Banque de France (banque-france.fr) (in French)

[84] https://acpr.banque-france.fr/sites/default/files/medias/documents/20200728_communique_presse_recommandation_esrb_dividendes_1.pdf (in French)

[85] L'ACPR demande aux institutions financières sous sa supervision de demeurer d'une grande prudence en matière de distributions (dividendes, rachats d'action, rémunérations variables) jusqu'au 30 septembre 2021 | Banque de France (banque-france.fr) (in French)

[86] Assouplissement temporaire des dates de remise des états de reporting prudentiel européens, des exigences nationales complémentaires et de publication des informations destinées au public - Contexte du Coronavirus/COVID-19 | Banque de France (banque-france.fr) (in French)

[87] Communications de l'ACPR dans le contexte de la pandémie COVID-19 | Banque de France (banque-france.fr) (in French)

[88] Ordonnance n° 2020-322 du 25 mars 2020 adaptant temporairement les conditions et modalités d'attribution de l'indemnité complémentaire prévue à l'article L. 1226-1 du code du travail et modifiant, à titre exceptionnel, les dates limites et les modalités de versement des sommes versées au titre de l'intéressement et de la participation - Légifrance (legifrance.gouv.fr) (in French)

[89] Épargne salariale, participation et intéressement | service-public.fr (in French)

[90] Loi Madelin et PER: déblocage anticipé porté à 8000 € LégiFiscal (legifiscal.fr) (in French)

[91] BaFin - Aktuelles zum Corona-Virus - Auslegungsentscheidung zur Erklärung zu den Grundsätzen der ... (in German)

[92] https://www.bafin.de/SharedDocs/Veroeffentlichungen/EN/Meldung/2020_21_Corona/meldung_2020_03_24_corona_virus4_aktien_en.htmlhttps://www.bafin.de/SharedDocs/Veroeffentlichungen/EN/Meldung/2020/meldung_2020_07_15_CEO-Fraud_en.html

[93] https://www.mnb.hu/letoltes/vezetoi-korlevel-a-penztari-szektor-szamara-a-koronavirus-terjedese-altal-okozott-helyzetben-elvart-kockazatmerseklo-lepesekrol.pdf

[94] Measures undertaken by the IcelandicGovernment in response to COVID-19 - LEX Lögmannsstofa

[95] Quarantine payments | Directorate of Labour (vinnumalastofnun.is)

[96] Questions and answers regarding quarinte payments | Directorate of Labour (vinnumalastofnun.is)

[97] Reduced employment ratio | Directorate of Labour (vinnumalastofnun.is)

[98] Government of Iceland | Covid-19 information

[99] Partial Compensation/Reduced Employment Rate | Bureau of Labor Statistics (vinnumalastofnun.is)

[100] 54/2006: Lög um atvinnuleysistryggingar | Lög | Alþingi (althingi.is) (in Icelandic)

[101] Questions and answers regarding reduced employment ratio | Directorate of Labour (vinnumalastofnun.is)

[102] Statement by the Central Bank of Iceland on extension of the hiatus in pension funds' foreign currency purchases (cb.is)

[103] Aðgerðir stjórnvalda til að mæta tímabundnu ástandi á vinnumarkaði - LEX Lögmannsstofa (in Icelandic)

[104] Ábendingar til aðila á lífeyrismarkaði vegna COVID-19 (sedlabanki.is) (in Icelandic)

[105] Statement_financial_supervision_april2020.pdf (cb.is)

[106] Government of Iceland | Covid-19 information

[107] Stjórnarráðið | COVID-19: Aðgerðir og ráðstafanir (stjornarradid.is) (in Icelandic)

[108] 902e83dc-f3db-40ca-a1a3-f2d508ae8338.pdf (hagstofan.s3.amazonaws.com) (in Icelandic)

[109] Statement_financial_supervision_april2020.pdf (cb.is)

[110] https://www.pensionsauthority.ie/en/news_press/news_press_archive/COVID-19_announcement_by_the_pensions_authority.html

[111] The Pensions Authority - COVID-19 - Update from the Pensions Authority

[112] https://www.pensionsauthority.ie/en/news_press/news_press_archive/pensions_authority_annual_report_and_accounts_2020.pdf

[113] ביטוח ,ההון שוק רשות | הנבחרות הפנסיה קרנות על ומטעה שגוי מידע מפני הציבור את להזהיר מבקשת ההון שוק רשות וחיסכון (www.gov.il) (in Hebrew)

[114] וחיסכון ביטוח ,ההון שוק רשות | שיקרי פיננסי ייעוץ - החוסכים לציבור אזהרה (www.gov.il) (in Hebrew)

[115] https://en.globes.co.il/en/article-self-employed-can-take-unemployment-pay-from-pension-1001345766

[116] שוק רשות | הקורונה משבר בתקופת הפקדות שהפסיקו לחוסכים ניהול דמי תקרת לאימוץ ביוזמה יוצאת ההון שוק רשות וחיסכון ביטוח ,ההון (www.gov.il) (in Hebrew)

[117] Audizione del Presidente COVIP - 11° Commissione Senato. "Affare assegnato riguardante ricadute occupazionali dell'epidemia da COVID-19, azioni idonee a fronteggiare le situazioni di crisi e necessità di garantire la sicurezza sanitaria nei luoghi di lavoro (atto n. 453)" | COVIP (in Italian)

[118] COVID-19_circolare_ania_revfinale.pdf (covip.it) (in Italian)

[119] Contributo di vigilanza per l'anno 2020 - Deliberazione COVIP dell'11 marzo 2020 | COVIP (in Italian)

[120] annual_report_2020_main_data.pdf (covip.it)

[121] Press Releases - Financial Services Commission (fsc.go.kr)

[122] Press Releases - Financial Services Commission (fsc.go.kr)

[123] Press Releases - Financial Services Commission (fsc.go.kr)

[124] With an outbreak of COVID-19, in supervising the financial market participants the FCMC will ensure an individual and flexible approach (fktk.lv)

[125] Bankas un apdrošināšanas sabiedrības tiek aicinātas ierobežot dividenžu izmaksu (fktk.lv) (in Latvian)

[126] Lietuvos bankas dėl koranoviruso atideda dalį planuotų tikrinimų | Lietuvos bankas (lb.lt) (in Lithuanian)

[127] Kaupiantiesiems pensijų fonduose patariama likti ramiems | Lietuvos bankas (lb.lt) (in Lithuanian)

[128] http://www.caa.lu/uploads/documents/files/LC20_15.pdf (in French)

[129] https://www.caa.lu/uploads/documents/files/LC21_1.pdf (in French)

[130] Regulatory reporting - CSSF

[131] FAQ_COVID-19_eng.pdf (cssf.lu)

[132] http://www.caa.lu/uploads/documents/files/Calendrier_Reportings_CAA_2020_F_3.pdf (in French)

[133] FAQ_COVID-19_eng.pdf (cssf.lu)

[134] http://www.caa.lu/fr/actualites/avertissement-general-contre-les-arnaques (in French)

[135] Otras Disposiciones, Calendario, Acuerdos y Lineamientos | Comisión Nacional del Sistema de Ahorro para el Retiro | Gobierno | gob.mx (www.gob.mx) (in Spanish)

[136] Medidas temporales y extraordinarias para garantizar la ejecución de actividades esenciales de las AFORE | Comisión Nacional del Sistema de Ahorro para el Retiro | Gobierno | gob.mx (www.gob.mx) (in Spanish)

[137] 10 razones por las que no debes preocuparte por las minusvalías en el SAR | Comisión Nacional del Sistema de Ahorro para el Retiro | Gobierno | gob.mx (www.gob.mx) (in Spanish)

[138] COMUNICADO | Comisión Nacional del Sistema de Ahorro para el Retiro | Gobierno | gob.mx (www.gob.mx) (in Spanish)

[139] NOW-regeling compenseert volledige pensioenpremie met extra 30% op loonsom (pensioenfederatie.nl) (in Dutch)

[140] The top-up was a contribution for all employer expenses on top of gross wages, including pension contributions, but also holiday pay, and premiums for employee insurance for unemployment and disability.

[141] Coronavirus: DutchGovernment adopts package of new measures designed to save jobs and the economy | News item | Government.nl

[142] Regeling NOW 2.0 gepubliceerd (pensioenfederatie.nl) (in Dutch)

[143] Het kabinet presenteert NOW III (pensioenfederatie.nl) (in Dutch)

[144] Government extends coronavirus support for jobs and the economy into 2021 | News item | Government.nl

[145] Dutch Labor, Employment, and Pensions Update - Lexology

[146] Support and recovery package substantially expanded | News item | Government.nl

[147] This wage bill exemption at 10% was introduced in Q4 2020.

[148] Support package for jobs and economy to be continued in third quarter | News item | Government.nl

[149] End of support package for jobs and economy | News item | Government.nl

[150] overzicht-aanvraagperiodes-now.pdf (uwv.nl) (in Dutch)

[151] Postponement of the reporting period for annual statements of pension funds due to Coronavirus (dnb.nl) (in Dutch)

[152] Minister biedt helderheid over pensioen op de korte termijn (pensioenfederatie.nl) (in Dutch)

[153] Riding out COVID-19 in KiwiSaver » Sorted

[154] How to stay safe from scams during COVID-19 » Sorted

[155] COVID-19 and your money: 7 things to do right now » Sorted

[156] Thinking of making a KiwiSaver hardship withdrawal? Here's what you need to know | FMA

[157] 2020 COVID-19 Wage Subsidy - Work and Income

[158] COVID-19 LeaveSupport Scheme - Work and Income

[159] The only way to stop contributions is for the employee to request a savings suspension from Inland Revenue.

[160] COVID-19 Wage Subsidy Extension - Work and Income

[161] COVID-19 Resurgence Wage Subsidy - Work and Income

[162] COVID-19 Wage Subsidy March 2021 - Work and Income

[163] COVID-19 Essential Workers Leave Support Scheme - Work and Income

[164] Essential companies could apply to a Wage Subsidy or a Leave Support for an employee if they met the eligibility conditions of the respective subsidies. However, they would only receive one of the two for the same employee.

[165] https://www.workandincome.govt.nz/about-work-and-income/news/2020/leave-support-scheme-changes.html

[166] COVID-19 Short-Term Absence Payment - Work and Income

[167] https://www.ird.govt.nz/COVID-19/business-and-organisations/COVID-19-support-payment

[168] https://www.fma.govt.nz/assets/Uploads/CoFR-table-of-deferred-regulatory-initiatives-April-2020.pdf

[169] https://www.justice.govt.nz/about/news-and-media/COVID-19-news/oaths-affirmations-or-declarations/

[170] COVID-19: KiwiSaver significant financial hardship applications | FMA

[171] https://www.fma.govt.nz/news-and-resources/COVID-19/hardship-withdrawals-a-last-resort-rob-everett/

[172] 'No action' relief as a result of COVID-19 | FMA

[173] https://www.regjeringen.no/en/aktuelt/additional-financial-measures-to-mitigate-the-economic-effects-of-the-coronavirus-crisis/id2696548/

[174] Regler om permitterte ansatte i private tjenestepensjonsordninger trer i kraft - regjeringen.no (in Norwegian)

[175] Regler om permitterte ansatte i private tjenestepensjonsordninger forlenges - regjeringen.no (in Norwegian)

[176] Regler om permitterte ansatte i private tjenestepensjonsordninger forlenges - regjeringen.no (in Norwegian)

[177] Regler om permitterte ansatte i private tjenestepensjonsordninger forlenges - regjeringen.no (in Norwegian)

[178] Regler om permitterte ansatte i private tjenestepensjonsordninger forlenges - regjeringen.no (in Norwegian)

[179] https://www.regjeringen.no/no/aktuelt/banker-og-forsikringsforetak-bor-holde-tilbake-overskudd/id2695014/ (in Norwegian)

[180] Oppfølging av ESRBs anbefaling om utbytterestriksjoner mv. - Finanstilsynet.no (in Norwegian)

[181] Banker og forsikringsforetak må orientere Finanstilsynet om planlagt utbytte - Finanstilsynet.no (in Norwegian)

[182] https://www.finanstilsynet.no/nyhetsarkiv/nyheter/2020/utsettelse-av-rapporteringsfrister/ (in Norwegian)

[183] https://www.finanstilsynet.no/nyhetsarkiv/nyheter/2020/finanstilsynet-folger-eiopas-anbefaling-om-lettelser-i-rapporteringskrav/ (in Norwegian)

[184] https://www.knf.gov.pl/o_nas/komunikaty?articleId=69462&p_id=18 (in Polish)

185 Koronawirus. Komunikat: zmiana terminów wdrożenia PPK - oficjalny portal Pracowniczych Planów Kapitałowych PPK (mojeppk.pl) (in Polish)

186 Zwolnienie z finansowania wpłat do PPK: kto może uzyskać? (bezprawnik.pl) (in Polish)

187 OFE to be eliminated. The government adopted a draft law | RSM Poland (EN)

188 https://www.asf.com.pt/NR/rdonlyres/58DAE1BA-D274-4C2D-87C5-ED043E9A0784/0/CartaCircularnr42020.pdf (in Portuguese)

189 https://www.asf.com.pt/NR/rdonlyres/58DAE1BA-D274-4C2D-87C5-ED043E9A0784/0/CartaCircularnr42020.pdf

190 CartaCircular10_2020_COVID-19_EGFP_AtualizaçãoMedidas.pdf (asf.com.pt) (in Portuguese)

191 ASF - Entidades Gestoras de Fundos de Pensões - Recomendações relativamente a distribuições de dividendos ou outras medidas que afetem os capitais próprios no âmbito da situação excecional relacionada com o surto pandémico COVID-19 (in Portuguese)

192 ASF - Empresas de Seguros - Recomendações relativamente a distribuições de dividendos ou outras medidas que afetem fundos próprios no âmbito da situação excecional relacionada com o surto pandémico COVID-19 (in Portuguese)

193 https://www.asf.com.pt/NR/rdonlyres/58DAE1BA-D274-4C2D-87C5-ED043E9A0784/0/CartaCircularnr42020.pdf (in Portuguese)

194 CartaCircular10_2020_COVID-19_EGFP_AtualizaçãoMedidas.pdf (asf.com.pt) (in Portuguese)

195 https://www.asf.com.pt/NR/exeres/DA3C0127-02DF-45FA-A945-A2A45D74FD60.htm (in Portuguese)

196 CartaCircular10_2020_COVID-19_EGFP_AtualizaçãoMedidas.pdf (asf.com.pt) (in Portuguese)

197 https://www.asf.com.pt/NR/rdonlyres/58DAE1BA-D274-4C2D-87C5-ED043E9A0784/0/CartaCircularnr42020.pdf (in Portuguese)

198 PPR pension funds are personal retirement saving schemes in the form of pension funds.

199 https://dre.pt/application/file/a/131347485 (in Portuguese)

200 ASF - Regras excecionais para o reembolso antecipado de Planos de Poupança (in Portuguese)

201 isp_first_aid_nov2020.pdf (gov.sk)

202 285482_2150149_71_2.pdf (europa.eu)

203 First aid PLUS - changes in State contributions from 1October 2020 - TPA the SlovakRepublic (tpa-group.sk)

204 Higher contributions for employers and self-employed individuals - “First Aid ++” - TPA the SlovakRepublic (tpa-group.sk)

205 First Aid ++ the SlovakRepublic | Auditorea

[206] Microsoft Word - 23112021_Complex memo on agreed measures regarding Coronavirus pandemic_EN (vgd.eu)

[207] Changes in First Aid from 1July 2021 | KPMG Slovensko (danovky.sk)

[208] UZ672020_752020.pdf (nbs.sk) (in the Slovak Republic)

[209] Sociálna poisťovňa - Ako požiadať o jednotlivé dávky bez návštevy pobočky počas koronakrízy (socpoist.sk) (in the Slovak Republic)

[210] ATVP v skladu s priporočilom OFS izdala mnenje glede izplačil dividend in dobičkov finančnih družb, ki jih nadzira | ATVP - Agencija za trg vrednostnih papirjev (a-tvp.si) (in Slovenian) for the SMA and https://www.a-zn.si/sporocilo-za-javnost-zacasno-zadrzanje-izplacila-dividend-v-zavarovalnicah-pozavarovalnicah-pokojninskim-druzbah-je-v-interesu-vseh-deleznikov/ (in Slovenian) for the ISA

[211] https://www.a-zn.si/sporocilo-za-javnost-zagotavljanje-financne-stabilnosti-v-okoliscinah-epidemije-COVID-19-z-zacasnim-zadrzanjem-izplacila-dividend/ (in Slovenian)

[212] Sporočilo za javnost: AZN pričakuje, da dividende ne bodo izplačane do konca septembra 2021 (a-zn.si) (in Slovenian)

[213] Spremembe pri vodenju postopkov ATVP zaradi interventnih ukrepov (COVID-19) | ATVP - Agencija za trg vrednostnih papirjev (a-tvp.si) (in Slovenian)

[214] Spremembe pri vodenju upravnih postopkov ATVP zaradi začasnih interventnih ukrepov (COVID-19) | ATVP - Agencija za trg vrednostnih papirjev (a-tvp.si) (in Slovenian)

[215] ATVP svari pred nepremišljenimi naložbami | ATVP - Agencija za trg vrednostnih papirjev (a-tvp.si) (in Slovenian)

[216] 20210122 Nota publica dividendos_v ESP.pdf (mineco.es) (in Spanish)

[217] https://www.boe.es/diario_boe/txt.php?id=BOE-A-2020-4208 (in Spanish)

[218] https://www.oecd.org/daf/fin/private-pensions/Financial-Incentives-for-Funded-Pension-Plans-in-OECD-Countries-2019.pdf

[219] Boletín de información trimestral segundo trimestre.pdf (mineco.es) (in Spanish)

[220] Short-time work allowance 2020 - Tillväxtverket (tillvaxtverket.se)

[221] Short-time work allowance 2021 - Tillväxtverket (tillvaxtverket.se)

[222] Questions and Answers - Tillväxtverket (tillvaxtverket.se)

[223] The support was calculated on employees' salary capped at SEK 44 000 per month.

[224] Short-time working allowance - verksamt.se

[225] https://www.fi.se/sv/publicerat/nyheter/2020/forsakringsforetag-och-tjanstepensionskassor-bor-anvanda-sina-buffertar/ (in Swedish)

[226] https://www.riksdagen.se/sv/dokument-lagar/dokument/_sfs-2020-198 (in Swedish)

[227] https://www.ipe.com/news/sweden-eases-iorp-ii-rules-for-covid-hit-pension-funds/10046486.article

[228] https://svenskforfattningssamling.se/doc/2020935.html (in Swedish)

[229] https://www.fi.se/sv/publicerat/nyheter/2020/bedragare-utger-sig-att-ringa-fran-fi/ (in Swedish)

[230] Finansiella företag ska vara återhållsamma med utdelningar till och med september 2021 | Finansinspektionen

[231] https://www.bsv.admin.ch/bsv/fr/home/publications-et-services/medieninformationen/nsb-anzeigeseite-unter-aktuell.msg-id-81044.html (in French)

[232] https://www.admin.ch/opc/fr/official-compilation/2020/3835.pdf (in French)

[233] https://www.finma.ch/fr/news/2020March 20200325-mm-garantiepaket/ (in French)

[234] https://www.finma.ch/fr/news/2020April 20200407-meldung-finma-aufsichtsmitteilung-03-2020/ (in French)

[235] https://www.thepensionsregulator.gov.uk/en/COVID-19-coronavirus-what-you-need-to-consider/db-scheme-funding-and-investment-COVID-19-guidance-for-trustees

[236] COVID-19 DB scheme funding investment trustees | The Pensions Regulator

[237] DC trustees: COVID-19 scheme management and investment guidance | The Pensions Regulator

[238] Need help paying this year's levy invoice? | Pension Protection Fund (ppf.co.uk)

[239] PPF extends 90-day levy payment window for schemes impacted by COVID-19 | Pension Protection Fund

[240] https://www.gov.uk/guidance/claim-for-wage-costs-through-the-coronavirus-job-retention-scheme

[241] https://www.gov.uk/government/news/chancellor-extends-furlough-scheme-until-october

[242] https://www.gov.uk/government/publications/changes-to-the-coronavirus-job-retention-scheme/changes-to-the-coronavirus-job-retention-scheme

[243] The date changed and been brought forward as the CJRS was extended.

[244] https://www.gov.uk/government/publications/job-support-scheme

[245] Who is claiming furlough? HMRC publishes its first list - Lexology

[246] Automatic enrolment and DC pension contributions: COVID-19 guidance for employers | The Pensions Regulator

[247] Salary sacrifice for employers - GOV.UK (www.gov.uk)

[248] PS19/1: Retirement Outcomes Review: feedback on CP18/17 and our final rules and guidance | FCA

[249] PS19/21: Retirement Outcomes Review: feedback on CP19/5 and our final rules and guidance | FCA

[250] Pension schemes to issue COVID-19 transfer warning to savers | The Pensions Regulator

[251] Pensions and Retirement income: our guidance for firms | FCA

[252] https://www.ppf.co.uk/sites/default/files/file-2020-05/COVID-19-and-your-pension.pdf

[253] New measures to protect pension savers from scam transfers - GOV.UK (www.gov.uk) and New regulations empower trustees to halt suspicious transfers | The Pensions Regulator

[254] P.L. 116-136 (27 March, 2020). John J. Topelski, Elizabeth A. Myers, Cong. Research Serv., IF 1 142 Retirement and Pension Provisions in the Coronavirus Aid, Relief, and Economic Security Act (CARES Act) (April 2020).

[255] The SECURE Act, passed as part of the Further Consolidated Appropriations Act, 2020, (P.L. 116-94), increased the age at which RMDs must begin from 70.5 to 72.

[256] https://www.irs.gov/pub/irs-drop/n-20-51.pdf

[257] IRS: Seniors, retirees not required to take distributions from retirement accounts this year under new law | Internal Revenue Service

[258] Notice 2020-61 (irs.gov)

[259] N-2020-82 (irs.gov)

[260] Notice 2020-61 (irs.gov)

[261] Adverse consequences from COVID-19 may occur as a result of being quarantined, furloughed, or laid off, or of having work hours reduced due to such virus or disease, being unable to work due to lack of child care due to such virus or disease, closing or reducing hours of a business owned or operated by the individual due to such virus or disease, or other factors as determined by US regulatory authorities.

[262] Text - H.R.133 - 116th Congress (2019-2020): Consolidated Appropriations Act, 2021 | Congress.gov | Library of Congress https://www.lexology.com/library/detail.aspx?g=ffeb6b14-3b1e-4739-8eab-1bbe776b0804&utm_source=lexology+daily+newsfeed&utm_medium=html+email+-+body+-+general+section&utm_campaign=lexology+subscriber+daily+feed&utm_content=lexology+daily+newsfeed+2021-03-16&utm_term=

[263] Money Purchase Pension Plan Definition (investopedia.com)

[264] Text - H.R.1319 - 117th Congress (2021-2022): American Rescue Plan Act of 2021 | Congress.gov | Library of Congress

[265] PBGC to Provide Special Financial Assistance to Troubled Multiemployer Plans | Pension Benefit Guaranty Corporation and hwaysandmeansreconciliation.pdf (cbo.gov)

[266] American Rescue Plan Includes Significant Relief for Troubled Multiemployer Pension Plans - Lexology

[267] PBGC to Provide Special Financial Assistance to Troubled Multiemployer Plans | Pension Benefit Guaranty Corporation

[268] American Rescue Plan Act FAQs | Pension Benefit Guaranty Corporation (pbgc.gov)

[269] Not all previous benefit cuts are undone and restored under the statute. The only benefit cuts subject to reinstatement are benefit suspensions under the Multiemployer Pension Reform Act and benefit suspensions to the PBGC guaranteed benefit level stemming from a plan's insolvency. Other types of benefit cuts (e.g. to "adjustable benefits") allowable to Critical Status plans are not restored.

[270] New COVID-19 Stimulus Bill Includes Significant Pension Reforms and Expands Scope of 162(m) Compensation Deduction Limit - Lexology

[271] Text - H.R.1319 - 117th Congress (2021-2022): American Rescue Plan Act of 2021 | Congress.gov | Library of Congress

[272] New COVID-19 Stimulus Bill Includes Significant Pension Reforms and Expands Scope of 162(m) Compensation Deduction Limit - Lexology

[273] US. Pension relief paves way for more de-risking - Pension Policy International

[274] EmergencyPensionPlanReliefActof2021Summary.pdf (jacksonlewis.com)

[275] US. DOL Issues Cybersecurity Best Practices for Retirement Plans - Pension Policy International

3 Assessing country responses to COVID-19 based on OECD policy guidelines

This chapter assesses whether the policies implemented by OECD countries to address the impact of the COVID-19 crisis on asset-backed pension arrangements have been in line with the initial OECD policy guidelines. It uses evidence up to the end of 2021 to analyse the effects of the OECD member countries' policy responses.

Nearly three years after the outbreak of the COVID-19 crisis, it is possible to take stock of the effects of this crisis on asset-backed pension systems and to assess the policies implemented by different countries in response to it. Chapter 1 describes the main challenges posed by COVID-19 on asset-backed pension systems and the main policy guidelines put forward by the OECD as early as June 2020 to assist pension policy makers, regulators and supervisors. Chapter 2 presents the main policy and supervisory responses that countries have implemented during 2020-21 to address the impact of COVID-19 on asset-backed pension arrangements.

This chapter assesses whether the policy responses to the COVID-19 crisis implemented by OECD countries in asset-backed pension systems have been in line with the initial OECD policy guidelines. The chapter recalls the issue that the policy guidelines were meant to address and describes the policy responses put in place by OECD countries considering their alignment or not with the guidelines. The chapter also looks at the evolution of the main parameters of asset-backed pension systems since the start of the crisis to get an understanding of the impact of the policy measures implemented.

Overall, OECD countries' policy responses to the COVID-19 crisis have been in line with the OECD policy guidelines. Most countries put measures in place to avoid the materialisation of investment losses when financial markets were low, they provided temporary flexibility into funding and solvency rules for defined benefit (DB) plans, they supported the continuation of contributions through job-retention schemes, and they supervised pension entities following a flexible, pragmatic, proportionate and risk-based approach. These policy responses helped pension funds to achieve positive investment returns, they reduced pressure on DB plan sponsors, they helped maintain contributions during 2020, and they avoided disruptions in the delivery of key services by pension entities. However, a few policy responses have not been aligned with the OECD policy guidelines. In particular, some countries temporarily reduced the flow of contributions paid into asset-backed pension arrangements and facilitated early withdrawals from defined contribution (DC) plans even for individuals who may not have been in dire need to tap into their retirement assets. These measures aimed to provide short-term relief to employers and individuals during the crisis, but they led to lower assets accumulated, jeopardising the adequacy of future retirement income. Overall, available evidence supports the relevance of the OECD policy guidelines, which could assist policy makers in addressing the shock of future crises.

Section 3.1 looks at the measures implemented to maintain investment strategies during market volatility in order to avoid the materialisation of investment losses. Section 3.2 analyses the measures supporting the solvency of DB plans and their sponsors. Section 3.3 assesses how different measures affected the level of contributions paid into retirement savings plans. Section 3.4 examines supervisory responses. Section 3.5 looks at the measures that facilitated early withdrawals from asset-backed pension arrangements. Finally, Section 3.6 concludes.

3.1. Countries avoided the materialisation of investment losses

COVID-19 initially led to a large fall in stock markets, reducing the value of retirement assets. Major stock markets suffered setbacks between mid-February and end-March 2020 as governments were taking precautionary measures to limit the spread of the virus and shutting down parts of the economy (Figure 3.1). Consequently, pension funds in most OECD countries experienced negative investment returns in the first quarter of 2020, leading to a decline in the value of retirement assets at the end of March compared to end-2019 ranging from -24.3% in Poland to -0.4% in Iceland (Figure 3.2).

However, saving for retirement is for the long term, and short-term volatility in financial markets should not derail plan members and providers from their long-term objective. As such, the OECD policy guidelines recommend plan members and providers to stay the course and maintain portfolio investments when markets are low to avoid selling and materialising value losses. Fluctuations in the value of assets are inevitable during the life of a portfolio. Selling assets when shocks occur leads to materialising the reduction in value and precluding opportunities to recover the losses. As Figure 3.1 shows, stock markets have recovered in many countries after the downturn in the first quarter of 2020. Staying the course would have allowed to recover the initial losses.

Figure 3.1. Evolution of selected MSCI indices between Q4-2019 and Q4-2021

Base: 100 at end-2019

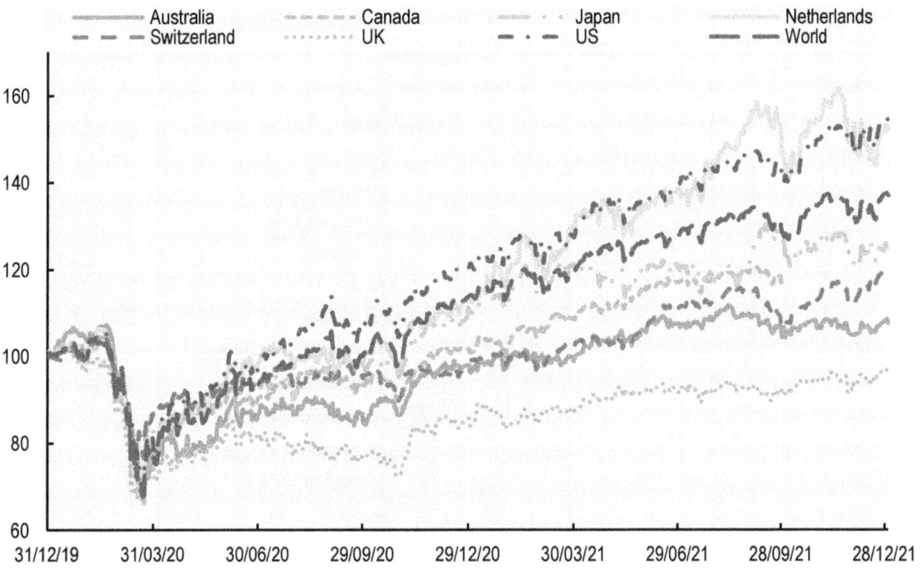

Source: www.investing.com

OECD countries have implemented a range of measures aligned with the objective of maintaining portfolio investments and avoiding the sale of assets during market volatility. Some countries, such as Hungary, Lithuania, Mexico, New Zealand and Portugal, endeavoured to limit switches to more conservative investment strategies and early withdrawals of funds by warning plan members about the risk of materialising investment losses. Other countries, including Canada, Costa Rica, Türkiye and the United Kingdom suspended the possibility to transfer assets across pension plans or providers. Additionally, Chile, Germany, Israel and Poland relaxed certain quantitative investment rules in order to avoid the sale of assets due to unintended breaches of investment limits or massive withdrawal requests. Finally, Sweden encouraged pension funds to refrain from selling assets to meet internal buffer requirements.

OECD countries also implemented measures to protect plan members close to or already in retirement. These individuals may be particularly vulnerable during shocks in financial markets as they may need to buy an annuity with their accumulated assets, or they may be required to withdraw funds during retirement. These situations may force them to sell when markets are low. Flexibility in the timing of buying an annuity and in drawdown rules could prevent people from locking in losses. In line with this, Latvia postponed the start of the pay-out phase for people about to retire during the crisis. Chile protected the value of assets from market volatility for plan members in the process of receiving retirement benefits by transferring their assets to a guaranteed account at the start of the process. Finally, Australia, Canada and the United States reduced or suspended minimum drawdown requirements for retirees.

Figure 3.2. Change in asset values at the end of Q1-2020 and Q4-2020 as compared to the end of Q4-2019 in selected OECD countries

In percent

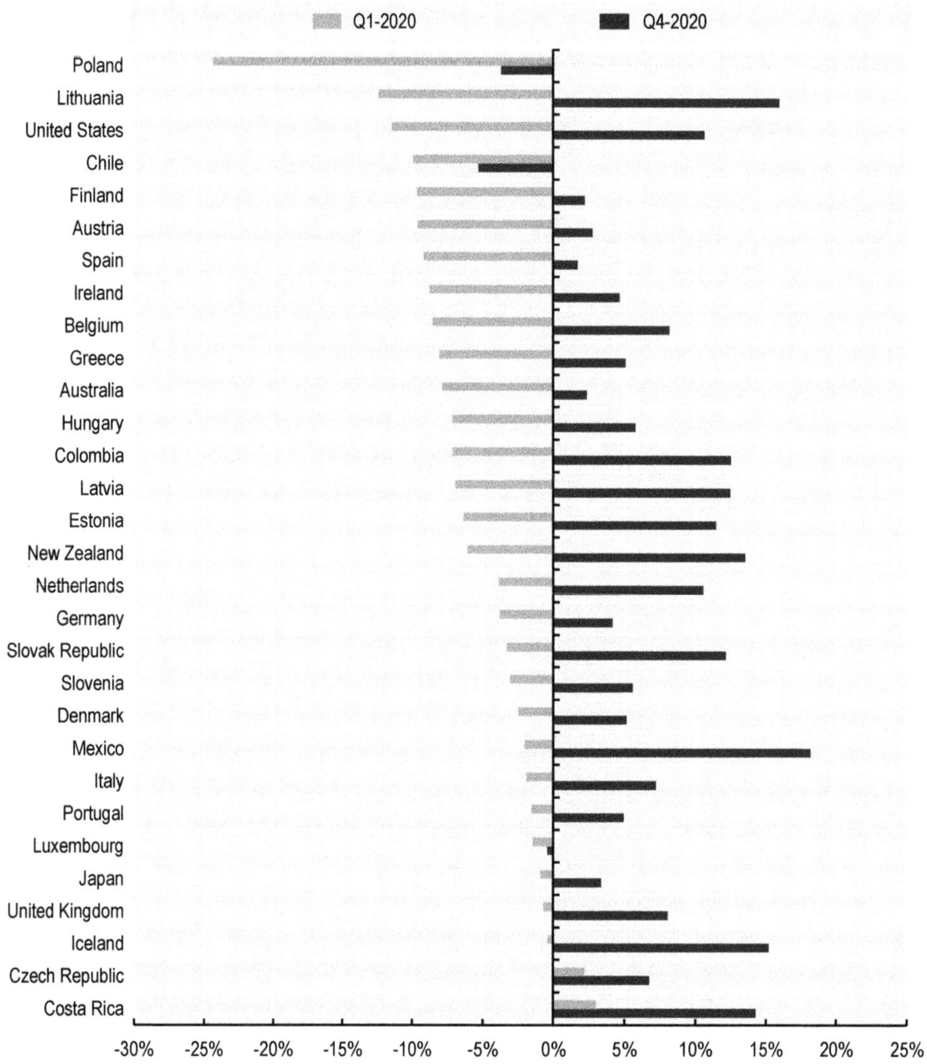

Source: ECB data for Austria, Belgium, Estonia, Germany, Greece, Ireland, Italy, Latvia, Lithuania, Luxembourg, the Netherlands, Portugal, the Slovak Republic, Slovenia and Spain; AIOS data for Costa Rica; National data sources for the other countries.

By contrast, transferring the assets of retirees taking programmed withdrawals to a public entity in Colombia may have crystallised investment losses. In April 2020, the government introduced a decree transferring the duty to pay pension benefits from pension fund administrators (AFPs) to the state pension fund (*Colpensiones*) when the balance in the account of pensioners using programmed withdrawals as of 31 March 2020 was not enough to guarantee the lifetime payment of a monthly minimum wage. In this case, AFPs were required to transfer the assets to *Colpensiones*, which then had the responsibility to pay a lifetime pension equivalent to the monthly minimum wage to retired members. In June 2020, the requirement to transfer the balance of eligible pensioners to *Colpensiones* was transformed into a voluntary option for AFPs. The measure was later declared unconstitutional in July 2020 and pensioners under the programmed withdrawal option who had been transferred to *Colpensiones* had to be brought back in their AFP. Although the intention of the transfer to *Colpensiones* was to protect the level of benefits of pensioners and to relieve AFPs from the guarantee, this measure may have prevented retirees from benefitting from the recovery of financial markets and receiving benefits greater than the monthly minimum wage going forward.

In most countries, the measures to avoid the sale of assets were temporary. As financial markets bounced back after the lows of March 2020 and assets had recovered in most countries, policy makers could revert to the usual rules. For example, Canada lifted the portability freeze of federally regulated DB plans at the end of August 2020. The possibility to change pension operators in Costa Rica resumed at the beginning of September 2020. The possibility for individuals to postpone their retirement option decision in Latvia ended on 30 November 2021. Finally, the loosening of minimum drawdown requirements stopped at the end of 2020 in Canada and the United States.

Overall, the measures taken seem to have helped to avoid the materialisation of short-term investment losses. Despite the negative developments in stock markets during the first quarter of 2020, most countries recorded positive real investment rates of return in 2020 overall (OECD, 2021[1]). As a result, for all countries in Figure 3.2 except two (Chile and Poland), assets in asset-backed pension arrangements at the end of 2020 had recovered or exceeded the levels observed at the end of 2019. The yearly increase in assets during 2020 was even larger than 10% in Colombia, Estonia, Iceland, Latvia, Lithuania, Mexico, the Netherlands, New Zealand, the Slovak Republic, and the United States. In the case of Chile, while the level of pension assets at the end of June 2020 was already above its December 2019 level, it subsequently fell due to the two rounds of early withdrawals permitted in July and November 2020.[1] Pension funds in Poland suffered the largest losses in Q1-2020 due to their large investment in equities (82% at the end of 2019) (OECD, 2021[1]), and had to wait until March 2021 to recover their 2019 level.[2]

However, switching behaviours remained problematic during the peak of market volatility in some countries. For example, in New Zealand, within a sample of 1.5 million *KiwiSaver* members, 58 356 (3.9%) changed their investment strategy between February and April 2020, at the height of market volatility (PWC, 2021[2]). This is 2.7 times more than during the same period in 2019. Of all the switches, 70.5% were to a lower risk fund, 11.0% to an equivalent fund and 18.5% to a higher risk fund. In comparison, in the same period in 2019, only 27.0% of switches were to a lower risk fund. Members aged 26 to 35 were more likely to switch, especially to lower risk funds. In addition, the vast majority (90.9%) of people who switched to a lower risk fund were still in this fund by August 2020, effectively locking in their losses. These results are consistent with international evidence showing that frequent switches typically result in worse investment outcomes (OECD, 2020[3]). Communications by *KiwiSaver* providers and the regulator (the Financial Market Authority) to encourage members to stay calm and keep their investment strategy were not fully successful. Other policy measures, such as implicit or explicit barriers to switching, may be necessary to deter frequent switching (OECD, 2020[3]).

3.2. Countries provided temporary flexibility towards funding and solvency rules for DB plans

The COVID-19 crisis exposed DB plans to a greater risk of underfunding, putting further pressure on plan sponsors. On the one hand, the fall in stock markets in Q1 2020 reduced the value of assets that should back up the liabilities arising from the benefit promises. On the other hand, liabilities rose in 2020 due to declining interest rates. For example, the UK's Pension Protection Fund uses conventional and index-linked gilt yields to calculate the liabilities of the DB plans in the scope of its index (PPF 7 800).[3] The 10, 15 and 20-year fixed interest gilt yields all declined in 2020, contributing to a 12% increase in the liabilities of the DB plans in the index. Meanwhile, the impact of mortality developments on the liabilities of DB plans has been marginal in the short term and is ambiguous over the long term (see Chapter 4). As a result, funding ratios deteriorated in a number of countries in Q1 2020 (Figure 3.3), putting pressure on plan sponsors to cover the shortfall following funding and solvency rules.

Figure 3.3. Evolution of the funding ratio of DB plans in selected OECD countries between end-2019 and end-2021

In percent

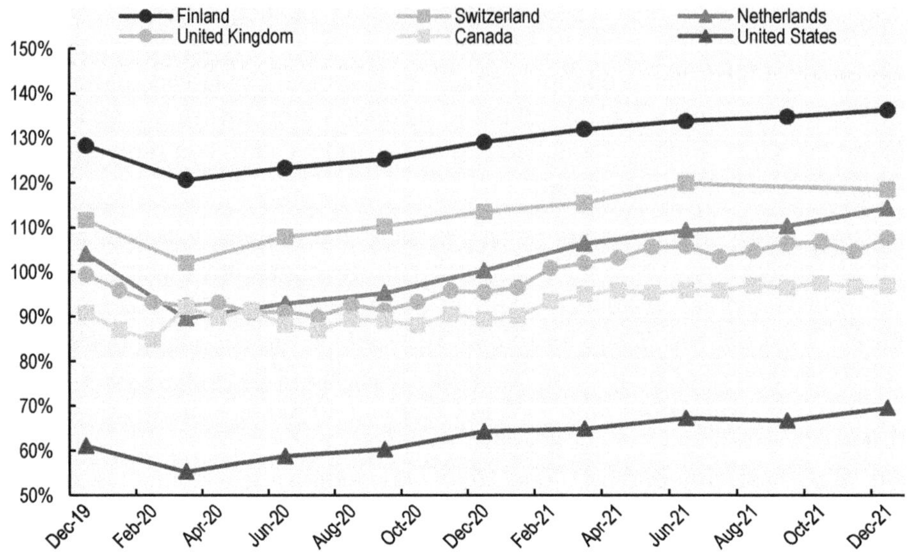

Note: Funding ratios are not comparable across countries as the methodologies used to derive them vary for the different sources. There are breaks in series in October 2020 and October 2021 for the United Kingdom, due to a change of sample (the impact of the change increased the funding ratio at 31 October 2020 by 2.1 percentage points and the one at 31 October 2021 by 0.9 percentage point).
Source: Aon's Pension Risk Tracker (S&P/TSX) for Canada; the Finnish Financial Supervisory Authority for Finland; *De Nederlandsche Bank* (DNB) for the Netherlands; the Occupational Pension Supervisory Commission for Switzerland; the Pension Protection Fund's 7 800 index for the United Kingdom; OECD calculations based on Federal Reserve Board data for the United States.

Temporary flexibility into funding and solvency rules for DB plans is necessary to account for short-term volatility in asset and liability valuations. While the primary goal of a DB pension plan is to provide secure benefits to members, funding regulations should aim to avoid undue pressure on plan sponsors to increase their contributions at times when their own profitability or even continuity is under pressure. In addition, funding regulations should also avoid the forced sells of equities during a downturn, crystallising any losses and driving markets further down. As such, funding regulations should aim to be counter-cyclical in nature (Yermo and Severinson, 2010[4]). The OECD policy guidelines, therefore, recommend introducing flexibility in funding and solvency rules for DB plans, while making sure to remove this flexibility once the emergency is over to continue protecting benefit promises in the long term.

Countries used different approaches to provide flexibility to DB plans and their sponsors. For example, Germany and the United Kingdom extended the deadline for submitting recovery plans for underfunded plans, while Finland extended the deadline for implementing recovery plans. The Netherlands extended by one year the minimum funding requirement of 90%. Additionally, Canada and the United Kingdom suspended deficit-reduction contributions by plan sponsors, while Germany and Japan allowed plan sponsors to defer the payment of these contributions.

Countries have reversed the temporary flexibility as funding ratios improved following the rebound in financial markets. Funding ratios have been improving in several countries since the market bottom at the end of Q1 2020, sometimes exceeding the 2019 level at the end of 2020, as in Finland, Switzerland and the United States (Figure 3.3).[4] Improvements also continued during 2021. This evolution allowed countries to revert to the usual funding and solvency rules. For example, in Germany, since 1 October 2020, employers again have to submit a recovery plan within three months from the onset of a funding shortfall (of 10% or more) in a *Pensionsfond*. In Canada, the suspension of deficit-reduction contributions ended at the end of December 2020.

By contrast, it was only in March 2021 that the United States introduced measures to support underfunded DB plans with the American Rescue Plan Act (ARPA). Some of these measures may last beyond COVID-19. They intend to tackle underfunding issues that existed before COVID-19, but that the pandemic exacerbated. As Figure 3.3 shows, DB plans in the United States were already highly underfunded before COVID-19. The ARPA provides a wide range of measures. For example, it allows multiemployer pension plans to keep the funding status of the year before the plan year starting between 1 March 2020 and 28 February 2021. It extends the recovery period by five years for underfunded multiemployer plans and by eight years for single-employer plans. It also maintains a narrow interest rate corridor until 2026 to protect plans from extreme interest rate movements and ensure liabilities are stable and predictable over the medium term. Moreover, the ARPA provides financial assistance to underfunded multiemployer plans by granting eligible plans a one-off payment worth 30 years of benefit payments to their members.

3.3. Governments have provided support to help workers and employers contribute to asset-backed pension plans

The situation in the labour market has been challenging since March 2020, potentially impeding people's ability to save for retirement. COVID-19 has created a labour market slump, putting millions of people out of work. To contain the spread of the virus and its variants, governments shut down parts of the economy, resulting in a drop in activity and unprecedented job losses (OECD, 2020[5]). As a result, the unemployment rate soared in the OECD area between January and April 2020, from 5.3% to 8.8%. The rate has fallen since then, going back to the pre-pandemic rate of 5.3% in January 2022.[5] Spells of full or partial unemployment could lead to contribution gaps if employees or employers stop contributing to asset-backed pension plans.

Regular contributions are key to increasing people's chances of reaching their desired retirement income. In particular, contributions made early in the career benefit from the effect of compound interest for longer. The OECD policy guidelines, therefore, recommend policy makers to support workers and employers so that they can keep contributing to asset-backed pension arrangements, thereby avoiding a long-term shortage of assets to finance retirement.

Many OECD countries have supported the continuation of contributions to asset-backed pension arrangements by introducing job-retention schemes where the government subsidises wages. The subsidies allow workers to get part of their salary, on which contributions to asset-backed pension plans are taken. In some cases, the subsidies do not cover pension contributions that remain due by the employer (e.g. Australia, Sweden and the United Kingdom). However, as they reduce staff costs, they make it easier for employers to keep their employees and pay the contributions. By contrast, in Denmark, Iceland, the Netherlands and the Slovak Republic, the subsidies cover employer contributions to asset-backed pension plans, either by including a top-up corresponding to the employer contribution or by calculating the subsidy based on a salary including the employer contribution.

Job-retention schemes have been extended in most countries as the different waves of the virus hit, but the terms have evolved with respect to the eligibility conditions and the amount of the subsidies. For example, in Iceland, support for employees with reduced working hours due to the pandemic was initially granted when working hours were reduced by 20% but still represented at least 25% of a full-time job. From 1 June 2020, only employees with a minimum reduction of working hours of 20% but representing at least 50% of a full-time job could be eligible. In the Netherlands, the government subsidy initially covered up to 90% of the wage bill of eligible companies, but this was reduced to 80% in October 2020, before increasing to 85% in January 2021. In addition, the top-up to cover pension contributions and other payroll charges increased from 30% to 40% of the compensation amount in June 2020. In the United Kingdom, employers have always been required to pay the 3% minimum employer contribution for employees enrolled automatically in a pension plan. The grant for temporarily laid-off employees initially covered that minimum contribution, but this ended in August 2020 and since then employers have been required to pay these contributions themselves.

Other measures have been implemented by countries to support pension contributions and the build-up of rights and assets. For example, Belgium, Norway and Switzerland (for people aged 58 or above) considered temporarily laid-off employees as covered by their occupational pension plan during spells of temporary unemployment. In Canada, employers have been allowed to make catch-up contributions to compensate for required contributions not paid in full in 2020 and 2021. Employers have also been allowed to pay contributions based on the full salary (i.e. before reduction) even for periods when employees were receiving a reduced wage. In Chile, access to unemployment benefits was extended to employees with a contract suspension. This allowed the unemployment insurance fund to pay the mandatory pension contributions on behalf of workers, while the employer was still liable for other compulsory social security contributions. Moreover, Finland and Switzerland allowed employers to use reserves to pay for contributions or to compensate for a reduction in contributions. Finally, Israel capped management fees for savers who had to stop contributing because of COVID-19.

By contrast, several countries have implemented measures that temporarily reduced the flow of contributions to asset-backed pension plans. For example, Belgium, Estonia, Finland, Greece and the Slovak Republic allowed employees and employers to defer the payment of contributions. Colombia and Finland reduced mandatory contribution rates, even though in Colombia, this measure was later on declared unconstitutional.[6] Moreover, Canada, Estonia, Poland and the Slovak Republic temporarily suspended the payment of contributions to certain plans.[7] The rationale for deferring, reducing or suspending contributions was to provide temporary relief to workers and employers, but this comes at the cost of reduced future retirement income. Indeed, deferred contributions are invested later in capital markets and do not earn a return during the deferral period. Moreover, reduced contributions (at the extreme to zero) lower the amount invested to finance future retirement income.

To limit the negative impact of deferred or reduced contributions on future retirement income, some countries put compensation mechanisms in place. For example, in Finland, employers could postpone the payment of pension contributions into earnings-related pension plans by three months, but had to pay a 2% interest on the delayed contributions. In addition, employer contributions will increase again between 2022 and 2025 to make up for the reduced contributions between May and December 2020 and replenish buffer funds. In Estonia, the 4% employer contributions to the statutory funded pension scheme (second pillar) were retained in the public pay-as-you-go scheme between 1 July 2020 and 31 August 2021. The government will put back the missing contributions with a return in the funded scheme between 2023 and 2024, as long as employees continued to pay their own 2% contribution into it between 1 July 2020 and 31 August 2021.[8]

Overall, the different measures have helped people to continue saving for retirement in some countries. For example, in the United Kingdom, data from the Treasury show that the proportion of contributing eligible jobholders and the employee pension contribution rates remained stable in recent years up to March 2021. In addition, the proportion of savers stopping their employee contribution decreased in the financial year April 2020 – March 2021, mainly driven by a fall in those stopping due to ending their employment, partly as a result of the job-retention scheme (Department for Work and Pensions, 2021[6]). These results are confirmed among members of NEST, the workplace pension scheme set up by the UK government (Nest Insight, 2021[7]). A number of countries recorded an overall increase in contributions in 2020, such as Australia, Germany, Lithuania, Poland and Switzerland (OECD, 2021[1]). One of the largest pension funds in Denmark (PFA) observed extra voluntary contributions from plan members in 2020 amid a consumption fall spurred by fewer spending opportunities.[9] Similarly, in Ireland, contributions grew by 13% in 2020 and some of these additional contributions may represent an example of transfers from increased levels of household deposits to retirement savings (Devine et al., 2021[8]). In the United States, according to the 2021 Retirement Confidence Survey conducted by the Employee Benefit Research Institute (EBRI), 69% of workers did not make changes to their workplace retirement plan contribution in 2020, and among those who did, 58% increased their contributions, 22% reduced their contributions and 23% stopped contributing (Employee Benefit Research Institute, 2021[9]).

However, some countries saw the opposite trend of declining contributions in 2020, such as Estonia, Finland, Luxembourg and Norway (OECD, 2021[1]). For Estonia and Finland, the measures to defer, reduce or suspend contributions may explain this fall in contributions compared to 2019. In Estonia, 9 575 individuals in total (around 1.3% of all participants) applied for a temporary suspension of their contributions to the second pillar, of which 60% were women.[10]

3.4. Pension supervisory authorities provided flexible, pragmatic, proportionate and risk-based supervisory oversight

COVID-19 has created operational disruptions as staff of pension providers had to work remotely. The pandemic may have complicated the delivery of key operational activities by pension providers, such as the timely investment of contributions, the management of assets and the timely payment of retirement benefits. Providers have had to put in place business continuity plans, adapt their processes and tackle the challenges from the COVID-19 outbreak (e.g. market fall in Q1 2020, liquidity issue due to early withdrawal requests), on top of their regular duties towards their members and supervisors (e.g. reporting, actuarial valuation). Dealing with this situation could have led to delays.

The International Organisation of Pension Supervisors (IOPS) supported a flexible, pragmatic, proportionate and risk-based supervisory approach to deal with the COVID-19 crisis (IOPS, 2020[10]). In particular, the IOPS acknowledged the relevance of easing some regulatory constraints and providing temporary relief from certain requirements, while emphasising the importance of addressing risks emerging from the COVID-19 crisis. The OECD policy guidelines are in line with the IOPS statement.

As a response to the COVID-19 crisis, pension supervisory authorities in most OECD countries have provided flexibility to supervised entities so they could prioritise the continuity of service provision and focus on key processes and day-to-day operations. Different approaches were followed. Most countries extended reporting deadlines or refrained from regulatory action in case of failure to meet the usual deadlines.[11] Some countries suspended on-site inspections or other planned supervisory actions (e.g. Australia, Austria, Belgium, Lithuania, Mexico, New Zealand, Poland and Portugal). Other countries provided temporary relief for selected requirements. For example, Mexico allowed private pension fund administrators to send simplified reports instead of the regular ones, Poland postponed the transformation of open pension funds into specialised open-end investment funds, and the United Kingdom gave a delay to firms to comply with the new rules to engage with members starting their pay-out phase. Some countries waived the requirement for personal presence to annual general meetings or committee meetings (e.g. Austria, Belgium, Israel, Japan, Mexico and Sweden). Finally, Italy and the United Kingdom extended deadlines to pay the levy to the supervisory commission (COVIP) and to the Pension Protection Fund, respectively.

Meanwhile, pension supervisory authorities in some OECD countries also intensified their activities to address new emerging risks at the height of the crisis. COVID-19 triggered specific risks for pension entities, related for instance to liquidity, investments, fund sustainability, operational and processing matters, scams and cybersecurity. To monitor these risks, some pension supervisory authorities introduced extraordinary monitoring and reporting (e.g. Australia, Denmark, Greece, Hungary, Iceland, Ireland, the Netherlands, Portugal, and the Slovak Republic). In addition, most supervisors in Europe asked supervised entities, in particular insurance companies, to suspend dividend payments, share buy backs and variable remuneration policies, in order to improve liquidity.[12]

As pension providers overcame the initial shock from COVID-19 and managed to adapt their processes, pension supervisory authorities have returned to their usual monitoring and rules, and policy reforms resumed. For example, APRA in Australia resumed public consultations on selected policy reforms and started a phased resumption of the issuing of new licenses in August 2020. Extensions for reporting deadlines usually only applied in 2020. For instance, the Office of the Superintendent of Financial Institutions Supervisors in Canada cancelled on 25 February 2021 the extensions in place since April 2020 to submit various reports. The recommendation to supervised entities to suspend dividend payments was removed from 30 September 2021 in most European countries. Additionally, some of the extraordinary monitoring stopped. For example, the request to Danish pension companies to report the solvency coverage and carry out a simplified stress test on a weekly basis ended on 17 June 2020. Moreover, reforms resumed, such as the one in Poland transforming open pension funds (OFE) into specialised open-end investment funds. The new Act came into force on 1 June 2021 and gave OFE participants until 2 August 2021 to submit declarations regarding transferring their savings to the Social Insurance Institution or to an Individual Retirement Pension Account.[13]

By contrast, pension supervisors increased their focus on fighting cybercrime and scams. While these risks are not new, COVID-19 has heightened them as people have been relying more on digital tools and scammers may have played on the fears of members in a context of volatile financial markets. For example, 24 000 members in Australia had their personal data stolen between January and mid-August 2020.[14] Data from Action Fraud in the United Kingdom suggest that savers had lost GBP 1.8 million to pension fraud in Q1 2021.[15] Regulators and supervisors have taken actions to raise awareness about scams and frauds and to address the issue more broadly. For example, the United Kingdom took a multi-pronged approach. It launched a national awareness campaign in April 2021 encouraging savers to remain vigilant before making changes to their pension arrangements.[16] It asked the pensions industry to sign up to its Pledge campaign to help combat pension scams and to encourage better reporting.[17] It also gave new powers to trustees and scheme managers to intervene and halt suspicious transfers.[18] In the United States, the Department of Labor issued a guidance on cybersecurity to employee retirement plans on 14 April 2021, stressing the obligation of plan fiduciaries to ensure proper mitigation of cybersecurity risks.

3.5. Repeated possibilities to access funds early may jeopardise long-term retirement security in a few countries

Many individuals lost their jobs due to the pandemic and may have been tempted to access their retirement savings to address short-term needs. Retirement assets belong to plan members, who may have seen them as a source to compensate for income losses resulting from the economic lockdown. However, providing short-term relief by allowing early access to retirement savings is at the cost of reduced retirement income down the line.

Retirement savings should be earmarked for the financing of future retirement income. As such, leakages from pension plans, i.e. access to savings before retirement, should be avoided. The OECD policy guidelines recommend that early access to funds should be allowed only as a measure of last resort and based on individuals' specific and exceptional circumstances. Additionally, the portability of funds upon changes of employers should be improved to avoid another source of leakage, in particular in times of economic crises. Access to loans may address the temporary liquidity needs of plan members, but could still affect future retirement income if the funds are not paid back.

Regulations in some countries were already in line with the principle of granting access to funds as a measure of last resort before the COVID-19 crisis. For example, several countries have been allowing members to withdraw their funds in case of serious illness, such as Australia, Canada, Denmark, Ireland, Italy, New Zealand, Poland, Spain and the United Kingdom (OECD, 2019[11]). Some countries have also permitted withdrawals in the case of financial hardship (e.g. Australia, Canada, France, Korea,

New Zealand) or unemployment (e.g. France, Italy, Mexico and Spain) (OECD, 2019[11]). Finally, some countries also have accounts, which are financed separately from pension accounts and to which individuals can access under specific circumstances (e.g. the Labour Capitalisation Fund in Costa Rica and the housing subaccount in Mexico).

Among these countries, some adjusted their regulations to COVID-19. For example, Mexico and New Zealand adapted the process to apply for funds to the distancing measures. Australia, Costa Rica (for the Labour Capitalisation Fund) and Portugal broadened the eligibility conditions to access to funds. For example, in Australia, only members being unemployed or receiving selected benefits and allowances could access funds early under the existing regulations. In 2020, employees made redundant or who had experienced a 20% or more reduction in working hours, as well as sole traders whose business had been suspended or had suffered a decline in turnover by 20% or more, could additionally access funds early. Moreover, Australia also increased the amount that eligible members could withdraw due to COVID-19, from a maximum of AUD 10 000 in any 12-month period usually, to two tranches of up to AUD 10 000 between April and December 2020.

Other countries introduced new early access possibilities specific to COVID-19. Spain and the United States conditioned early withdrawals on members suffering from the economic or health consequences of COVID-19.[19] By contrast, Chile, Iceland and France (for the self-employed) allowed unconditional early access to funds.

Despite the potential long-term consequences on retirement income adequacy, several countries have extended or repeated their COVID-19 early access policies. Iceland and Portugal both extended the initial period to apply for an early release of savings in voluntary personal pension plans by one year. Chile allowed plan members to withdraw up to 10% of their mandatory savings unconditionally three times, in July 2020, November 2020 and April 2021. By contrast, COVID-19 early withdrawals ended as planned in Australia, France, Spain and the United States.

Measures allowing early access to funds started when financial markets were still volatile in some countries, driving some individuals to sell at the bottom of the market and miss out on the recovery. For example, the early access policies started in March 2020 in Spain and the United States, and in April 2020 in Australia, Iceland and Portugal. For individuals who took advantage of the withdrawal possibility immediately, the timing may not have played well and they may have materialised investment losses by withdrawing funds during this period. In Australia for example, individuals withdrawing the maximum allowed (AUD 20 000) at their first opportunity could have foregone AUD 3 164 in returns from market recovery according to estimates from the McKell Institute.[20] People in Chile and France may have been less impacted, as the early withdrawal possibilities started in July 2020, when markets had already bounced back, at least partially.

Unconditional withdrawals may also increase volatility in financial markets, due to important changes in the portfolio of pension funds. The Central Bank of Chile considered that the three withdrawal possibilities involved a significant liquidation of assets by pension funds and that the orderly liquidation of such assets was essential to preserve the stability of financial markets and the efficiency of price formation processes. Therefore, it took a range of measures to mitigate volatility in financial markets (e.g. the establishment of a special cash purchase and term sale programme, open to banking companies and other financial institutions). The Central Bank also ensured that pension funds had access to market mechanisms that are open and available to provide liquidity and facilitate an orderly adjustment of their portfolios.

In some countries, early access to funds was already granted during the 2008 global financial crisis. This is the case, for example, in Australia, Iceland and Spain (Antolín and Stewart, 2009[12]). In Iceland for instance, individuals were allowed to access their voluntary savings to pay down mortgage loans in 2009.[21] In 2020, access to voluntary savings was unconditional. Accessing savings twice in the course of 11 years may have reduced significantly the resources available to finance future retirement income for some individuals.

As expected, the amounts withdrawn from asset-backed pension plans due to COVID-19 have been larger when access has been unconditional (Figure 3.4). The largest withdrawals have been observed in Chile (24.2% of assets) where people have had the possibility to access their savings unconditionally three times. In Iceland, unconditional withdrawals from voluntary plans are also significant; in September 2021, they represented 4.0% of the assets in these plans at the end of 2019. In both countries, the numbers may still go up as the withdrawal policy was going on beyond end-2021 (until April 2022 in Chile and June 2023 in Iceland). In the other countries, where early withdrawals were conditional on suffering from financial hardship, unemployment or a decline in activity due to COVID-19, the amounts withdrawn so far represent less than 1.5% of assets.

Figure 3.4. Amount of assets withdrawn before retirement during the COVID-19 crisis in selected countries, by type of access

As a percentage of total assets at end-2019

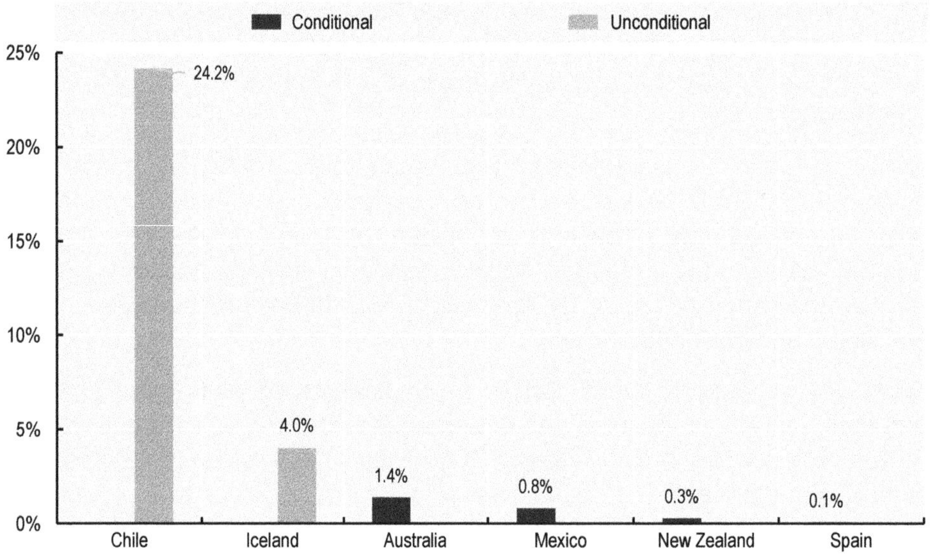

Note: Data refer to early withdrawals between 20 April 2020 and 31 January 2021 for Australia, between 30 July 2020 and 1 October 2021 for Chile, between March 2020 and September 2021 for Iceland, between March 2020 and August 2021 for Mexico (due to unemployment), between March 2020 and May 2021 for New Zealand (due to financial hardship), and between 14 March 2020 and 30 September 2020 for Spain.
Source: National data sources.

The characteristics of people who accessed their funds early during the COVID-19 crisis are similar in Australia and Chile. In Australia, 25% of members making an early withdrawal had a small balance, with less than AUD 1 000 left in the account after the withdrawal(s) (APRA, 2020[13]). Men have had a higher take-up rate than women across all age and account balance brackets, as 57% of payments went to men versus 43% for women in the third and fourth quarter of 2020. Additionally, around 62% of all early withdrawals were paid to members aged 25 to 44. Moreover, the average amount withdrawn by people who accessed the scheme twice was AUD 16 377 (i.e. 82% of the maximum allowed), and the funds were mainly used for mortgage or rent payments (31%) or household bills (29%).[22] In the case of Chile, across all three withdrawals, most of the payments by 27 August 2021 were made to men (53% for the first withdrawal, 55% for the second and 58% for the third), and between 70% and 74% of the withdrawals were made by members aged 26 to 55.[23] In addition, 35% of those who withdrew funds at least once have emptied their account balance. These are mostly women and individuals younger than 35.[24]

Some countries have implemented measures that may mitigate the effect of early withdrawals on future retirement income. In Chile, the government introduced a state-funded CLP 200 000 bonus for those who emptied their mandatory savings accounts due to the first two rounds of withdrawals between 30 July 2020 and 31 March 2021, and those with a balance of less than CLP 200 000 as of 31 March 2021. Only members who have been participating in the system since at least 1 January 2021 are eligible for this bonus, which is paid by the Treasury in the individuals' accounts. Although members can withdraw the money, they are not required to do so and can leave it untouched to replenish their accounts. In the United States, individuals who accessed their funds are allowed to put some or all of their withdrawals back into their plans within three years. If they do so, the amounts withdrawn will not be considered as taxable income, and the repayments will not be counted towards their annual contribution limits.

Facilitating loans from pension plans rather than allowing early withdrawals may have been another way to provide temporary relief while mitigating the effect on future retirement income. For example, Israel increased the loan repayment period from 7 to 15 years. The United States increased the amount members could borrow from their DC plan. The loan could amount to the full balance of the plan (instead of 50%) up to USD 100 000 (instead of USD 50 000). Members could also delay the repayment of their outstanding loan from their DC plan by one year, although interest continued to accrue on delayed payments.

Finally, it is worth noting that the lack of portability of pension plans increases leakages from the system in times of economic crises. Access to funds when leaving the employer is allowed in some countries, in particular when individuals have small account balances. For example, in Australia, Austria, Germany, Luxembourg, the Netherlands, Switzerland and the United States, small entitlements are directly paid to the individual rather than kept as deferred rights or transferred to another plan (OECD, 2019[11]). As the COVID-19 crisis increased unemployment, in particular during the first quarter of 2020, more individuals than usual may have received their savings as cash. This money will not be available to finance retirement, unless individuals actively transfer it to another pension plan. Improving plan portability would ensure that all contributions paid into asset-backed pension plans are eventually used to finance future retirement income.

3.6. Conclusion

This chapter has assessed whether the policy responses to the COVID-19 crisis implemented by OECD countries in their asset-backed pension systems have been aligned with the OECD policy guidelines published in the *OECD Pensions Outlook 2020* (OECD, 2020[14]) and presented in Chapter 1 of this monograph. It focused on five of the main policy guidelines and uses available evidence to assess the impact that OECD countries' policy responses have had on asset-backed pension systems.

Overall, OECD countries' policy responses to the COVID-19 crisis have been in line with the OECD policy guidelines and contributed to cushion the impact of the crisis on asset-backed pension systems.

Most countries put measures in place to avoid the materialisation of investment losses when financial markets were low. For example, some countries limited switches to lower-risk investment options, relaxed quantitative investment rules in case of unintended breaches, or reduced minimum drawdown requirements for retirees. These measures contributed to the growth of assets during 2020 in most countries, despite the negative investment returns recorded in the first quarter of 2020.

Countries with DB plans provided temporary flexibility towards funding and solvency requirements to avoid undue pressure on plan sponsors to increase their contributions. For example, some countries extended the deadline for submitting or implementing recovery plans, or extended the recovery period for underfunded plans. Other countries reduced, deferred or suspended deficit-reduction contributions by plan sponsors. As assets grew faster than liabilities after the market fall in the first quarter of 2020, funding ratios had recovered or exceeded their 2019 level by the end of 2020. This positive development allowed countries to revert to their usual funding and solvency rules and fully justifies the flexibility provided.

Many countries have supported the continuation of contributions to asset-backed pension arrangements by workers and employers. Some countries introduced job-retention schemes where the government subsidised wages and sometimes even pension contributions. Other countries considered temporarily laid-off employees as covered by their occupational pension plan during spells of temporary unemployment. These countries managed to sustain the level of contributions paid to asset-backed pension plans during 2020 or even recorded an increase in contribution levels, potentially triggered by fewer spending opportunities during lockdown periods.

Finally, pension supervisory authorities in most countries provided flexible, pragmatic, proportionate and risk-based supervisory oversight. They temporarily adapted their supervisory practices, extended the deadline for reporting, and provided temporary relief for selected requirements. This allowed pension entities to focus on key processes and day-to-day operations. At the same time, some pension supervisory authorities intensified their activities to monitor new emerging risks, in particular regarding scams and cybercrimes.

By contrast, some OECD countries implemented policy responses that have not been aligned with the OECD policy guidelines.

Several countries temporarily reduced the flow of contributions paid into asset-backed pension arrangements. They deferred, reduced or suspended contributions to provide short-term relief to employers and individuals. As a result, some of these countries saw a decline in the volume of contributions paid in 2020 compared to 2019. This will reduce the amount set aside to finance future retirement income, unless delayed contributions are paid later with interest.

Finally, some countries facilitated individuals' early access to their funds. Some countries only eased the process to apply for already existing release mechanisms for individuals in financial hardship or with serious health conditions. However, other countries allowed unconditional access to savings, such that even individuals who may not have been in dire need for money could withdraw their assets. In Chile for example, these early withdrawals led to a notable 24% fall in assets by October 2021, while 35% of those who withdrew funds had emptied their account balance. This will significantly reduce the resources available to finance future retirement income.

The analysis, therefore, confirms that the OECD policy guidelines developed in the context of the COVID-19 crisis have been and are still relevant. They could assist pension policy makers, regulators and supervisors in addressing the shock of future crises.

References

Antolín, P. and F. Stewart (2009), "Private Pensions and Policy Responses to the Financial and Economic Crisis", *OECD Working Papers on Insurance and Private Pensions*, No. 36, OECD Publishing, Paris, https://dx.doi.org/10.1787/224386871887. [12]

APRA (2020), "The superannuation Early Release Scheme: Insights from APRA's Pandemic Data Collection", *APRA Insight*, Vol. Issue 4, https://prod.apra.shared.skpr.live/superannuation-early-release-scheme-insights-from-apra%E2%80%99s-pandemic-data-collection. [13]

Department for Work and Pensions (2021), *Workplace pension participation and savings trends of eligible employees: 2009 to 2020*, https://www.gov.uk/government/statistics/workplace-pension-participation-and-savings-trends-2009-to-2020/workplace-pension-participation-and-savings-trends-of-eligible-employees-2009-to-2020. [6]

Devine, K. et al. (2021), "New Insights from Irish Pension Fund", *Quarterly Bulletin 3 - July 2021 - Central Bank of Ireland*, https://www.centralbank.ie/docs/default-source/publications/quarterly-bulletins/quarterly-bulletin-signed-articles/new-insights-from-irish-pension-funds-statistics.pdf. [8]

Employee Benefit Research Institute (2021), *2021 Retirement Confidence Survey*, https://www.ebri.org/retirement/retirement-confidence-survey. [9]

IOPS (2020), *IOPS statement on pension supervisory actions to mitigate the consequences of the Covid-19 crisis*, http://www.iopsweb.org/IOPS-statement-on-pension-supervisory-actions-Covid-19-crisis.pdf. [10]

Nest Insight (2021), *Retirement savings in the UK 2020*, https://www.nestinsight.org.uk/wp-content/uploads/2021/02/Retirement-saving-in-the-UK-2020.pdf. [7]

OECD (2021), *Pension Markets in Figures*, https://www.oecd.org/pensions/pensionmarketsinfocus.htm. [1]

OECD (2020), *OECD Employment Outlook 2020: Worker Security and the COVID-19 Crisis*, OECD Publishing, Paris, https://dx.doi.org/10.1787/1686c758-en. [5]

OECD (2020), *OECD Pensions Outlook 2020*, OECD Publishing, Paris, https://doi.org/10.1787/67ede41b-en. [14]

OECD (2020), "Retirement savings and old-age pensions in the time of COVID-19", in *OECD Pensions Outlook 2020*, OECD Publishing, Paris, https://dx.doi.org/10.1787/b698aae4-en. [15]

OECD (2020), "Retirement savings in the time of COVID-19", *OECD Policy Responses to Coronavirus*, https://www.oecd.org/coronavirus/policy-responses/retirement-savings-in-the-time-of-covid-19-b9740518/. [16]

OECD (2020), "Switching investments in defined contribution retirement savings arrangements", in *OECD Pensions Outlook 2020*, OECD Publishing, Paris, https://dx.doi.org/10.1787/ed47ae07-en. [3]

OECD (2019), "Are funded pensions well designed to adapt to non-standard forms of work?", in *Pensions at a Glance 2019: OECD and G20 Indicators*, OECD Publishing, Paris, https://dx.doi.org/10.1787/1231a36d-en. [11]

PWC (2021), *Lockdown: A review of KiwiSaver member behaviour in response to COVID-19*, https://www.fma.govt.nz/assets/Reports/KiwiSaver-switching-behaviour-150621.pdf. [2]

Yermo, J. and C. Severinson (2010), "The Impact of the Financial Crisis on Defined Benefit Plans and the Need for Counter-Cyclical Funding Regulations", *OECD Working Papers on Finance, Insurance and Private Pensions*, No. 3, OECD Publishing, Paris, https://dx.doi.org/10.1787/5km91p3jszxw-en. [4]

Notes

[1] A third round was allowed in May 2021, see Section 3.5.

[2] The "security slider" mechanism, by which the assets of members within ten years of the retirement age are gradually transferred from open pension funds to the public pay-as-you-go scheme, may also explain the slowest asset recovery in Poland.

[3] The PPF 7800 index | Pension Protection Fund

[4] This evolution is despite the decline in interest rates that occurred in some countries in 2020.

[5] Unemployment Rates, OECD - Updated: March 2022 - OECD

[6] Employees and employers who benefitted from the reduction of the contribution rate for April and May 2020 have 36 months from 1 June 2021 to pay the missing contributions.

[7] In the case of Poland, according to Article 25(4) of the PPK Act, employers fulfilling certain criteria can benefit from the exemption of contributions to an employee capital plan. This provision is not specific to the COVID-19 crisis but is particularly relevant in this case.

[8] The credited return will correspond to the average return of second pillar pension plans between 1 July 2020 and 31 December 2022.

[9] Rekordmange indbetaler ekstra til pensionsopsparingen i denne tid (pfa.dk) (in Danish).

[10] Sissemaksed peatas ajutiselt 9575 inimest - Pensionikeskus (in Estonian).

[11] In addition, the timing for the provision of information on occupational pensions to EIOPA was extended by two weeks for the information regarding the first quarter of 2020 and by eight weeks for the information regarding annual reporting with reference to the year-end 2019 (Statement on principles to mitigate the impact of Coronavirus/COVID-19 on the occupational pensions sector | Eiopa (europa.eu)).

[12] They followed the call from EIOPA towards insurers and reinsurers to suspend dividend payments, share buy backs and variable remuneration policies (EIOPA statement on dividends distribution and variable remuneration policies in the context of COVID-19 | Eiopa (europa.eu)). This call was extended to pension providers in the Czech Republic, Denmark, Portugal, Slovenia and Sweden.

[13] By default, their money was transferred to an Individual Retirement Pension Account (IKE).

[14] Identity theft soars during COVID-19 as scammers target government payments, superannuation - ABC News

[15] Warning from Action Fraud to #ProtectYourPension as GBP1.8 million lost to pension fraud so far this year | Action Fraud

[16] Warning from Action Fraud to #ProtectYourPension as GBP1.8 million lost to pension fraud so far this year | Action Fraud

[17] Pension schemes reporting stop scammers | The Pensions Regulator

[18] New measures to protect pension savers from scam transfers - GOV.UK (www.gov.uk)

[19] In the United States, some pension plans but not all allow members to take financial hardship withdrawals. The COVID-19 related withdrawals applied to all qualified members of DC and money purchase pension plans.

[20] Buy High, Sell Low? The early super access scheme and foregone returns on investment - McKell Institute

[21] Since June 2014 and until June 2023, active members in voluntary personal pension plans can withdraw assets tax free to pay down residential housing debt or invest in residential housing.

[22] Household financial resources, December 2020 | Australian Bureau of Statistics (abs.gov.au)

[23] Ficha Estadística Ley N° 21.248-Primer retiro de fondos - SP. Superintendencia de Pensiones - Gobierno de Chile (spensiones.cl) for the first withdrawal, Ficha Estadística Ley N° 21.295-Segundo retiro de fondos - SP. Superintendencia de Pensiones - Gobierno de Chile (spensiones.cl) for the second and Ficha Estadística Ley N° 21.330-Tercer retiro de fondos - SP. Superintendencia de Pensiones - Gobierno de Chile (spensiones.cl) for the third (in Spanish).

[24] Ficha Estadística Ley N° 21.330-Tercer retiro de fondos - SP. Superintendencia de Pensiones - Gobierno de Chile (spensiones.cl) (in Spanish).

4 The impact of the COVID-19 pandemic on mortality and life expectancy

This chapter first discusses the direct and indirect impacts of the COVID-19 pandemic on mortality and life expectancy, and the effects that these impacts may continue to have going forward. It describes differences in the impact of pandemic on the mortality for entire populations and across demographic groups. It also looks at the indirect effects of responses to the pandemic, in particular relating to healthcare access, lockdown measures imposed by governments, and any overall economic fallout. It then considers the potential long-term impacts that the pandemic may have on mortality before discussing how mortality assumptions should account for this shock to longevity going forward.

The understanding and modelling of longevity is central to the ability of the providers of lifetime retirement income to ensure that they will be able to continue to make retirement income payments. Mortality assumptions are the basis on which retirement income calculations are made, and their accuracy is crucial to ensure the solvency of providers and their resilience to face longevity risk.

The COVID-19 pandemic has been one of the largest shocks to longevity in recent history. Mortality was not only impacted directly by the virus, but also indirectly from the measures that governments imposed to combat the virus and the broader economic and social consequences that those have had. The immediate death toll from the virus itself was significant, but people also suffered indirect consequences of the pandemic, such as the impact to healthcare access and the effects that lockdown measures had on personal well-being and behaviour as well as on the economy. Hospitals that were overwhelmed with COVID patients may not have been able to provide needed care for individuals with other illnesses, while the fear of catching COVID-19 may have also led individuals not to seek needed medical care at all. Lockdown measures took a toll on personal well-being, with negative consequences manifesting themselves through substance abuse, declines in mental health, and violence. Nevertheless, it also resulted in some behavioural changes that were positive for mortality, such as less driving and better hygiene. The broader economic consequences of lockdowns are intertwined with both healthcare and well-being, and could also have an impact on mortality in the near term. In the long-term the impact on mortality is much more uncertain. There could be additional impacts on mortality for those who have been exposed to the virus, or potentially negative consequences on mortality linked to the shifting social and political trends emerging in the wake of the pandemic.

Understanding the broad impact of the COVID-19 pandemic on mortality is important to be able assess the impact of COVID-19 on the value of pension and annuity liabilities and to inform the setting of mortality assumptions for both current mortality and future mortality improvements. It will also provide lessons for managing and responding to the impact of similar events in the future.

This chapter looks at the wide-ranging impacts that COVID-19 has had already on mortality, focusing on the peak years of the pandemic in 2020 and 2021, and the effects that we may continue to observe going forward. The first section investigates the short-term impact of the pandemic on mortality. It looks at the direct impact of the COVID-19 virus on mortality and how the impact has varied across different groups of the population. It also considers the indirect effects of responses to the pandemic, in particular relating to healthcare, lockdown measures imposed by governments, and the overall economic fallout. The second section discusses the potential implications for mortality in the longer term. It considers the possible long-term consequences on mortality from the virus itself. It also discusses the potential indirect effects that could be felt from social and political shifts. The chapter concludes with a discussion of the implications that these impacts have for setting mortality assumptions used in the context of asset-backed pension systems.

4.1. The short-term impact of COVID-19 on mortality

The official count of COVID-19 deaths globally over the peak years of the pandemic of 2020 and 2021 totalled around 5.5 million lives lost (The Economist, 2022[1]).[1,2] However, this figure does not accurately reflect the total number of lives that the pandemic took during that time. The official count includes only the deaths where the individual tested positive for the virus, or in some countries where the individual demonstrated a probable infection, yet the deaths of many more individuals who were never tested or suspected of being infected can likely be attributed to COVID-19. In addition, this figure ignores the indirect impact that the pandemic has had on mortality, due for example to reduced access to healthcare or the negative consequences that lockdown measures had on well-being.

To capture the real death toll of the pandemic, a more useful figure is the level of excess mortality experienced. Excess mortality measures the level of mortality experienced compared to what otherwise would have been expected, with expectations normally based on the average experience over recent years. As this figure accounts for all deaths experienced during the pandemic, it captures both the deaths directly related to the virus as well as the indirect effects the pandemic has had on mortality. While many of these indirect effects have likely resulted in additional deaths, there has also been some positive impact, such as the reduction of traffic accidents and improved hygiene, which would serve to offset the total mortality cost of COVID-19.

On a global scale, excess mortality figures present a significantly grimmer picture of the lives lost from COVID-19 than the official numbers indicate. One estimate puts global excess deaths at 19.2 million in 2020 and 2021, more than three times the level of officially reported COVID deaths (The Economist, 2022[1]).[3] Few countries were spared. Figure 4.1 shows the average percentage of weekly excess deaths and the maximum weekly excess deaths experienced in OECD countries over the period from January 2020 to December 2021, or the latest available data. The average excess mortality across OECD jurisdictions over the period was just under 10%, with the average maximum excess during any week at 62.5%.[4] Nevertheless, several countries managed to keep excess deaths during the pandemic to a minimum. New Zealand and Australia experienced fewer deaths on average during the pandemic than expected in normal times due to their zero-COVID policies, and Japan, Iceland, Korea, Denmark, Luxembourg, and Norway managed to keep average excess deaths under 1.5%. The relative severity of the pandemic waves differs across countries, with some like Spain experiencing significant spikes, while in others such as Israel the peak in mortality was more moderate. At the right end of the figure, the heavy death toll of the pandemic can be observed in Latin America, particularly in Colombia and Mexico where the average weekly excess mortality exceeded 35%, and the worst wave caused excess mortality of over 160% in Mexico.

Figure 4.1. Average weekly excess mortality during the COVID-19 pandemic

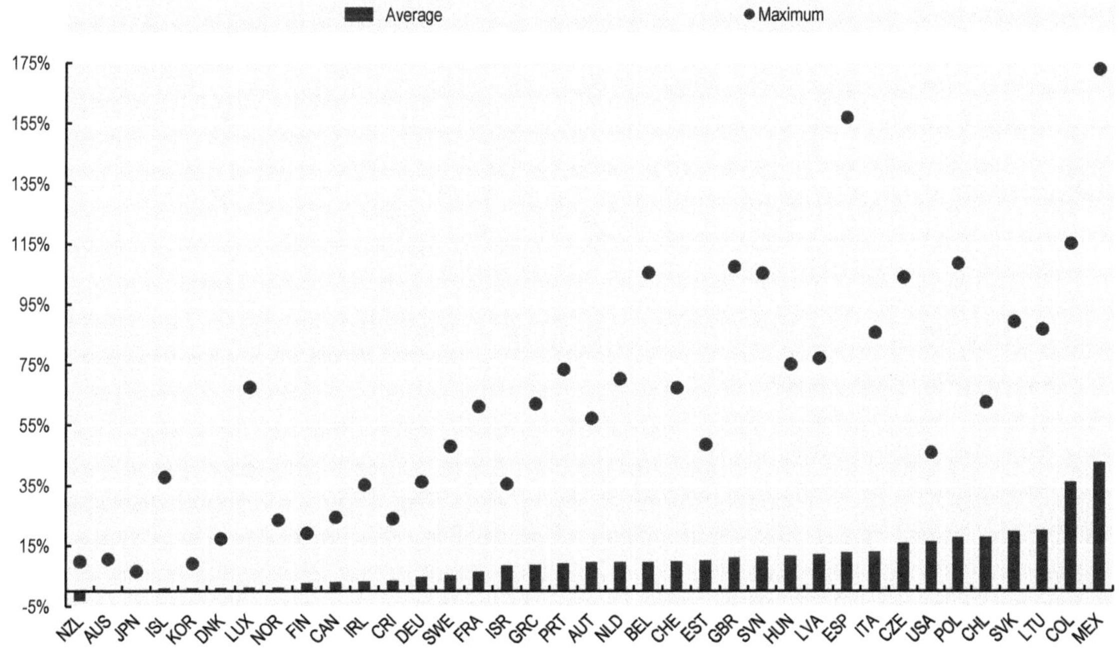

Note: From January 2020 through December 2021 or latest available data. Before 20 September 2021, expected deaths based on the average deaths over 2015-2019. After September 2021, expected deaths calculated based on an extrapolation of a regression over the same period. Average excess mortality calculated as a simple average across weekly reported data for each country.
Source: Adapted from Giattino et al. (2022[2]), *Excess mortality during the Coronavirus pandemic (COVID-19)*, https://ourworldindata.org/excess-mortality-covid.

The excess mortality experienced over 2020 led to a significant reduction in period life expectancy in most jurisdictions. Figure 4.2 shows the change in period life expectancy at age 60 in 2020 compared to 2019 in selected jurisdictions. The results are broadly consistent with the observed total excess mortality, with all jurisdictions shown experiencing a decline in life expectancy except Norway, Iceland, and Denmark, who all experienced very low levels of total excess mortality. In most jurisdictions, males suffered a larger drop in period life expectancy than females, in line with observations that men had a higher mortality risk from COVID-19. Polish males observed the largest decline in period life expectancy in 2020, losing 1.5 years for men, followed by US males and Spaniards of both genders for whom the observed decrease was over 1.4 years.

Figure 4.2. Change in period life expectancy at age 60 in 2020 compared to 2019

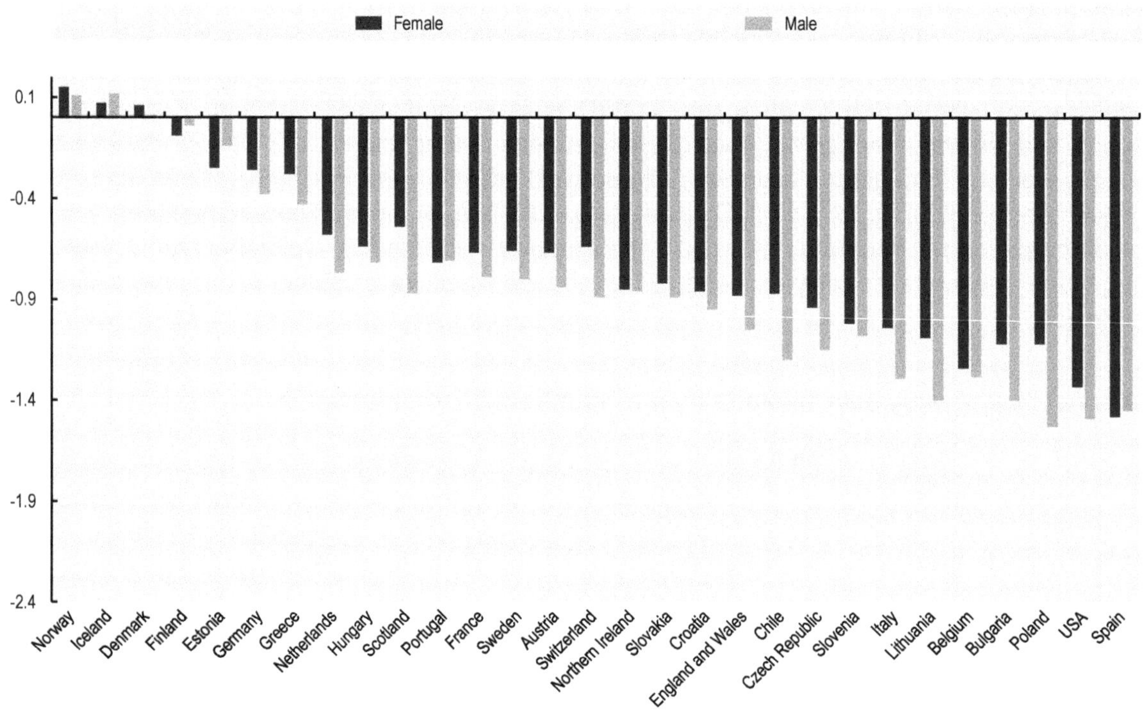

Note: Period life expectancy describes the mortality experience of a specific year, and does not take into account future expectations of mortality.
Source: Adapted from Aberto et al. (2021[3]), *Quantifying impacts of the COVID-19 pandemic through life-expectancy losses: a population-level study of 29 countries*, DOI: 10.1093/ije/dyab207.

Nevertheless, these estimates do not take into account future trends in mortality, and only capture the impact that COVID-19 had on mortality during a single year. The impact on cohort life expectancies – accounting for mortality improvements and a return to 'normal' levels of mortality – would be substantially smaller, even insignificant. For example, Figure 4.2 shows that period life expectancy for Dutch males aged 60 fell by 9.24 months (0.77 years). However, assuming that excess mortality continues only through 2020-2022, the impact on cohort life expectancy is only 15 days (0.5 months).[5]

Within countries, different age groups did not experience the same relative magnitude of excess mortality. The differences observed across age groups may provide an indication as to what extent indirect effects may have had a disproportionate effect on some age groups. For example, the youngest age group may have experienced a net reduction in mortality because of fewer deaths caused by traffic accidents. Other age groups may have modified their behaviour more, such as by being stricter with social distancing.

Additional explanations for observed differences across age groups could be differences in access to health care or testing. Figure 4.3 shows the excess mortality experienced during the pandemic by age group. Those aged 15-64 experienced negative excess deaths in several countries, indicating that positive indirect effects on mortality may have outweighed the negative impact of the COVID-19 virus. Surprisingly, those aged 85 and over did not experience the highest excess mortality in any jurisdiction, and in some countries such as the United States experienced substantially lower excess mortality than other age groups. In the United States, those aged 15-24 actually experienced the highest levels of excess mortality (Leavitt, 2021[4]). The age group 75-84 was the most severely impacted in half of the jurisdictions shown. The relative impact for different age groups has also changed over time. In the United Kingdom, for example, excess deaths for ages 45-64 were somewhat higher in 2021 compared to 2020 (Continuous Mortality Investigation, 2021[5]).

Figure 4.3. Average weekly excess mortality during the COVID-19 pandemic by age group

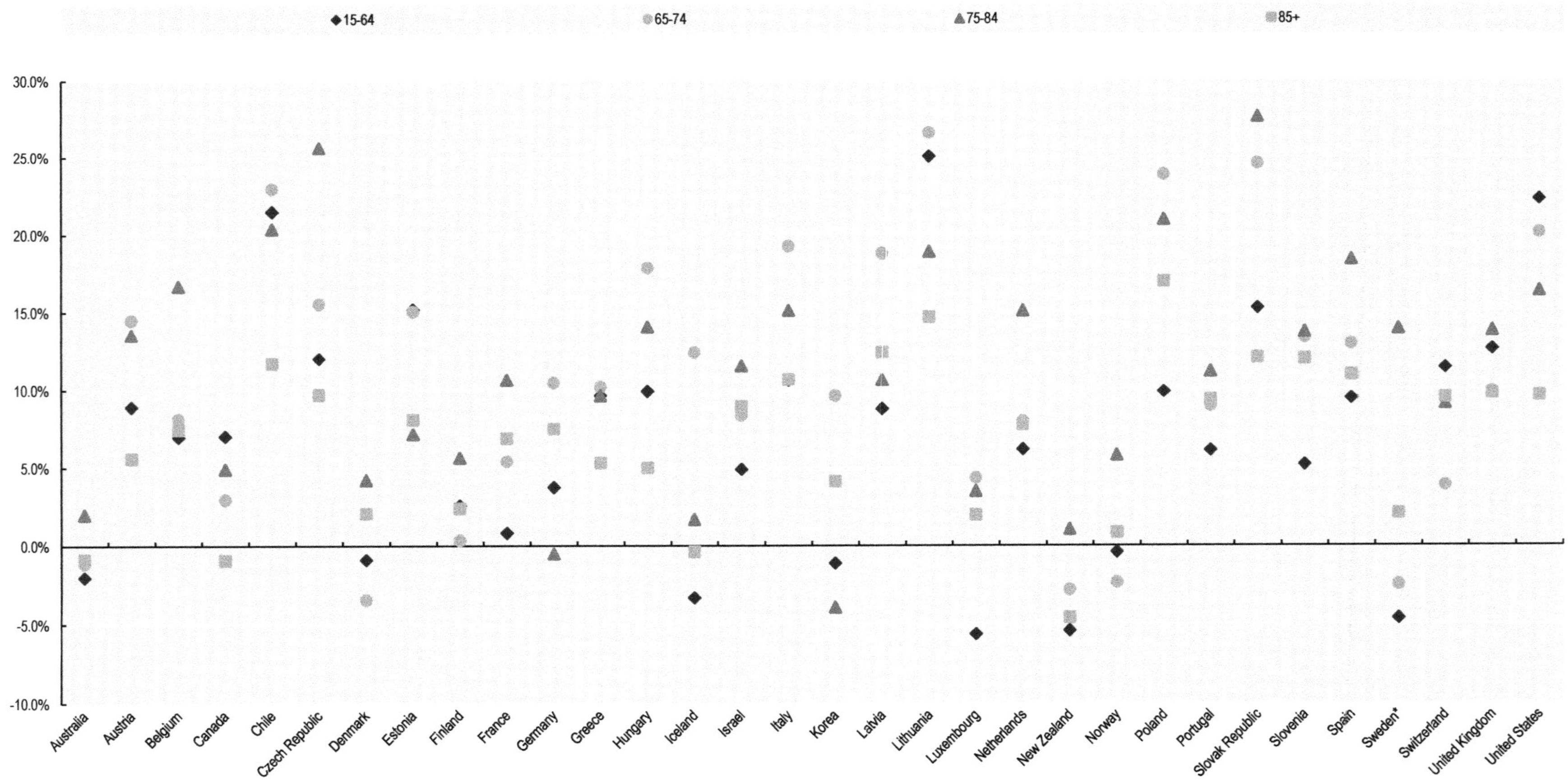

Note: From January 2020 to December 2021 or latest data available as of January 14, 2022, except Sweden where data is that available as of August 2021. In 2020, Mexicc (not shown) experienced 61% excess mortality for ages under 65 compared to 65% for ages over 65 (Gobierno de México, 2021[6]).
Source: Adapted from Giattino et al. (2022[2]), *Excess mortality during the Coronavirus pandemic (COVID-19)*, https://ourworldindata.org/excess-mortality-covid.

It is not easy to distinguish between the deaths caused directly by the COVID-19 virus, and those resulting from the indirect effects of the pandemic. The gap between the COVID deaths officially reported and the observed excess mortality can provide some indication of the indirect cost of lives, as shown in Figure 4.4. Countries on the right side of the figure experienced higher excess mortality than officially reported COVID deaths. While this could indicate that some of the indirect effects of the pandemic have had a negative effect on mortality, this would also capture any of deaths that were from COVID-19 but not reported as such. On the left side of the figure, several countries experienced lower total excess deaths than the number of COVID deaths officially reported. This would capture deaths that were classified as being due to COVID-19 because of a recent positive test result, but were actually due to other causes. This could also indicate that indirect impacts such as behavioural changes may have had a positive impact on mortality.

Figure 4.4. Excess mortality relative to officially reported COVID-19 deaths

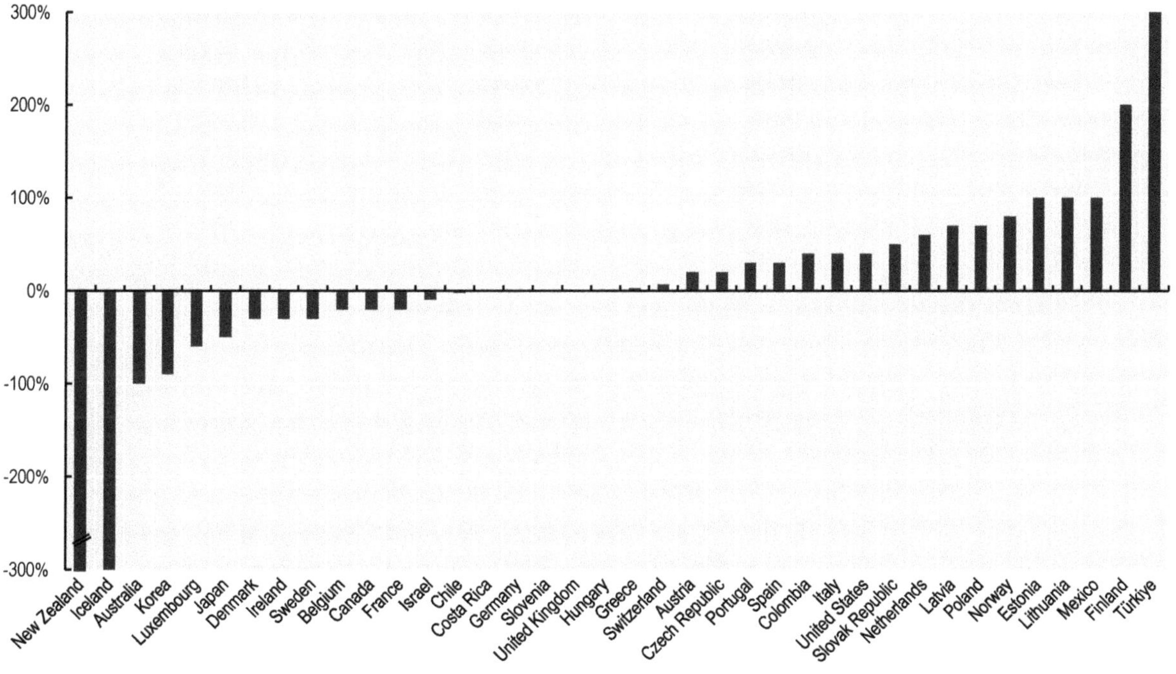

Note: Data available as of 13 January, 2022. Figure truncated at -300%, with the relative excess mortality for New Zealand at -5000%.
Source: Adapted from The Economist (2022[11]), *The pandemic's true death toll*, https://econ.st/3yE7flu.

Another way to understand the direct and indirect impact of COVID-19 on mortality is to look at the decomposition of the change in life expectancy from 2019 to 2020. Figure 4.5 shows the decomposition of this change in life expectancy at birth (contrary to Figure 4.2 that shows life expectancy at age 60) between the direct impact of COVID-19 and the impact from other causes. Chileans experienced the largest reduction in life expectancy attributed directly to COVID-19, whereas those from the United States experienced the largest total reduction in life expectancy. Other causes of mortality actually had a positive impact on life expectancy in Chile, particularly for females.

Figure 4.5. Decomposition of the change in period life expectancy at birth from 2019 to 2020

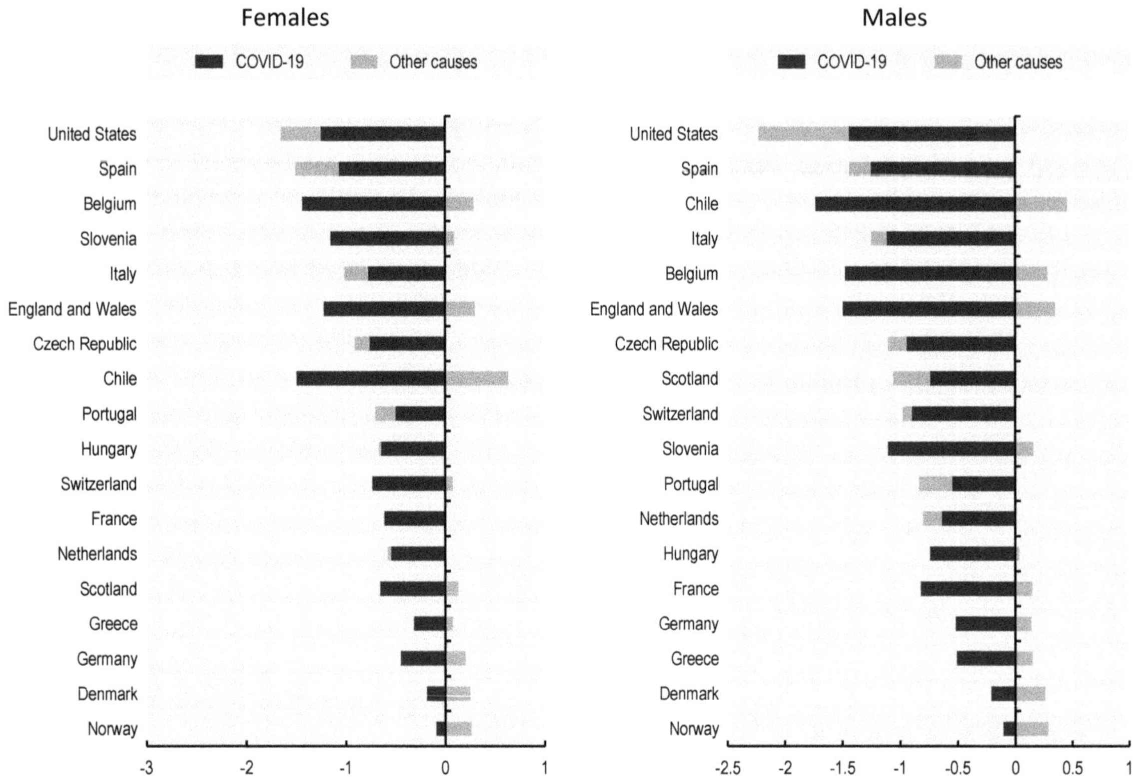

Note: Period life expectancy describes the mortality experience of a specific year, and does not take into account future expectations of mortality.
Source: Adapted from Aberto et al. (2021[3]), *Quantifying impacts of the COVID-19 pandemic through life-expectancy losses: a population-level study of 29 countries*, DOI: 10.1093/ije/dyab207.

Nevertheless, average figures may hide that indirect effects may still have had a net negative impact for many groups of the population, even if they were positive overall. Disadvantaged groups who have experienced higher mortality from COVID-19 have also experienced higher excess mortality during the pandemic from other causes. One study in the United States estimates that 17% of excess deaths were attributable to causes other than COVID-19, and this figure was substantially higher for counties having lower socioeconomic levels, poorer health, and a larger Black population (Stokes et al., 2021[7]).

While official statistics for COVID-19 deaths may not provide an accurate estimate of the total impact it has had on mortality, they do provide important insights regarding relative mortality risk for various groups of the population. The following section describes these differences and their potential drivers.

4.1.1. The direct impact of the COVID-19 virus

The mortality risk from COVID-19 seems to generally follow a similar pattern to the mortality risk from all causes, so those at higher risk of dying during regular times are also at higher risk of dying from COVID-19. As with baseline mortality, the mortality risk from COVID-19 differs substantially across ages, genders, baseline health, socioeconomic status, and ethnicity.

Differences across ages

The mortality risk from COVID-19 increases exponentially with age, similarly to the normal mortality pattern observed across ages. The Gompertz model, which is commonly used to define mortality rates across ages and assumes that mortality increases exponentially with age, provides an adequate fit for the mortality from COVID-19. Indeed, the pattern of the mortality risk from COVID-19 has followed a similar pattern as that for other causes of death related to ageing, including pneumonia and influenza. However, the relative mortality risk for adults from COVID-19 has been much higher, at between 2.8 to 8.2 times higher than pneumonia and influenza (Sasson, 2021[8]).

Given the exponential pattern of mortality risk across ages, the age structure of a population is clearly a determinant in the overall mortality for COVID-19 experienced in any given jurisdiction. However, the starting point of mortality also matters. Older people are at higher relative risk in high-income countries, who have lower baseline mortality at adult ages, than in low and middle-income countries. This is because high-income countries have experienced more significant longevity gains at younger to middle ages, so the mortality curve for high-income countries is much steeper (see Figure 4.6 for an illustration). This means that individuals 'age' more quickly than in low and middle-income countries where the mortality curve is flatter. As such, the mortality risk from COVID-19 increases on average by 12.6 percent with each year of age in high-income countries, compared to only 7.1 percent in low and middle-income countries (Demombynes, 2020[9]). Younger individuals in the latter countries are therefore at higher relative risk of dying from COVID-19.

Figure 4.6. Illustration of slope of mortality curves for higher and lower income countries

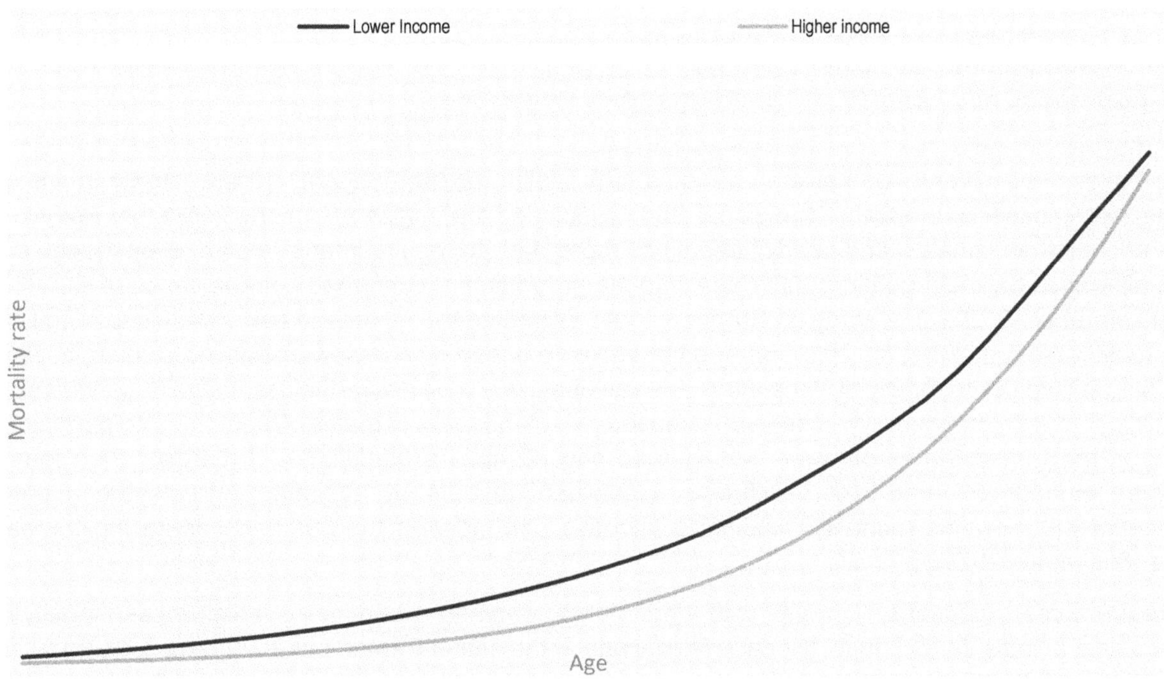

Differences between genders

Males have been at a higher risk of dying from COVID-19 than females on average. Males have represented slightly less than half of confirmed positive cases – though they have been also less likely to get tested – but have made up a higher proportion of confirmed deaths (The Sex, Gender, and COVID-19 Project, 2021[10]). Figure 4.7 shows that this is generally true in a sample of 30 OECD countries where sex-disaggregated data is available. While men represent on average 48.3% of confirmed COVID-19 cases in the sample, weighted by the number of cases, they make up 55% of the deaths (The Sex, Gender, and COVID-19 Project, 2021[10]).

Figure 4.7. Percent of male confirmed COVID-19 cases and deaths in OECD countries

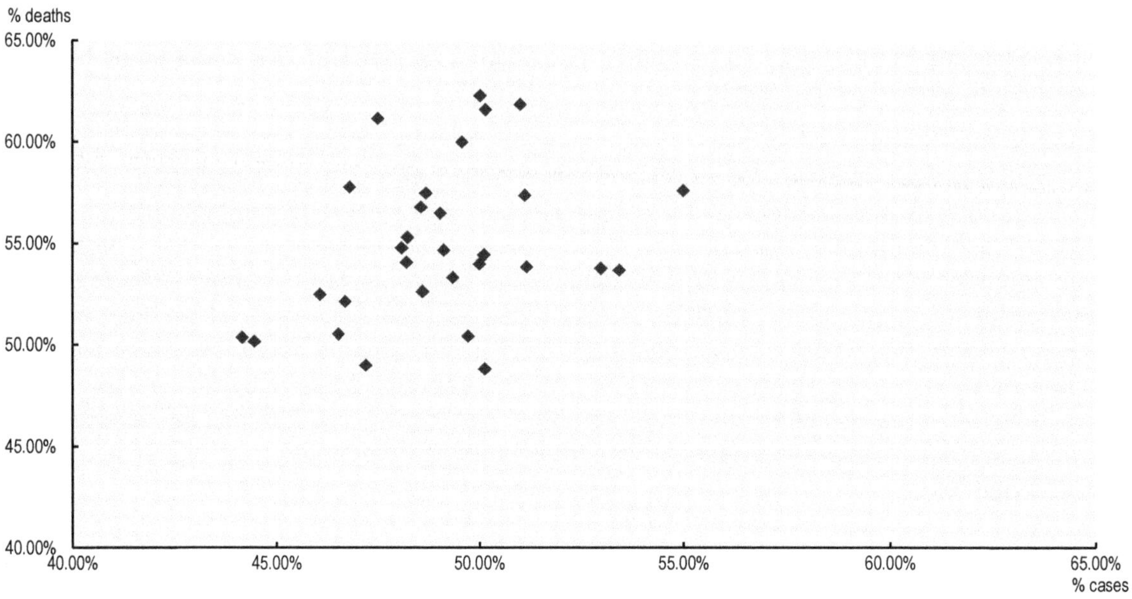

Note: Data from 30 OECD countries available as of 24 August 2021.
Source: Adapted from The Sex, Gender, and COVID-19 Project (2021[10]), *The COVID-19 Sex-Disaggregated Data Tracker*, https://globalhealth5050.org/the-sex-gender-and-covid-19-project/the-data-tracker/.

Nevertheless, the differences between genders in mortality risk from COVID-19 are largely in line with differences in baseline mortality. One global study concluded that males are nearly 40% more likely to die of COVID-19 than females, and nearly three times more likely to require intensive care, even though there is no difference between genders with respect to the proportion of confirmed positive cases of COVID-19 (Peckham et al., 2020[11]). A study on European data estimated the increased risk of males to range from 11% to 54% (Ahrenfeldt et al., 2020[12]). Another estimate based on a review of existing studies, however, puts the relative risk to males higher at 86% (Biswas et al., 2020[13]). Nevertheless, these observations are mostly in line with the generally observed increased risk of mortality of males. To put this into perspective, males in the United States between the ages 55 and 80 have a higher risk of mortality than females between around 35% and 70%.[6] Differences between genders by age also demonstrate a pattern consistent with baseline mortality, tending to increase until ages in the 60s and decreasing thereafter (Ahrenfeldt et al., 2020[12]).

There are some exceptions, however, with a handful of countries experiencing a higher case fatality rate for females. In India, for example, the case fatality rate at the end of September 2020, was 3.3% for women compared to 2.9% for men. Nepal, Slovenia, and Vietnam have also demonstrated higher case fatality rates for females. Nevertheless, it is difficult to determine whether these are the true differences in mortality or whether they may be caused by biases in reporting, testing or access to healthcare (Dehingia and Raj, 2021[14]).

Differences by underlying health conditions

Having an underlying comorbidity significantly increases the mortality risk of COVID-19. Kidney disease is among the most deadly, increasing the risk of death by nearly five times. Other comorbidities identified as significant risk factors include, in order of descending risk, cardiovascular disease (~3x), respiratory disease (2-3x), diabetes (~2x), hypertension (~2x), dementia (~2x), cancer (~2x), and liver disease (1.5x) (Biswas et al., 2020[13]; Cho, Yoon and Lee, 2021[15]).

Indeed, the vast majority of people who have died from COVID-19 have had at least one comorbidity, and multiple comorbidities are common. Among those who died of COVID-19 in Canada, for example, 90% had at least one other underlying condition, nearly two-thirds had at least two comorbidities and nearly half had three or more (Statistics Canada, 2021[16]). One study on a care home in Sweden showed that deaths during the first wave of the pandemic were mainly the frailest of the population having multiple comorbidities, with 92% of deaths having three or more comorbidities (Nilsson, Andersson and Sjödahl, 2021[17]).

Death among the population under 65 with no comorbidities has remained rare. Less than 3.6% of COVID-19 fatalities under age 65 in France, Italy, the Netherlands, Sweden, Georgia (USA), and New York City (USA) had no comorbidities, though Mexico presents an exception to this with nearly 18% of those dying under 65 having no comorbidity (Ioannidis, Axfors and Contopoulos-Ioannidis, 2020[18]). However, this could at least partially driven by lower levels or reporting or diagnosis of comorbidities in Mexico.

Frail populations are clearly more at risk of dying from COVID-19. This leads to the somewhat counterintuitive observation that countries having better health care systems also have higher COVID-19 death rates. This is because in these countries people are more likely to survive life-threatening events such as heart attacks and strokes, making the overall population frailer on average. One study found that for every 1% increase in the size of a country's population surviving heart conditions or stroke, the death rate from COVID increased by 19% (Botly et al., 2020[19]).

That frailer populations are more at risk supports the hypothesis that many of the deaths from COVID-19 are accelerated deaths that may well have occurred in the short-term regardless. This phenomenon has been observed in past pandemics as well. Following the Spanish Flu of 1918-1919, the gap in life expectancy between males and females significantly decreased. This is likely because many of those dying during that pandemic also had tuberculosis. Indeed, tuberculosis rates dropped in the years following the Spanish Flu, and disproportionately so for males (Noymer and Garenne, 2000[20]).

Differences by socioeconomic status

There is mixed evidence as to whether more disadvantaged groups have been at higher risk of dying from COVID-19. The link between socioeconomic status and COVID-19 mortality risk varies from one country to the next, therefore local context seems to play an important role in the difference in outcomes.

Higher levels of deprivation have been associated with higher COVID-19 mortality in several jurisdictions. In England, a one percentage point increase in the proportion of the population experiencing income deprivation was found to lead to a 2% increase in COVID-19 mortality rates (Rose et al., 2020[21]). In Scotland as well, mortality rates were two times higher for those from the most deprived areas, controlling for age and sex (Lone et al., 2021[22]). A strong gradient of excess mortality and socioeconomic status was also found in Santiago, Chile (Mena et al., 2021[23]).

Nevertheless, other studies have not shown a conclusive link between socioeconomic status and COVID-19 mortality. In Germany, one study found no evidence of a link between poverty and COVID-19 mortality during the first wave of the pandemic (Ettensperger, 2021[24]). In Wisconsin, USA, poverty was found to be associated with higher rates of admission to the Intensive Care Unit, but not higher rates of death (Muñoz-Price et al., 2020[25]). Supporting these results, a study using US Census data did not show income or poverty to be a significant factor in predicting mortality (McLaren, 2020[26]).

The drivers of these disparities and the potential increased mortality risk for lower socioeconomic groups vary across countries. A common explanation put forward is that lower socioeconomic groups have a higher incidence of comorbidities that increase the mortality risk from COVID-19. In the United States, those with either lower education or lower incomes have higher rates of every medical risk factor (Wiemers et al., 2020[27]). In Chile, people living in lower socioeconomic areas are more likely to be overweight and live in crowded conditions (Mena et al., 2021[23]). However, in England, the higher mortality risk for more deprived groups was not significantly explained by medical risk factors (Williamson et al., 2020[28]).

Access to medical care and health services is another potential driver of observed differences. In Chile, lower socioeconomic neighbourhoods experienced more testing delays (Mena et al., 2021[23]).

Higher rates of infection may also play a role. Lower socioeconomic groups may be more likely to have occupations that do not allow for teleworking, increasing their risk of infection. In Chile, lockdown measures were less effective at reducing people's mobility in more disadvantaged areas (Mena et al., 2021[23]). Lower socioeconomic groups in Korea were also shown to be at higher risk of contracting COVID-19, particularly for those over the age of 60 (Oh, Choi and Song, 2021[29]).

Difference by ethnicity

Large disparities of mortality rates due to COVID-19 across ethnic groups have been observed in some jurisdictions. In the United States, Black, Hispanic, and Native populations have been at least twice as likely to die of COVID-19 compared to the White population (Center for Disease Control and Prevention, 2021[30]). This led to a reduction in life expectancy in 2020 for Blacks and Hispanics that was two to three times greater than for Whites (Woolf, Masters and Aron, 2021[31]). In England, the Black male population's mortality risk was 3.7 times that of the White population during the first wave of the pandemic, and nearly all ethnic minorities were at higher risk of death than Whites. During the second wave, the mortality risk for the Bangladeshi population increased substantially to 4-5 times that of the White population (Office for National Statistics, 2021[32]).

The higher risk to ethnic minorities is clear, though factors other than ethnicity are likely driving these results. One study in Louisiana confirmed that while Blacks had a much higher rate of hospitalisation and deaths than Whites, race itself was not an explanatory factor in the conditional survivor probability when controlling for other factors (Price-Haywood et al., 2020[33]).

There are several explanations put forward to explain observed differences across ethnic groups, including that they tend to be from more disadvantaged backgrounds, have higher rates of comorbidities, or have higher rates of infection. However, there is not strong evidence supporting the explanation that these populations tend to more often be from lower socioeconomic backgrounds. One study in England showed that only a small part of the excess risk could be attributed to higher levels of deprivation (Williamson et al., 2020[28]). Another study in Wisconsin, USA found no strong relationship between socioeconomic status and race (Muñoz-Price et al., 2020[25]). An analysis using US Census data also found no evidence that income, poverty rates, or educational differences were driving the racial disparities for Black and Native populations, though education did seem to be a factor for differences observed for the Hispanic and Asian populations (McLaren, 2020[26]).

That minority populations suffer from higher rates of comorbidities seems to be a more plausible explanation for their increased mortality risk. In the United States, Blacks have a higher prevalence of most of the COVID-19 risk factors than Whites (Wiemers et al., 2020[27]). In one study in Louisiana, USA, Black patients had a higher prevalence of obesity, diabetes, hypertension, and chronic kidney disease (Price-Haywood et al., 2020[33]). In contrast, another study in England showed that a higher prevalence of medical problems did not fully explain observed disparities (Williamson et al., 2020[28]).

Higher infection rates may be another explanatory factor for observed ethnic disparities. In the Wisconsin study, Blacks were more likely to test positive for COVID-19, even when controlling for demographics, health and geography (Muñoz-Price et al., 2020[25]). Another study linked the increased risk to the use of public transportation and to the prevalence of heath support workers in the population (e.g. home aids, nursing assistants), in line with the theory of increased exposure leading to higher rates of infection (McLaren, 2020[26]).

4.1.2. The indirect impacts of responses to the COVID-19 pandemic

The indirect consequences of the COVID-19 pandemic on mortality have potentially been large. The gap between officially reported COVID-19 deaths and the number of excess deaths presented in Figure 4.4 and Figure 4.5 provided some indication of the magnitude of this impact. This section aims to better understand the drivers of excess deaths not directly related to the COVID-19 virus itself. Drivers identified include reduced healthcare access, the impact of lockdown measures on well-being and behaviour, and the broader economic impact that the response to the pandemic had.

Healthcare access

The COVID-19 pandemic caused significant disruptions to health services, including essential and emergency care that could have led to excess mortality from health problems other than COVID-19. A survey by the World Health Organization (WHO) found that 94% of the 135 responding countries experienced some disruption to essential health services, and over a third of the countries experienced disruptions to over half of their services. This included potentially lifesaving emergency, critical and operative interventions, which were disrupted in 20% of the countries. Over 40% of countries had disruptions to mental, neurological and substance abuse services, and a third experienced disruptions related to pre- and post-natal care. While less impacted, 26% of high-income countries still experienced disruptions (World Health Organization, 2021[34]).

Disruptions to health services, in particularly urgent care services, likely led to an increase in mortality for those unable to obtain needed treatment. One survey in the United States indicated that 1-2% of individuals surveyed were not able to access needed urgent care in the prior two months specifically because of the pandemic (Center for Disease Control and Prevention, 2021[35]). Deaths from Alzheimer's and heart disease significantly increased in the United States during the peaks of the pandemic (Woolf et al., 2021[36]). The United Kingdom estimated that 6 000 of the excess non-COVID-19 deaths in March and April 2020 were due to changes in emergency care, compared to 42 000 deaths attributed directly to COVID-19. Another 10 000 are estimated to have died as a result of changes to adult social care, including early discharge, lack of emergency health care, and changes in the quality of care (Office for National Statistics, 2020[37]).

Avoidance of health care facilities because of a fear of being infected also likely played a significant role in the increased deaths among those not receiving needed care. In Northern Italy, emergency visits and hospitalisations decreased across all age groups and all types of diagnoses shortly after the first confirmed COVID-19 case in Italy. However, out-of-hospital mortality from neoplasms, cardiovascular and endocrine diseases significantly increased during lockdown, indicating that these individuals were not seeking needed care at the hospital (Santi et al., 2021[38]). Similarly, in Denmark, non-COVID-19 hospital admissions decreased by 30% after the first lockdown, and by 22% following the second lockdown after trends had returned to baseline levels. Despite this, mortality rates for non-COVID-19 diseases increased by over 20% during the lockdowns, and mortality rates from respiratory diseases, cancer, pneumonia, and sepsis remained higher over the entire period (Bodilsen et al., 2021[39]). In England and Wales, deaths from ischaemic heart disease, asthma, and diabetes increased, despite a reduction of these deaths in hospitals, indicating that many of these deaths were due to not receiving care (Kraindler, Barclay and Tallack, 2020[40]).

Disadvantaged groups of the population were in many cases more likely to experience reduced access to health care services. In Europe, a strong socioeconomic gradient was observed by socioeconomic status and previous health conditions for those experiencing foregone, postponed, or unavailable care, meaning that those who were more economically vulnerable and in poor health had less access to the health system (Börsch-Supan, 2021[41]). In the United States, the proportion of individuals not having access to urgent care because of the pandemic was negatively correlated with education level (Center for Disease Control and Prevention, 2021[35]). In addition, Black, Hispanic, and disabled populations were more likely to avoid urgent or emergency care during the first wave of the pandemic (Czeisler et al., 2020[42]). Hospital restrictions also seem to have been unbalanced in some cases, with sites caring more for Black populations being more impacted by lockdown measures. In a study on US patients with prostate cancer, prostatectomies decreased by over 90% for Blacks compared to only 17% for Whites, a difference not explained by the clinical parameters such as risk factors and age. While surgical treatments were restricted during lockdowns to prioritize those needing emergency care, some sites experienced increased surgical volume while those treating a higher proportion of Black patients paused surgeries completely (Vince, 2021[43]).

Capacity constraints and diminished resources could also put developing countries at increased mortality risk, especially children. Vaccination programmes against diseases other than COVID-19 in particular have been significantly disrupted. As of April 2021, vaccination programmes in 50 countries were still postponed, meaning that 228 million people faced an additional risk of contracting life threatening diseases such as measles, polio, and yellow fever (WHO, 2021[44]). Missed vaccinations may also reduce herd immunity, presenting a larger risk to these populations as a whole. This is not without precedent. During the Ebola outbreak in 2014, vaccinations for infants under one year fell by 75%, vaccinations for measles fell by 20%, and around half of the children in the three most affected countries did not receive all of their routine vaccinations (Elston et al., 2017[45]).

Past experience has shown that the unavailability of healthcare or the reluctance to seek healthcare during health crises can be particularly detrimental to pregnant women and children, especially in developing countries. At the height of the Ebola outbreak in 2014 in Sierra Leone, maternal mortality increased by 170%, and still births increased by 40%. Over that year, reduced access to routine health services increased maternal and child mortality by 22% and 25%, respectively, with preventable and treatable infectious diseases being a major contributor to the latter (Elston et al., 2017[45]). Applying this experience to the COVID-19 pandemic, one theoretical model estimated that child mortality could increase by up to 45%, and maternal mortality by up to 39%, in low-income and middle-income countries. 60% of the increase in maternal deaths were due to reduced access to key childbirth interventions, while 40% of the increase in child deaths were due to reduced access to treatments for pneumonia, sepsis, and diarrhea (Roberton et al., 2020[46]).

Lockdown measures

The strict lockdown measures that many governments implemented during the peak waves of the COVID-19 pandemic had a significant toll on the mental health and well-being of the populations impacted. In the United Kingdom, the proportion of adults experiencing some form of depression in early 2021 doubled from pre-pandemic levels, with young adults and women more impacted (Office of National Statistics, 2021[47]). Similarly, the proportion of adults having symptoms of anxiety or depression increased by 5 percentage points over the period from August 2020 to February 2021, with young adults being particularly impacted (Vahratian et al., 2021[48]). Such declines in wellbeing can lead to potentially fatal detrimental behaviour linked to substance abuse or even suicide. Declines in well-being at home may also pose a threat to those in abusive relationships. On the positive side, in some jurisdictions social distancing may have reduced the number of homicides during lockdown periods, reduced traffic fatalities, and reduced fatalities from other contagious diseases such as seasonal influenza.

Substance abuse

The boredom and reductions in well-being that accompanied lockdown measures exacerbated existing negative trends with respect to substance abuse and fatalities from drug overdoses. In the United States, deaths from drug overdoses increased by 29% in 2020 compared to 2019. That amounted to 93 000 people, or to put this into perspective, about 25% of the number of deaths due directly to COVID-19 (OSF Healthcare, 2021[49]). In 2020, more than twice the number of people in San Francisco, California died of overdoses than of COVID-19 (The Economist, 2021[50]). Ontario, Canada experienced an increase of 75% in deaths from opioid overdoses in 2020 compared to 2019, with an 82% increase for the 25 to 44 age group (Gomes et al., 2021[51]). Alcohol-related deaths also increased substantially in Canada in 2020, increasing by more than 20% for those under the age of 65, and by nearly 50% for those under the age of 45 (Statistics Canada, 2021[52]).

The alarming increase in overdoses has been directly linked with the lockdown orders imposed in certain areas. Weekly median death rates from overdoses in San Francisco, California increased by 50% following the shelter in place order (Appa et al., 2021[53]). Overdose deaths in Ohio, USA increased by over 70% within two months following the declaration of a national emergency before decreasing again by August 2020. The largest increase was for ages under 25, whose death rates more than doubled compared to 2018-2019, and ages over 65 where the increase was just under 90% (Currie et al., 2021[54]).

However, the impact of lockdowns on substance abuse varies across countries. While the data is less conclusive, some evidence indicates that drug use declined during the strict lockdown periods in Europe, largely due to disruptions in the supply chain and less opportunity to use. Overdose deaths seem to have been lower in Italy and Portugal. However, they may have been higher in Finland, and they increased in Spain once lockdown restrictions eased. Other worrisome trends indicate that there could be an increase in problems linked to substance abuse in the coming years. Cocaine shipments seem to have increased substantially in Europe, and the product has also become more potent (UNODC, 2021[55]).

Suicide

While depression and anxiety rose during the pandemic, this did not seem to lead to an immediate increase in suicide mortality in most countries. In one study of 21 high- and upper-middle-income countries, no significant increase in suicides was observed through the end of July, 2020 (Pirkis et al., 2021[56]). Suicides even declined in some jurisdictions, such as the United States where suicides in 2020 were 6% lower than in 2019 (Ahmad and Anderson, 2021[57]). One explanation for this could be that significant efforts were put into offering support to those at risk, in recognition of the impact that lockdown could have on mental health. Another, observed in previous epidemics, is the feeling of community and everyone going through hard times together. The economic assistance that many governments provided in high-income countries could have also mitigated any increase in the short term (John et al., 2020[58]).

Indeed, there is some evidence that the impact of the pandemic on suicide rates could still be observed going forward. Japan, Puerto Rico and Vienna, Austria all showed signs of an increase in suicides following the initial wave (Pirkis et al., 2021[56]). Following an initial decline of 14% in Japan during the first five months of the pandemic, suicides increased by 16% during the second wave, particularly for females and adolescents (Tanaka and Okamoto, 2021[59]). In Peru, the downward trend in suicides seemed to reverse in the post-lockdown period (Calderon-Anyosa and Kaufman, 2021[60]).

In addition, suicide rates may have increased for certain groups of the population. There were some signs that child suicide rates increased in the United Kingdom during the first lockdown period (Odd et al., 2021[61]). During the first wave of the pandemic, suicides among the Black population in Maryland, USA appeared to have doubled compared to previous years, while among the White population suicides nearly halved (Bray et al., 2021[62]). In the United States, emergency room visits due to suicide attempts by adolescent girls increased by 51% in early 2021 compared to 2019, while rising only by 4% for boys (U. S. Surgeon General, 2021[63]).

Femicide

Lockdown measures may have increased violence against women, as those in abusive relationships became trapped at home with their abusers. Data early in the pandemic showed a worrying increase in the reports of domestic violence and calls to emergency and helplines, with observed increases between

25% to 33% in Argentina, Cyprus, France and Singapore (UN Women, 2020[64]).[7] In Peru, calls to helplines for domestic violence increased by 48% (Calderon-Anyosa and Kaufman, 2021[60]). In South Africa, gender-based violence cases increased by 37% during the first week of lockdown in April 2020 (Warah, 2021[65]).

This increase in domestic violence has not necessarily translated into increased femicides, however. Femicides have decreased slightly in Mexico after remaining constant during the lockdown period, and have also decreased in Argentina, France, Peru, and Portugal, though in the latter the number of attempted femicides has not decreased (Hoehn-Velasco, Silverio-Murillo and de la Miyar, 2021[66]; Statistica, 2021[67]; Le Monde, 2021[68]; Calderon-Anyosa and Kaufman, 2021[60]; OMA-UMAR, 2020[69]).

Nevertheless, femicides have increased in some jurisdictions, and for others there are signs that an increase is yet to come. Femicide rates nearly doubled in the United Kingdom during the first weeks of the pandemic (Guerra Lund, Manica and Mânica, 2020[70]). A significant increase was also observed in Quebec, Canada (Laou, 2021[71]). Femicides followed a steady increasing trend between March and August, 2020 in Colombia (Statistica, 2021[67]). In Peru, over 900 women, of which two-thirds were children, were reported missing during the three and a half months of lockdown, and many missing person reports later end up being femicides (Charrier, 2020[72]). In addition, a significant portion of femicides occur at the moment of separation from the partner, whereas women were not able to leave during lockdown periods (Shiloh Vidon, 2021[73]). Lockdown measures may also have reduced the opportunity for femicide. In Peru, for example, bodies are most frequently found outside of the home (Casana-Jara, 2020[74]). It may therefore be the case that femicides could increase in the months following lockdowns.

Homicide

While lockdown measures had a significant positive influence on crime rates, which experienced sharp reductions, homicide rates seem to have been less impacted. While overall crime reduced by 37% in European cities, the reduction was lowest for homicides, which went down by only 14% (Nivette et al., 2021[75]). Homicides in Mexico did not experience a big change, even though other types of crime reduced during lockdown before returning to pre-pandemic levels (Balmori de la Miyar, Hoehn-Velasco and Silverio-Murillo, 2021[76]). Other areas in Latin America experienced a more significant drop, with homicides reducing by 24%, 29% and 76% in large cities in Brazil, Colombia and Peru, respectively, though in Peru rates started to pick back up following the lockdown period (Nivette et al., 2021[75]) (Calderon-Anyosa and Kaufman, 2021[60]). Despite a significant drop in crime in large cities in the United States during lockdown orders, homicides actually increased in the summer of 2020 (Abrams, 2021[77]).

Traffic accidents

Lockdown measures led to a significant drop in traffic, though this did not always translate into a reduction in traffic fatalities. Nevertheless, many countries did experience a substantial drop in traffic deaths. Peru experienced a larger drop in fatalities related to traffic accidents than the reduction in suicides and homicides (Calderon-Anyosa and Kaufman, 2021[60]). Stay-at-home orders in March and April, 2020, reduced traffic deaths in Türkiye by 72% (Oguzoglu, 2020[78]). Across Europe, traffic fatalities decreased by 17% on average, although fatalities actually increased in Finland, Ireland, Latvia, Estonia, Luxembourg, Switzerland, and Iceland (European Commission, 2021[79]). Only a slight decrease was observed in Japan, and fatalities increased in certain prefectures such as in Tokyo (Tauchi, 2021[80]).

Globally, the change in traffic fatalities was not proportional with the change in traffic. In April 2020 the International Transport Forum found a decrease in road deaths by only a third, even though traffic was halved (ITF, 2020[81]). Other jurisdictions experienced an increase in traffic fatalities, despite less driving. In Ontario, Canada, traffic fatalities increased by 22% despite a reduction in accidents of 26% (The Canadian Press, 2021[82]). In the United States, traffic deaths increased by 7.2% compared to 2019 despite a 13.2% decrease in miles driven (NHTSA, 2021[83]). The increase in fatalities in both jurisdictions was attributed to an increase in reckless driving practices.

Contagious disease

Improved hygiene and social distancing measures, including the use of masks, have not only helped in preventing the spread of COVID-19, but have also led to a significant reduction in the transmission of contagious diseases, in particular seasonal influenza. In normal years, seasonal influenza is a significant cause of mortality globally, with around 300 to 500 thousand deaths each year associated with influenza (Paget et al., 2019[84]). During the 2020-2021 influenza season, samples testing positive for influenza fell to practically zero in the WHO European Region (the European Influenza Surveillance Network, 2021[85]). It has also reached historical lows in the United States, Australia, Chile, and South Africa during 2020 (Olsen et al., 2020[86]).

While fewer people certainly lost their lives to influenza, the net benefits are less clear. The elderly more susceptible to seasonal influenza would be also more at risk for COVID-19. In addition, the absence of the seasonal influenza epidemic could lead to a reduction in herd immunity, leading to more severe and longer epidemics in coming flu seasons (Sanz-Muñoz et al., 2021[87]).

Economic variables

Economic cycles can have an impact on mortality because of changes in employment situations, daily behaviour and habits, and public spending. During the first year of the pandemic, many governments provided economic aid that shielded people from the full impact of the economic fallout resulting from lockdown requirements and business closures. However, the effects of any enduring unemployment and cuts to public spending may continue to be felt in the near to medium term, which could have possible ramifications on mortality. Countries providing less economic aid during the crisis likely already felt some of these effects. Additionally, negative effects on mortality can persist for years following a recession (Doerr and Hofmann, 2020[88]).

Many of the potential impacts on mortality from difficult economic environments are similar to the indirect effects on mortality already discussed in the context of COVID-19, although the drivers and dynamics of these impacts are subtly different so are worth discussing separately. Access to healthcare can be impacted through a reduction in public spending, as opposed to capacity constraints and fear of infection. As with lockdowns, increased unemployment can change daily habits and behaviours, and have important impacts on well-being, but without the accompanying social restrictions. As with COVID-19, disadvantaged populations tend to be more negatively impacted, as they are more likely to experience a loss of income from unemployment that will impact access to food and healthcare, with particularly harmful consequences for the young and the elderly.

Counterintuitively, recessions have actually been shown to be beneficial for mortality in many developed economies, and in the United States in particular. One widely cited study of the period 1972-1991 finds evidence that mortality increases in periods of higher growth, which the author attributes to higher rates of smoking and obesity, less physical activity and a poorer diet. In contrast, during periods of unemployment, people have more time to dedicate to their health. A reduction in accidents also significantly contributes to reduced mortality in recessions – as was also expected during COVID lockdowns – that primarily impacts young to middle ages. Overall, the study finds that a single percentage point increases in state unemployment rates reduce mortality by 2% (Rhum, 2000[89]). Reductions in mortality from accidents during recessions, particularly for younger men, have also been observed in Australia, France, Greece, Korea (Brüning and Thuilliez, 2019[90]; Laliotis, Ioannidis and Stavropoulou, 2016[91]; Kim et al., 2003[92]).

Suicides, however, are an important exception to the pattern of pro-cyclicality of mortality with the economy. The same study demonstrating the pro-cyclicality of mortality in the United States finds that suicides rise by 1.3% for each percentage point rise in unemployment (Rhum, 2000[89]). Increased suicides during economic crises have also been observed in Greece, Hong Kong (China), Japan, and Korea (Laliotis, Ioannidis and Stavropoulou, 2016[91]; Chang et al., 2009[93]). In one longitudinal study in Sweden, unemployment increased the risk of death for the working age population by nearly 50%, controlling for other characteristics such as health (Gerdtham and Johannesson, 2003[94]). Across Europe, a one percentage point increase in unemployment corresponds to a 1% increase in suicides for the working age population, but there is no impact on those over the age of 65 (Breuer, 2014[95]). Contrary to some increases observed during the COVID-19 pandemic, however, suicides during periods of high unemployment tend to affect men the most. This could imply that suicide patterns during COVID lockdowns may be more linked to the social situation imposed by lockdowns rather than economic hardship per se.

The pattern of pro-cyclicality of mortality in developed countries seems to be reversing more recently. An extension of the US study to 2010 showed that mortality has become more disconnected from macroeconomic conditions. The author attributes this mainly to recent negative trends in drug overdoses, which was also observed during the COVID lockdowns. While mental health has always been counter-cyclical, access to drugs is now easier so these troubles are more frequently fatal (Ruhm, 2015[96]). Mortality has also gone from being pro-cyclical to counter-cyclical in France, where mortality no longer decreases when unemployment increases (Brüning and Thuilliez, 2019[90]). While some pro-cyclical drivers of mortality were observed in Greece following the 2008 financial crisis – such as fewer respiratory infections, reduced smoking, and increased physical activity – mortality improvements still slowed during this period (Filippidis et al., 2017[97]; Laliotis, Ioannidis and Stavropoulou, 2016[91]). Another notable observation occurred in Australia, where the introduction of universal healthcare eliminated pro-cyclical mortality for female infants (Atalay et al., 2021[98]). Pro-cyclical mortality among infants in developed countries has been attributed in part to mothers having more time available to attend to self-care and the health of their baby (Dehejia and Lleras-Muney, 2004[99]).

Taking a more global perspective, mortality is predominantly counter-cyclical, particularly in the developing world. In one study of 180 countries, mortality increased by 4% during years where GDP declined, and this increase lasted up to ten years following the recession. This result is driven mainly by emerging and developing economies, as the effect is often not significant in advanced economies (Doerr and Hofmann, 2020[88]). The negative effects of recession in developing countries are particularly detrimental to children. A 1% decrease in GDP per capita translates into 0.24-0.4 more deaths per 1 000 children in developing countries, and there is a larger impact on girls (Baird, Friedman and Schady, 2011[100]).

The loss of income is one factor driving increased mortality during recessions, particularly for poorer households who may then struggle to obtain enough food to feed their family or pay for needed medical care. In France, the negative impact of recessions on mortality is higher for more disadvantaged groups such as migrants and those with lower education (Brüning and Thuilliez, 2019[90]). In Mexico, an increase in elderly mortality following the 1995 crisis was associated with an increase in women entering the labour force. While this could be a result of women then being less able to care for elderly relatives, there is more evidence that this was a result of the drop in income that forced women to look for work (Cutler et al., 2000[101]). Similarly in France, increased unemployment is associated with increased mortality among the age group 65-74, particularly for men (Brüning and Thuilliez, 2019[90]).

Access to healthcare is another major contributor to excess mortality during recessions, even in more developed countries, and especially among the elderly. In Mexico, mortality for ages 70-79 increased by 1% during the 1995 crisis, driven by non-communicable diseases such as cardiovascular disease and chronic respiratory disease (Cutler et al., 2000[101]). Following the 2008 financial crisis in Greece, where healthcare expenditure decreased by 25%, mortality for ages over 65 increased mainly due to circulatory and digestive diseases (Filippidis et al., 2017[97]; Laliotis, Ioannidis and Stavropoulou, 2016[91]). Adverse events during medical treatments also increased, highlighting the importance of the quality of healthcare (Laliotis, Ioannidis and Stavropoulou, 2016[91]). In Spain, during this same period of high austerity, winter mortality increased for ages over 60, particularly for males (Benmarhnia et al., 2014[102]).

4.2. Potential long-term consequences of the COVID-19 pandemic on mortality

While the short-term impacts of COVID-19 on mortality continue to emerge, we can expect most of these impacts to be temporary as the drivers of excess mortality subside. Nevertheless, COVID-19 could also have some effects on mortality that could emerge over time. The COVID-19 virus itself may have a long-term impact on health or immunity. The pandemic situation may also have exacerbated political and societal trends that could have long-term implications for future trends in life expectancy.

4.2.1. Long-term effects of the COVID-19 virus

COVID-19 may have long-term health implications that could increase the mortality risk of survivors. Many people who contracted and survived COVID-19 have experienced symptoms for weeks or even months, even if their initial symptoms were mild to moderate, a situation which has now commonly become known as "Long COVID". While studies may be biased towards hospitalised patients, one review of current literature estimates that 56% of confirmed COVID-19 cases experience symptoms beyond 12 weeks, and that 10% of these were not able to return to work (Domingo et al., 2021[103]). A broader and ongoing study in the United Kingdom indicates that up to 12% of infected individuals report to have symptoms lasting beyond 12 weeks, and up to 18% for those having symptomatic acute infections (Office for National Statistics, 2021[104]). Nevertheless, long-term medical problems reported are not necessarily the same symptoms as for the acute infection, and can include respiratory issues, neurological problems, gastrointestinal disorders, cardiovascular disorders, and a higher risk of having mental health issues (Al-Aly, Xie and Bowe, 2021[105]).

There is evidence that COVID-19 can cause lasting damage to the kidneys, lungs, heart, and brain, which could potentially lead to increased mortality risk. Severe illness from COVID-19 can lead to a long-term reduction in kidney function, and even patients experiencing moderate illness were shown to be at increased risk of death over the next six months (Bowe et al., 2021[106]). In another study, a third of a sample of hospitalised patients experienced lung tissue death (Marshall, 2020[107]). Heart injury has been in a quarter of hospitalised patients, and 60% of patients having recovered from COVID-19 had lasting heart inflammation (Giustino et al., 2020[108]; Puntmann et al., 2020[109]). There is also evidence that COVID-19 blocks blood flow to the brain (Hirunpattarasilp et al., 2021[110]). Long-term health impacts of these clinical observations could include kidney or heart failure, chronic respiratory problems, strokes, or even an increased risk of Parkinson's and Alzheimer's disease (Mayo Clinic, 2021[111]).

Evidence of longer-term complications can be found in patients recovering from the related diseases of severe acute respiratory syndrome (SARS) and the Middle East respiratory syndrome (MERS). Abnormalities in lung functioning, reduced exercise capacity, and psychological problems are common in survivors of SARS and MERS even 12 months after they have been discharged from the hospital (Ahmed et al., 2020[112]). After 15 years, 4.6% of SARS patients still had visible scarring on their lungs, and 38% had diminished lung functioning (Zhang et al., 2018[113]).

Studies on the Spanish Flu of 1918 have shown that there may be lasting health impacts to individuals exposed to viruses around birth. Children born in Sweden in 1919 are estimated to have had three months shorter life expectancy than proximate cohorts. The 1919 cohort ultimately had worse health and socioeconomic outcomes in old age, and males exposed to the virus during the second trimester experienced higher rates of heart disease and cancer (Helgertz and Bengtsson, 2019[114]). Similarly, in the United States, cohorts exposed in late gestation and at birth experienced 8-9% higher mortality from all causes, translating into at least seven months lower life expectancy at age 70 compared to surrounding cohorts. Those born during the peaks of the pandemic had higher mortality in particular from respiratory and cardiovascular disease, but also fewer cancer deaths (Myrskylä, Mehta and Chang, 2013[115]). These outcomes could mean that the 2020-2022 cohorts born during the COVID-19 pandemic could experience specific patterns of future mortality improvements and lower life expectancies compared to surrounding cohorts.

There is also evidence that any immunity acquired during a flu pandemic can affect future immune responses to other viruses, especially immunity acquired in childhood. One recent and plausible explanation put forward for the high fatality rate for young adults during the Spanish flu is the concept of antigenic imprinting, where the body's antibody response is significantly influenced by the influenza strains exposed to in childhood. The ages experiencing the highest fatality during the Spanish flu would have been young children during the H3N8 Russian influenza in 1889-1890. The Spanish flu was caused by another type of influenza strain, the H1N1 strain. The antigenic imprinting theory proposes that the immune response of this cohort was dominated by antibodies responding to the earlier strain, and therefore not effective against the H1N1 strain (Gagnon et al., 2013[116]). This theory could also explain differences in the prevalence of infection from different flu strains for cohorts born before and after the Hong Kong flu of 1968 (Woo, 2019[117]).

Immune responses to coronaviruses may also be influenced by past exposure, which can have implications for future immunity. One study found that while the antibodies found in patients who had recovered from SARS were not effective against COVID-19 by themselves, these patients had a very strong immune response to the Pfizer vaccine, even after just one dose. The antibodies they developed were also effective against a broader range of coronavirus variants, which was not the case for others vaccinated for COVID-19 (Tan et al., 2021[118]). Other researchers have speculated that there may be some level of protection offered from T cells developed in response to other types of coronavirus, which seem to also be more effective than antibodies against different variants (Redd et al., 2021[119]; Tarke et al., 2021[120]; Geers et al., 2021[121]; Doshi, 2020[122]). Nevertheless, more research is needed to investigate the implications of the immune response to different strains of coronavirus.

4.2.2. Potential long-term political shifts

Populations in democratic countries generally have higher life expectancies. Countries scoring at least 0.7 on the Liberal Democracy Index all had life expectancies over 74, while those countries having life expectancies under 60 all score below 0.5 on the Index (Figure 4.8).

Figure 4.8. Life expectancy at birth vs. Liberal Democracy Index, 2019

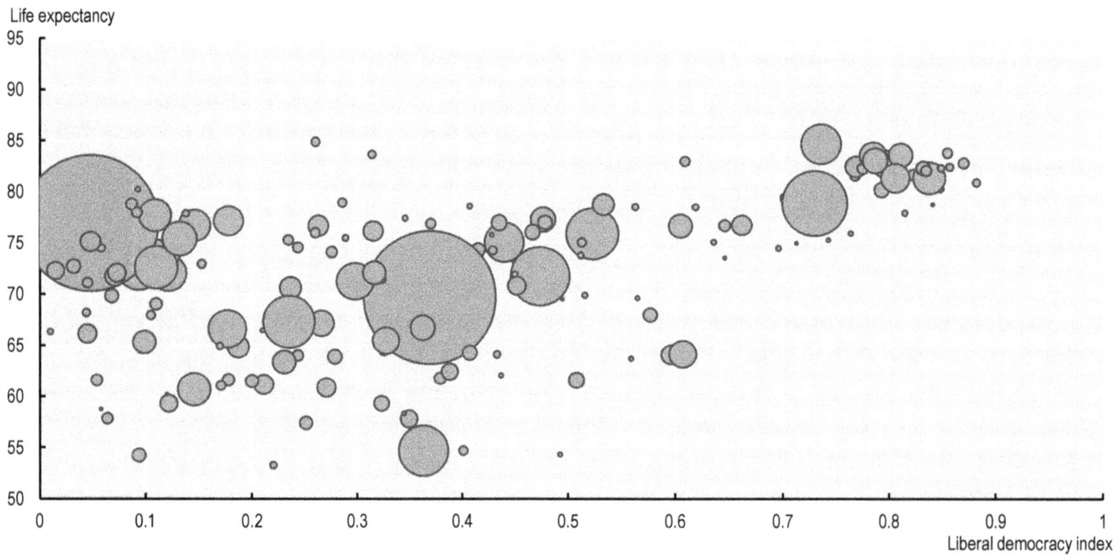

Source: Adapted from Ortiz-Ospina (2019[123]), *Does democracy lead to better health?*, https://ourworldindata.org/democracy-health.

Indeed, democracy seems to matter more than economic measures for measures of health of a population. Democracy is more strongly associated with higher life expectancy than a country's GNP, level of inequality, and public expenditure (Franco, Álvarez-Dardet and Ruiz, 2004[124]). Democratic experience also explains more of the variation in mortality from cardiovascular disease, transport injury, cancer, cirrhosis, and other non-communicable diseases than GDP does (Bollyky et al., 2019[125]).

Political shifts have led to significant changes in life expectancy in the past. Life expectancies in the Central and Eastern European and Baltic countries started improving in the 1990s following the collapse of the Soviet Union, after years of stagnation and even decreases in life expectancy. Following the German reunification of 1990, the life expectancy of East Germans rapidly caught up to that of West Germans. One estimate is that East German men and women would have had 5.7 years and 4 years lower life expectancy, respectively, if reunification had not occurred (Vogt, 2013[126]).

Over recent decades there have been trends in the opposite direction, indicating some reversal in trends towards democracy, even in established democracies. Since 2005, the number of countries classified as "Free" by Freedom House has gone from 89 to 82, while the number of "Not Free" countries has increased by 9 over the same period. The "Democracy Gap", or the number of countries whose aggregate Freedom score declined compared to those where it has increased, has been negative over the last 15 years and reached its highest level over that period in 2020 (Repucci and Slipowitz, 2021[127]). At an international level, some researchers have observed a decline in overt efforts to promote democracy, which has contributed to an increased willingness by some governments in developing democracies to violently oppose pro-democracy demonstrations and political opponents (Hyde, 2020[128]). Societal preferences have also moved away from democratic values in some areas. For example, in 2018, for the first time less than half of Latin Americans expressed full support for democracy, and nearly a third expressed indifference between a democratic or authoritarian regime, twice the proportion expressing an indifference two decades ago (UNDP, 2020[129]).

The COVID-19 pandemic exacerbated these trends. From January to August 2020, measures assessing the condition of human rights and democracy decreased in 80 out of 192 countries, or over 40% of the countries assessed, with struggling democracies and highly repressive states being the most impacted (Repucci and Slipowitz, 2020[130]). There is also evidence that the pandemic may have influenced public preferences for democracy, at least in the short term. At the beginning of the pandemic, Spaniards expressed higher preferences for strong leadership, technocracy, and authoritarian government, as well as more willingness to give up individual freedoms (Amat et al., 2020[131]).

Nevertheless, COVID-19 is unlikely to have an enduring negative impact on established democracies. To the contrary, public opinion may push these countries to place more weight on public health issues and the opinions of experts (Rapeli and Saikkonen, 2020[132]). However, social media has still facilitated the spread of misinformation that reinforces some groups' beliefs in the effectiveness of unproven treatments or the dangers of vaccination against COVID-19. This type of polarisation is likely to endure.

4.3. Implications for mortality assumptions in the context of asset-backed pension arrangements

COVID-19 has had a significant impact on mortality and life expectancy in the short term, but the impact on mortality assumptions used in the context of asset-backed pensions should be much lower. Many of the mortality shocks will be temporary, and mortality rates can be expected to return to their prior trajectories. Longer-term impacts are significantly less certain, however, thereby increasing the potential risk that experience will deviate from best estimate assumptions. This calls for the ongoing monitoring of longevity experience. Impacts will also vary widely from one country to the next, depending on factors such as the level of development, baseline health, and conditions during lockdown. These differences will need to be considered when assessing the impact of the COVID-19 pandemic on mortality assumptions.

4.3.1. Overall impact of the COVID-19 pandemic on mortality

The immediate impact of the COVID-19 virus itself will be a temporary shock to mortality. The evidence shows that across ages and genders, the shock to mortality seems to have been broadly parallel to the baseline curve. That is, the pattern of mortality across ages and genders was similar to a normal year, albeit at a higher level. Once the pandemic subsides, mortality rates should return to their baseline levels. This was the case following the Spanish Flu pandemic of 1918-1919. Figure 4.9 shows that life expectancy returned to its previous trend within three to four years, even exceeding the level observed prior to the pandemic.

Figure 4.9. Life expectancy at birth around the Spanish Flu of 1918-19 for selected countries

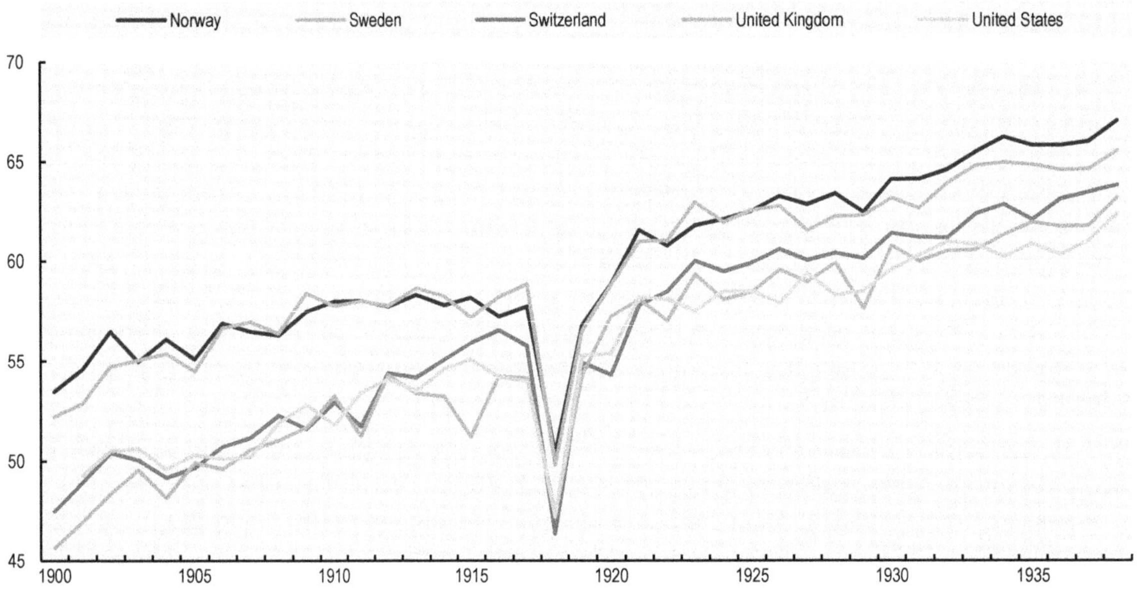

Source: Adapted from Roser, Ortiz-Ospina and Ritchie (2019[133]), *Life Expectancy*, https://ourworldindata.org/life-expectancy.

Indeed, the frailest of the population are more likely to have died during the COVID-19 pandemic, and we can expect the survivors to be relatively stronger on average, resulting in lower mortality in the years following the peak of the outbreak. Many of the deaths due to COVID-19 may have been accelerated deaths that would have occurred anyway over the next several years. This is supported by evidence that the specific groups experiencing higher mortality were also the ones having a higher mortality risk generally, in particular those with higher rates of comorbidities. This selection effect will likely be short-lived, however, with mortality levels returning to their previous trajectory within a few years, as they did following the Spanish Flu pandemic of 1918-1919 (Figure 4.9).

Nevertheless, the impact of COVID-19 on mortality will likely still be felt over the coming year or two, as new variants emerge that may be more contagious or able to evade vaccines. Indeed, elevated excess mortality continues, at least in cycles, in many jurisdictions. Nevertheless, while variants of the virus continue to infect even vaccinated individuals, increased immunity has led to lower rates of health complications and deaths.

Viruses causing past pandemics have eventually become endemic, as more people become exposed to the virus and it mutates and becomes less fatal, even if it manages to at least partially evade immunity (Callaway, 2021[134]) (Branswell, 2021[135]). If COVID-19 follows this trend as expected, the virus should eventually become endemic and continue to circulate among the population, likely causing milder symptoms like a seasonal cold, as with the other four coronavirus strains that currently circulate endemically among the human population. Nevertheless, while it is sure that the pandemic will eventually dissipate and large excess mortality levels will subside, uncertainty remains around the virulence of future variants and how long this process will take.

The impact of reduced healthcare access is also likely to be largely temporary. Disruptions to service should lessen as increased COVID-19 vaccination rates improve hospital capacity to care for other patients. Reductions in infections should also help assuage people's fear to seek needed medical attention, and healthcare provision will likely return to its normal levels. Nevertheless, delayed diagnosis of serious illness, such as cancer, may increase mortality in the short term to the extent that early preventative measures were not taken. In addition, high levels of stress and burnout among medical staff could present a challenge to maintaining the same levels of healthcare, as many individuals could exit the profession.

Lockdown measures have also been lifted, though some of the impacts that these will have on mortality may still emerge over the next year or two. Homicides and traffic accidents are likely to quickly return to their previous levels with the lifting of lockdown restrictions, though a spike in femicides may yet occur as women may be more likely to try to leave abusive relationships. Lingering mental health issues from the lockdown situation may endure in the short term, potentially increasing suicide rates, particularly if the widespread awareness and support offered during lockdown is eased during the post-lockdown period. While lockdown exacerbated the existing trends in drug overdoses in some cases, the change in trends generally seemed to be linked directly to lockdown. Nevertheless, the increasing trend in overdoses can certainly be expected to continue barring major changes in the facility to access drugs, and may even accelerate. The reduction in herd immunity from seasonal influenza will likely mean that the flu epidemics of the coming years will be more severe, and potentially have a larger impact on mortality than recent epidemics. Thus, any short-term gains from reduced influenza deaths are likely to be neutralised, or even net out to be negative.

Enduring impacts of the economic shock may have a more lasting impact on mortality in the medium term, particularly in developing countries. Disadvantaged households are likely to be more negatively impacted, and elderly mortality could increase even in advanced economies if unemployment remains high and there are cuts to public spending on healthcare. Any positive effects on mortality of the working age population from higher unemployment, such as reduced traffic accidents, are likely to be outweighed by the negative trends in substance abuse and potentially increased suicides.

Longer-term health impacts of the COVID-19 virus cannot be known in advance, and will only emerge in the decades to come. Ultimately, a cohort effect may emerge in the data for survivors or for those born during the COVID-19 pandemic. Disadvantaged populations that experienced higher infection rates could be more impacted. These trends will need to be monitored over time.

Political shifts will also need to be monitored, though there does not seem to be an immediate threat to mortality from changing political actions and public preferences for established democracies. There may nevertheless be a negative shift in the long-term trend in life expectancy for newer or less stable democracies if the current trends with respect to the support for democracy continue.

4.3.2. The impact of COVID-19 on mortality assumptions going forward

Overall, COVID-19 is likely to have a negligible impact on the mortality assumptions used in the context of asset backed pension arrangements. In most cases, mortality and life expectancy are likely to return to their previous trends within a year or two, with COVID-19 representing a temporary – albeit large – negative shock.

In assessing the impact of the COVID-19 pandemic on mortality assumptions, it is important to consider the purpose of these assumptions within the context of the asset-backed pension system. Here, best estimate mortality assumptions are needed to estimate how long pensioners can expect to receive their retirement income with the goal to ensure that there will be sufficient assets to finance that income over their remaining lifetime. As such, it is important that these assumptions reflect the best estimate life expectancy of current and future pensioners who have survived the pandemic. Nevertheless, significant uncertainty around the potential longer-term effects that COVID-19 will have on longevity remains, and the assessment and management of longevity risk will need to account for this uncertainty.

Historical mortality experience is frequently used as a basis on which to establish mortality assumptions for both current mortality and future mortality improvements. In selecting which historical data to use to calibrate the assumptions, it is necessary to consider whether the mortality experience during the period selected will be reflective of the current and future mortality of the population to which they will apply. When there have been anomalous shocks to mortality or clear changes in historical trends, judgement is needed to determine whether that data should be included in any calibration of mortality assumptions.

Current mortality assumptions

Current mortality assumptions are usually based on recent mortality data of a population that is expected to be representative of the population to whom the assumptions will apply. To reduce random volatility and increase the robustness of the assumptions, a span of several years (e.g. the last three to five years of data) is normally used.

In the context of the COVID-19 pandemic, the mortality experience from the years 2020-2021 should be adjusted or excluded from any calibration of current mortality assumptions, as their inclusion would significantly increase the calculated level of mortality.[8] Given that the main impacts of the virus and indirect effects of the pandemic such as reduced access to health care have likely already been realised, this experience should not be relevant for estimating the mortality of those who survived this period. Nevertheless, somewhat higher excess mortality has also continued into 2022, which could justify an adjustment to this year's assumed level of mortality to be higher than otherwise expected.

Going forward, basing current best estimate mortality assumptions on the average mortality excluding the shock from the pandemic seems reasonable. Additional adjustments could potentially be made based on any available measures or indices indicating changes in overall health or vulnerability for the currently surviving population relative to levels prior to 2020.

Future mortality improvements

The calibration of future mortality improvement assumptions normally relies upon a much longer period of historical experience, as these assumptions intend to capture the long-term trajectory that mortality will follow. As such, the period over which these trends are based should be reflective of the trends expected to influence mortality going forward.

Here again, the mortality experience of the year 2020-2021 is a clear disruption to the long-term trend, and should normally be disregarded for the purpose of calibrating future mortality improvement assumptions. Nevertheless, future expectations regarding how the pandemic will affect mortality trends in the medium to long term can still inform modelling choices, and in particular whether mortality improvements could slow.

While mortality should return to its prior trajectory over the next few years, it will likely be rather volatile in the near term and long-term uncertainty in the trend remains. Mortality rates may initially decrease beyond what their prior trend implied, as the surviving population is likely to be stronger and healthier on average (see Figure 4.10 for an illustration). This decrease could potentially be partially offset, however, by higher mortality from the indirect effects of the pandemic – such as health care interruptions and more severe flu seasons – that should gradually subside.

Figure 4.10. Illustration of the expected impact of COVID-19 on mortality

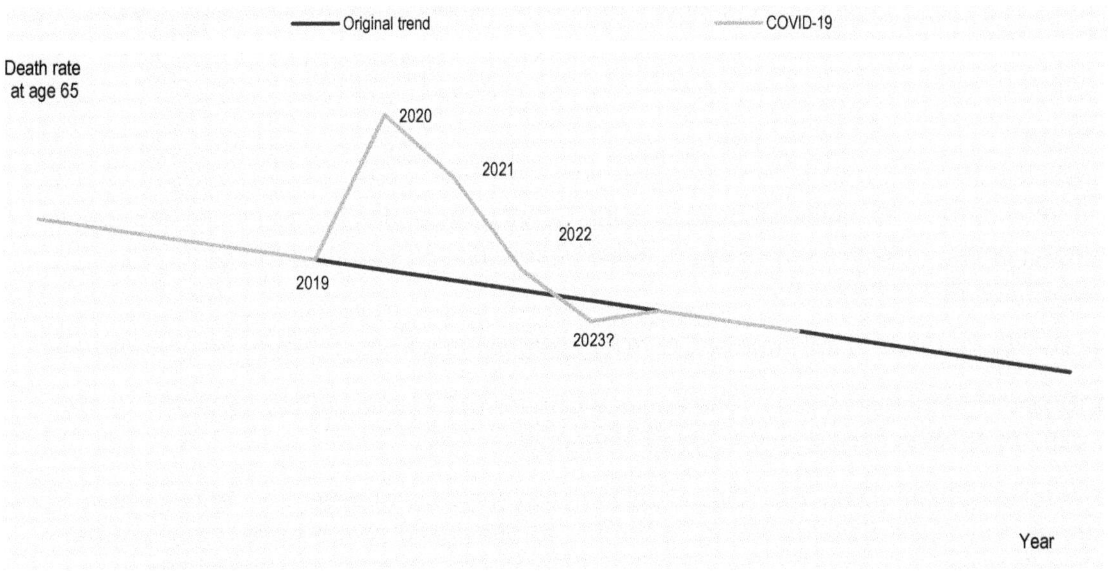

Note: Mortality in the near term may be below trend because of selection effects, while the long-term trend will also be influenced by factors such as the long-term health effects of COVID-19.
Source: Based on discussions and inputs from David Blake and Andrew Cairns.

The economic environment may have an additional impact on mortality over the medium term. In particular, if the higher public debt levels in advanced economies result in cuts to public healthcare spending, this could result in lower improvements to elderly mortality.

Nevertheless, in the longer term, the length of the historical period over which mortality improvement assumptions are calibrated should capture the expected trend in mortality going forward. Short-term volatility will be smoothed out and the effect of economic cycles on mortality captured, meaning that assumptions should be an appropriate best estimate on average.

Longevity risk management and monitoring

The potential long-term effects of the COVID-19 virus on mortality remain highly uncertain and cannot yet be reflected in best estimate mortality assumptions. Assumptions will need to be regularly monitored and updated to adjust to any continued excess mortality in the short term. It will also be important that risk assessments reflect and account for the increased uncertainty in the long term. Stress testing of the assumptions can help to ensure that the potential impact of higher long-term mortality is understood and accounted for in the risk management strategy.

The expected volatility of mortality experience in the near term also highlights the need to be prudent with respect to any gains realised from a reduction in liability value resulting from the higher realised mortality during the COVID-19 pandemic. While reserves will no longer be needed to finance the pensions of those who died during the pandemic, there is a meaningful risk of underestimating the mortality of survivors in the near term, so some of these reserves may be need to be retained to cover the remaining liabilities rather than fully realised as profit. Mortality assumptions will need to be monitored to make sure they continue to be in line with observed experience and future expectations to ensure that reserves remain adequate.

The COVID-19 pandemic will eventually come to an end, and the mortality assumptions used in the context of asset-backed pension arrangements must reflect the best estimate view of what is most likely to happen going forward. At this point in time, the most likely scenario seems to be that mortality levels will return to their previous trajectory. While there remains significant uncertainty as to the long-term impact that the pandemic will have on mortality, how to deal with this uncertainty has not changed. Indeed, this is the nature of managing longevity risk.

References

Aberto, J. et al. (2021), "Quantifying impacts of the COVID-19 pandemic through life-expectancy losses: a population-level study of 29 countries", *international Journal of Epidemiology*, https://doi.org/10.1093/ije/dyab207. [3]

Abrams, D. (2021), *Crime in the Time of COVID*, https://econofact.org/crime-in-the-time-of-covid. [77]

Ahmad, F. and R. Anderson (2021), "The Leading Causes of Death in the US for 2020", *JAMA*, Vol. 325/18, p. 1829, https://doi.org/10.1001/jama.2021.5469. [57]

Ahmed, H. et al. (2020), "Long-term clinical outcomes in survivors of severe acute respiratory syndrome and Middle East respiratory syndrome coronavirus outbreaks after hospitalisation or ICU admission: A systematic review and meta-analysis", *Journal of Rehabilitation Medicine*, p. 0, https://doi.org/10.2340/16501977-2694. [112]

Ahrenfeldt, L. et al. (2020), *Sex and age differences in COVID-19 mortality in Europe *, Research Square Platform LLC, https://doi.org/10.21203/rs.3.rs-61444/v1. [12]

Al-Aly, Z., Y. Xie and B. Bowe (2021), "High-dimensional characterization of post-acute sequelae of COVID-19", *Nature*, Vol. 594/7862, pp. 259-264, https://doi.org/10.1038/s41586-021-03553-9. [105]

Amat, F. et al. (2020), *Pandemics meet democracy. Experimental evidence from the COVID-19 crisis in Spain*, Center for Open Science, https://doi.org/10.31235/osf.io/dkusw. [131]

Appa, A. et al. (2021), "Drug Overdose Deaths Before and After Shelter-in-Place Orders During the COVID-19 Pandemic in San Francisco", *JAMA Network Open*, Vol. 4/5, p. e2110452, https://doi.org/10.1001/jamanetworkopen.2021.10452. [53]

Atalay, K. et al. (2021), "Lives saved during economic downturns: Evidence from Australia", *Epub*, Vol. 30/10, pp. 2452-2467, https://doi.org/10.1002/hec.4394. [98]

Baird, S., J. Friedman and N. Schady (2011), "Aggregate Income Shocks and Infant Mortality in the Developing World", *Review of Economics and Statistics*, Vol. 93/3, pp. 847-56, http://hdl.handle.net/10986/4916. [100]

Balmori de la Miyar, J., L. Hoehn-Velasco and A. Silverio-Murillo (2021), "The U-shaped crime recovery during COVID-19: evidence from national crime rates in Mexico", *Crime Science*, Vol. 10/1, https://doi.org/10.1186/s40163-021-00147-8. [76]

Benmarhnia, T. et al. (2014), "Impact of the economic crisis on the health of older persons in Spain: research clues based on an analysis of mortality. SESPAS report 2014", *Gaceta Sanitaria*, Vol. 28, pp. 137-141, https://doi.org/10.1016/j.gaceta.2014.02.016. [102]

Biswas, M. et al. (2020), "Association of Sex, Age, and Comorbidities with Mortality in COVID-19 Patients: A Systematic Review and Meta-Analysis", *Intervirology*, Vol. 64/1, pp. 36-47, https://doi.org/10.1159/000512592. [13]

Bodilsen, J. et al. (2021), "Hospital admission and mortality rates for non-covid diseases in Denmark during covid-19 pandemic: nationwide population based cohort study", *BMJ*, p. n1135, https://doi.org/10.1136/bmj.n1135. [39]

Bollyky, T. et al. (2019), "The relationships between democratic experience, adult health, and cause-specific mortality in 170 countries between 1980 and 2016: an observational analysis", *The Lancet*, Vol. 393/10181, pp. 1628-1640, https://doi.org/10.1016/s0140-6736(19)30235-1. [125]

Börsch-Supan, A. (2021), *The Multifaceted Effects of the Pandemic and the Lockdown Measures on EU Citizens*, https://www.cepar.edu.au/resources-videos/videos/multifaceted-effects-pandemic-and-lockdown-measures-eu-citizens. [41]

Botly, L. et al. (2020), "COVID-19 Pandemic: Global Impact and Potential Implications for Cardiovascular Disease in Canada", *CJC Open*, Vol. 2/4, pp. 265-272, https://doi.org/10.1016/j.cjco.2020.06.003. [19]

Bowe, B. et al. (2021), "Kidney Outcomes in Long COVID", *Journal of the American Society of Nephrology*, p. ASN.2021060734, https://doi.org/10.1681/asn.2021060734. [106]

Branswell, H. (2021), *How the Covid pandemic ends: Scientists look to the past to see the future*, https://www.statnews.com/2021/05/19/how-the-covid-pandemic-ends-scientists-look-to-the-past-to-see-the-future/. [135]

Bray, M. et al. (2021), "Racial Differences in Statewide Suicide Mortality Trends in Maryland During the Coronavirus Disease 2019 (COVID-19) Pandemic", *JAMA Psychiatry*, Vol. 78/4, p. 444, https://doi.org/10.1001/jamapsychiatry.2020.3938. [62]

Breuer, C. (2014), "Unemployment and Suicide Mortality: Evidence from Regional Panel Data in Europe", *Health Economics*, Vol. 24/8, pp. 936-950, https://doi.org/10.1002/hec.3073. [95]

Brüning, M. and J. Thuilliez (2019), "Mortality and Macroeconomic Conditions: What Can We Learn From France?", *Demography*, Vol. 56/5, pp. 1747-1764, https://doi.org/10.1007/s13524-019-00811-4. [90]

Calderon-Anyosa, R. and J. Kaufman (2021), "Impact of COVID-19 lockdown policy on homicide, suicide, and motor vehicle deaths in Peru", *Preventive Medicine*, Vol. 143, p. 106331, https://doi.org/10.1016/j.ypmed.2020.106331. [60]

Callaway, E. (2021), *Beyond Omicron: what's next for COVID's viral evolution*, https://www.nature.com/articles/d41586-021-03619-8. [134]

Casana-Jara, K. (2020), "Características de la muerte de mujeres por violencia según las necropsias realizadas en la morgue del Callao", *Revista Peruana de Medicina Experimental y Salud Pública*, Vol. 37/2, pp. 297-301, https://doi.org/10.17843/rpmesp.2020.372.5111. [74]

Center for Disaease Control and Prevention (2021), *Risk for COVID-19 Infection, Hospitalization, and Death By Race/Ethnicity*, https://www.cdc.gov/coronavirus/2019-ncov/covid-data/investigations-discovery/hospitalization-death-by-race-ethnicity.html (accessed on September 2021). [30]

Center for Disease Control and Prevention (2021), *Reduced Access to Care - RANDS during COVID-19*, https://www.cdc.gov/nchs/covid19/rands/reduced-access-to-care.htm. [35]

Chang, S. et al. (2009), "Was the economic crisis 1997–1998 responsible for rising suicide rates in East/Southeast Asia? A time–trend analysis for Japan, Hong Kong, South Korea, Taiwan, Singapore and Thailand", *Social Science & Medicine*, Vol. 68/7, pp. 1322-1331, https://doi.org/10.1016/j.socscimed.2009.01.010. [93]

Charrier, L. (2020), *Au Pérou, pourquoi les femmes disparaissent ?*. [72]

Chi-wai, M. et al. (2021), *HKUMed finds Omicron SARS-CoV-2 can infect faster and better than Delta in human bronchus but with less severe infection in lung*, http://www.med.hku.hk/en/news/press/20211215-omicron-sars-cov-2-infection. [141]

Cho, S., S. Yoon and H. Lee (2021), "Impact of comorbidity burden on mortality in patients with COVID-19 using the Korean health insurance database", *Scientific Reports*, Vol. 11/1, https://doi.org/10.1038/s41598-021-85813-2. [15]

Continuous Mortality Investigation (2021), *England & Wales mortality monitor – COVID-19 update – week 44 of 2021*, https://www.actuaries.org.uk/system/files/field/document/Mortality%20pandemic%20monitor%20Week%2044%202021%20v01%202021-11-16.pdf. [5]

Currie, J. et al. (2021), "Trends in Drug Overdose Mortality in Ohio During the First 7 Months of the COVID-19 Pandemic", *JAMA Network Open*, Vol. 4/4, p. e217112, https://doi.org/10.1001/jamanetworkopen.2021.7112. [54]

Cutler, D. et al. (2000), *Financial Crisis, Health Outcomes and Aging: Mexico in the 1980s and 1990s*, National Bureau of Economic Research, Cambridge, MA, https://doi.org/10.3386/w7746. [101]

Czeisler, M. et al. (2020), "Delay or Avoidance of Medical Care Because of COVID-19–Related Concerns — United States, June 2020", *MMWR. Morbidity and Mortality Weekly Report*, Vol. 69/35, https://doi.org/10.15585/mmwr.mm6935e3. [42]

Dehejia, R. and A. Lleras-Muney (2004), "Booms, Busts, and Babies' Health", *The Quarterly Journal of Economics*, Vol. 119/3, pp. 1091-1130, https://doi.org/10.1162/0033553041502216. [99]

Dehingia, N. and A. Raj (2021), "Sex differences in COVID-19 case fatality: do we know enough?", *The Lancet Global Health*, Vol. 9/1, pp. e14-e15, https://doi.org/10.1016/s2214-109x(20)30464-2. [14]

Demombynes, G. (2020), *COVID-19 Age-Mortality Curves Are Flatter in Developing Countries*, World Bank, https://openknowledge.worldbank.org/handle/10986/34028 License: CC BY 3.0 IGO. [9]

Digard, P. (ed.) (2013), "Age-Specific Mortality During the 1918 Influenza Pandemic: Unravelling the Mystery of High Young Adult Mortality", *PLoS ONE*, Vol. 8/8, p. e69586, https://doi.org/10.1371/journal.pone.0069586. [116]

Doerr, S. and B. Hofmann (2020), *Recessions and mortality: a global perspective*, https://www.bis.org/publ/work910.pdf. [88]

Domingo, F. et al. (2021), *Prevalence of long-term effects in individuals diagnosed with COVID-19: a living systematic review*, Cold Spring Harbor Laboratory, https://doi.org/10.1101/2021.06.03.21258317. [103]

Doshi, P. (2020), "Covid-19: Do many people have pre-existing immunity?", *BMJ*, p. m3563, https://doi.org/10.1136/bmj.m3563. [122]

Elston, J. et al. (2017), "The health impact of the 2014–15 Ebola outbreak", *Public Health*, Vol. 143, pp. 60-70, https://doi.org/10.1016/j.puhe.2016.10.020. [45]

Ettensperger, F. (2021), "The Relationship Between Poverty and COVID-19 Infection and Case-Fatality Rates in Germany during the First Wave of the Pandemic", *Statistics, Politics and Policy*, Vol. 0/0, https://doi.org/10.1515/spp-2021-0002. [24]

European Commission (2021), *Road safety: 4 000 fewer people lost their lives on EU roads in 2020 as death rate falls to all time low*, https://ec.europa.eu/transport/modes/road/news/2021-04-20-road-safety_en. [79]

Ferguson, N. et al. (2021), *Report 50 - Hospitalisation risk for Omicron cases in England*, https://www.imperial.ac.uk/mrc-global-infectious-disease-analysis/covid-19/report-50-severity-omicron/. [142]

Filippidis, F. et al. (2017), "Medium-term impact of the economic crisis on mortality, health-related behaviours and access to healthcare in Greece", *Scientific Reports*, Vol. 7/1, https://doi.org/10.1038/srep46423. [97]

Franco, Á., C. Álvarez-Dardet and M. Ruiz (2004), "Effect of democracy on health: ecological study", *BMJ*, Vol. 329/7480, pp. 1421-1423, https://doi.org/10.1136/bmj.329.7480.1421. [124]

García-Guerrero, V. and H. Beltrán-Sánchez (2021), "Heterogeneity in Excess Mortality and Its Impact on Loss of Life Expectancy due to COVID-19: Evidence from Mexico", *Canadian Studies in Population*, Vol. 48/2-3, pp. 165-200, https://doi.org/10.1007/s42650-021-00051-1. [143]

Geers, D. et al. (2021), "SARS-CoV-2 variants of concern partially escape humoral but not T-cell responses in COVID-19 convalescent donors and vaccinees", *Science Immunology*, Vol. 6/59, p. eabj1750, https://doi.org/10.1126/sciimmunol.abj1750. [121]

Gerdtham, U. and M. Johannesson (2003), "A note on the effect of unemployment on mortality", *Journal of Health Economics*, Vol. 22/3, pp. 505-518, https://doi.org/10.1016/s0167-6296(03)00004-3. [94]

Giattino, C. et al. (2022), *Excess mortality during the Coronavirus pandemic (COVID-19)*, https://ourworldindata.org/excess-mortality-covid. [2]

Giustino, G. et al. (2020), "Coronavirus and Cardiovascular Disease, Myocardial Injury, and Arrhythmia", *Journal of the American College of Cardiology*, Vol. 76/17, pp. 2011-2023, https://doi.org/10.1016/j.jacc.2020.08.059. [108]

Gobierno de México (2021), *Boletin estadistico sobre el excesso de mortalidad por todas las causas durante la emergencia por COVID-19*. [6]

Gomes, T. et al. (2021), *Changing Circumstances Surrounding Opiod-Related Deaths in Ontario during the COVID-19 Pandemic*, https://odprn.ca/wp-content/uploads/2021/05/Changing-Circumstances-Surrounding-Opioid-Related-Deaths.pdf. [51]

Guerra Lund, R., S. Manica and G. Mânica (2020), "COLLATERAL ISSUES IN TIMES OF COVID-19: CHILD ABUSE, DOMESTIC VIOLENCE AND FEMICIDE", *Revista Brasileira de Odontologia Legal*, Vol. 7/2, https://doi.org/10.21117/rbol-v7n22020-318. [70]

Helgertz, J. and T. Bengtsson (2019), "The Long-Lasting Influenza: The Impact of Fetal Stress During the 1918 Influenza Pandemic on Socioeconomic Attainment and Health in Sweden, 1968–2012", *Demography*, Vol. 56/4, pp. 1389-1425, https://doi.org/10.1007/s13524-019-00799-x. [114]

Hirunpattarasilp, C. et al. (2021), *SARS-CoV-2 binding to ACE2 triggers pericyte-mediated angiotensin-evoked cerebral capillary constriction*, Cold Spring Harbor Laboratory, https://doi.org/10.1101/2021.04.01.438122. [110]

Hoehn-Velasco, L., A. Silverio-Murillo and J. de la Miyar (2021), "The great crime recovery: Crimes against women during, and after, the COVID-19 lockdown in Mexico", *Economics & Human Biology*, Vol. 41, p. 100991, https://doi.org/10.1016/j.ehb.2021.100991. [66]

Hyde, S. (2020), "Democracy's backsliding in the international environment", *Science*, Vol. 369/6508, pp. 1192-1196, https://doi.org/10.1126/science.abb2434. [128]

Ioannidis, J., C. Axfors and D. Contopoulos-Ioannidis (2020), "Population-level COVID-19 mortality risk for non-elderly individuals overall and for non-elderly individuals without underlying diseases in pandemic epicenters", *Environmental Research*, Vol. 188, p. 109890, https://doi.org/10.1016/j.envres.2020.109890. [18]

ITF (2020), *Road Safety Annual Report 2020*. [81]

John, A. et al. (2020), "Trends in suicide during the covid-19 pandemic", *BMJ*, p. m4352, https://doi.org/10.1136/bmj.m4352. [58]

Kim, H. et al. (2003), "Changes in mortality after the recent economic crisis in South Korea", *Annals of epidemiology*, Vol. 14/6, pp. 442-6, https://doi.org/10.1016/j.annepidem.2003.09.018. [92]

Kraindler, J., C. Barclay and C. Tallack (2020), *Understanding changes to mortality during the pandemic*, https://www.health.org.uk/news-and-comment/charts-and-infographics/understanding-changes-to-all-mortality-during-the-pandemic. [40]

Laliotis, I., J. Ioannidis and C. Stavropoulou (2016), "Total and cause-specific mortality before and after the onset of the Greek economic crisis: an interrupted time-series analysis", *The Lancet*, Vol. 1/2, pp. e56-e65, https://doi.org/10.1016/S2468-2667(16)30018-4. [91]

Laou, S. (2021), *Hausse des féminicides : « C'est du jamais vu », s'alarment des organismes*, https://ici.radio-canada.ca/nouvelle/1778820/meurtres-femmes-violence-conjugale-canada-augmentation. [71]

Le Monde (2021), "Les féminicides en France : 90 femmes tuées en 2020, contre 146 en 2019, selon le ministère de la justice", https://www.lemonde.fr/societe/article/2021/02/02/90-feminicides-ont-ete-commis-en-2020-contre-146-en-2019-annonce-le-ministere-de-la-justice_6068512_3224.html. [68]

Leavitt, R. (2021), *2020 Excess Deaths in the U.S. General Population by Age and Sex Updated May 2021*, https://www.soa.org/globalassets/assets/files/resources/research-report/2021/05-excess-deaths-gen-population-update.pdf. [4]

Lewnard, J. et al. (2022), *Clinical outcomes among patients infected with Omicron (B.1.1.529) SARS-CoV-2 variant in southern California*, Cold Spring Harbor Laboratory, https://doi.org/10.1101/2022.01.11.22269045. [139]

Lone, N. et al. (2021), "Influence of socioeconomic deprivation on interventions and outcomes for patients admitted with COVID-19 to critical care units in Scotland: A national cohort study", *The Lancet Regional Health - Europe*, Vol. 1, p. 100005, https://doi.org/10.1016/j.lanepe.2020.100005. [22]

Manzoli, L. (ed.) (2021), "Non-COVID-19 patients in times of pandemic: Emergency department visits, hospitalizations and cause-specific mortality in Northern Italy", *PLOS ONE*, Vol. 16/3, p. e0248995, https://doi.org/10.1371/journal.pone.0248995. [38]

Marshall, M. (2020), "The lasting misery of coronavirus long-haulers", *Nature*, Vol. 585/7825, pp. 339-341, https://doi.org/10.1038/d41586-020-02598-6. [107]

Maslo, C. et al. (2021), "Characteristics and Outcomes of Hospitalized Patients in South Africa During the COVID-19 Omicron Wave Compared With Previous Waves", *JAMA*, https://doi.org/10.1001/jama.2021.24868. [138]

Mayo Clinic (2021), *COVID-19 (coronavirus): Long-term effects*, https://www.mayoclinic.org/diseases-conditions/coronavirus/in-depth/coronavirus-long-term-effects/art-20490351 (accessed on September 2021). [111]

McLaren, J. (2020), *Racial Disparity in COVID-19 Deaths: Seeking Economic Roots with Census data.*, National Bureau of Economic Research, Cambridge, MA, https://doi.org/10.3386/w27407. [26]

Mena, G. et al. (2021), "Socioeconomic status determines COVID-19 incidence and related mortality in Santiago, Chile", *Science*, Vol. 372/6545, p. eabg5298, https://doi.org/10.1126/science.abg5298. [23]

Muñoz-Price, L. et al. (2020), "Racial Disparities in Incidence and Outcomes Among Patients With COVID-19", *JAMA Network Open*, Vol. 3/9, p. e2021892, https://doi.org/10.1001/jamanetworkopen.2020.21892. [25]

Myrskylä, M., N. Mehta and V. Chang (2013), "Early Life Exposure to the 1918 Influenza Pandemic and Old-Age Mortality by Cause of Death", *American Journal of Public Health*, Vol. 103/7, pp. e83-e90, https://doi.org/10.2105/ajph.2012.301060. [115]

NHTSA (2021), *Early Estimate of Motor Vehicle Traffic Fatalities in 2020*, https://crashstats.nhtsa.dot.gov/Api/Public/ViewPublication/813115. [83]

Nilsson, L., C. Andersson and R. Sjödahl (2021), "COVID-19 as the sole cause of death is uncommon in frail home healthcare individuals: a population-based study", *BMC Geriatrics*, Vol. 21/1, https://doi.org/10.1186/s12877-021-02176-z. [17]

Nivette, A. et al. (2021), "A global analysis of the impact of COVID-19 stay-at-home restrictions on crime", *Nature Human Behaviour*, Vol. 5/7, pp. 868-877, https://doi.org/10.1038/s41562-021-01139-z. [75]

Noymer, A. and M. Garenne (2000), "The 1918 Influenza Epidemic's Effects on Sex Differentials in Mortality in the United States", *Population and Development Review*, Vol. 26/3, pp. 565-581, https://doi.org/10.1111/j.1728-4457.2000.00565.x. [20]

Odd, D. et al. (2021), *Child Suicide Rates During the COVID-19 pandemic in England*, Cold Spring Harbor Laboratory, https://doi.org/10.1101/2021.07.13.21260366. [61]

Office for National Statistics (2021), *Technical article: Updated estimates of the prevalence of post-acute symptoms among people with coronavirus (COVID-19) in the UK: 26 April 2020 to 1 August 2021*, https://www.ons.gov.uk/peoplepopulationandcommunity/healthandsocialcare/conditionsanddiseases/articles/technicalarticleupdatedestimatesoftheprevalenceofpostacutesymptomsamongpeoplewithcoronaviruscovid19intheuk/26april2020to1august2021. [104]

Office for National Statistics (2021), *Updating ethnic contrasts in deaths involving the coronavirus (COVID-19), England: 24 January 2020 to 31 March 2021*, https://www.ons.gov.uk/peoplepopulationandcommunity/birthsdeathsandmarriages/deaths/articles/updatingethniccontrastsindeathsinvolvingthecoronaviruscovid19englandandwales/24january2020to31march2021. [32]

Office for National Statistics (2020), *Direct and Indirect Impacts of COVID-19 on Excess Deaths and Morbidity*, https://assets.publishing.service.gov.uk/government/uploads/system/uploads/attachment_data/file/907616/s0650-direct-indirect-impacts-covid-19-excess-deaths-morbidity-sage-48.pdf. [37]

Office of National Statistics (2021), *Coronavirus and depression in adults, Great Britain: January to March 2021*, https://www.ons.gov.uk/peoplepopulationandcommunity/wellbeing/articles/coronavirusanddepressioninadultsgreatbritain/januarytomarch2021. [47]

Oguzoglu, U. (2020), *COVID-19 Lockdowns and Decline in Traffic Related Deaths and Injuries*. [78]

Oh, T., J. Choi and I. Song (2021), “Socioeconomic disparity and the risk of contracting COVID-19 in South Korea: an NHIS-COVID-19 database cohort study”, *BMC Public Health*, Vol. 21/1, https://doi.org/10.1186/s12889-021-10207-y. [29]

Olsen, S. et al. (2020), *Decreased Influenza Activity During the COVID-19 Pandemic — United States, Australia, Chile, and South Africa, 2020*, https://doi.org/10.15585/mmwr.mm6937a6. [86]

OMA-UMAR (2020), *Femicide in Portugal during the COVID-19 pandemic*, http://www.umarfeminismos.org/images/stories/oma/Femicide_in_Portugal_during_the_COVID-19_pandemic.pdf. [69]

Ortiz-Ospina, E. (2019), *Does democracy lead to better health?*, https://ourworldindata.org/democracy-health. [123]

OSF Healthcare (2021), *Drug overdose deaths during COVID: Worse than expected*, https://newsroom.osfhealthcare.org/covid-19-fallout-a-spike-in-drug-deaths/. [49]

Paget, J. et al. (2019), “Global mortality associated with seasonal influenza epidemics: New burden estimates and predictors from the GLaMOR Project”, *Journal of Global Health*, Vol. 9/2, https://doi.org/10.7189/jogh.09.020421. [84]

Peckham, H. et al. (2020), “Male sex identified by global COVID-19 meta-analysis as a risk factor for death and ITU admission”, *Nature Communications*, Vol. 11/1, https://doi.org/10.1038/s41467-020-19741-6. [11]

Pirkis, J. et al. (2021), “Suicide trends in the early months of the COVID-19 pandemic: an interrupted time-series analysis of preliminary data from 21 countries”, *The Lancet Psychiatry*, Vol. 8/7, pp. 579-588, https://doi.org/10.1016/s2215-0366(21)00091-2. [56]

Price-Haywood, E. et al. (2020), "Hospitalization and Mortality among Black Patients and White Patients with Covid-19", *New England Journal of Medicine*, Vol. 382/26, pp. 2534-2543, https://doi.org/10.1056/nejmsa2011686. [33]

Puntmann, V. et al. (2020), "Outcomes of Cardiovascular Magnetic Resonance Imaging in Patients Recently Recovered From Coronavirus Disease 2019 (COVID-19)", *JAMA Cardiology*, Vol. 5/11, p. 1265, https://doi.org/10.1001/jamacardio.2020.3557. [109]

Rapeli, L. and I. Saikkonen (2020), "How Will the COVID-19 Pandemic Affect Democracy?", *Democratic Theory*, Vol. 7/2, pp. 25-32, https://doi.org/10.3167/dt.2020.070204. [132]

Redd, A. et al. (2021), "CD8+ T-Cell Responses in COVID-19 Convalescent Individuals Target Conserved Epitopes From Multiple Prominent SARS-CoV-2 Circulating Variants", *Open Forum Infectious Diseases*, Vol. 8/7, https://doi.org/10.1093/ofid/ofab143. [119]

Repucci, S. and A. Slipowitz (2021), *Freedom in the World 2021: Democracy under Siege*, https://freedomhouse.org/report/freedom-world/2021/democracy-under-siege. [127]

Repucci, S. and A. Slipowitz (2020), *Democracy under Lockdown*, https://freedomhouse.org/report/special-report/2020/democracy-under-lockdown. [130]

Rhum, C. (2000), "Are Recessions Good for Your Health?", *The Quarterly Journal of Economics*, Vol. 115/2, pp. 617-650, http://www.jstor.org/stable/2587005. [89]

Roberton, T. et al. (2020), "Early estimates of the indirect effects of the COVID-19 pandemic on maternal and child mortality in low-income and middle-income countries: a modelling study", *The Lancet Global Health*, Vol. 8/7, pp. e901-e908, https://doi.org/10.1016/s2214-109x(20)30229-1. [46]

Roser, M., E. Ortiz-Ospina and H. Ritchie (2019), *Life Expectancy*, https://ourworldindata.org/life-expectancy. [133]

Rose, T. et al. (2020), *Inequalities in COVID19 mortality related to ethnicity and socioeconomic deprivation*, Cold Spring Harbor Laboratory, https://doi.org/10.1101/2020.04.25.20079491. [21]

Ruhm, C. (2015), "Recessions, healthy no more?", *Journal of Health Economics*, Vol. 42, pp. 17-28, https://doi.org/10.1016/j.jhealeco.2015.03.004. [96]

Sanz-Muñoz, I. et al. (2021), "Social Distancing, Lockdown and the Wide Use of Mask; A Magic Solution or a Double-Edged Sword for Respiratory Viruses Epidemiology?", *Vaccines*, Vol. 9/6, p. 595, https://doi.org/10.3390/vaccines9060595. [87]

Sasson, I. (2021), "Age and COVID-19 mortality: A comparison of Gompertz doubling time across countries and causes of death", *Demographic Research*, Vol. 44, pp. 379-396, https://doi.org/10.4054/demres.2021.44.16. [8]

Sheikh, A. et al. (2021), *Severity of Omicron variant of concern and vaccine effectiveness against symptomatic disease: national cohort with nested test negative design study in Scotland*, https://www.research.ed.ac.uk/en/publications/severity-of-omicron-variant-of-concern-and-vaccine-effectiveness-. [140]

Shiloh Vidon, T. (2021), *France announces sharp drop in femicides, but NGOs say it's too early to rejoice*, https://www.france24.com/en/europe/20210203-france-announces-sharp-drop-in-femicides-but-ngos-say-it-s-too-early-to-rejoice. [73]

Statistica (2021), *Argentina: femicide victims 2015-2020*, https://www.statista.com/statistics/1102274/number-femicide-victims-argentina/. [136]

Statistica (2021), *Number of femicides registered during the coronavirus (COVID-19) lockdown in Colombia from March to August 2020, by month*. [67]

Statistics Canada (2021), *Provisional death counts and excess mortality, January 2020 to April 2021*, https://www150.statcan.gc.ca/n1/daily-quotidien/210712/dq210712b-eng.htm. [52]

Statistics Canada (2021), *Provisional death counts and excess mortality, January 2020 to February 2021*, https://www150.statcan.gc.ca/n1/daily-quotidien/210514/dq210514c-eng.htm. [16]

Suthar, A. (ed.) (2021), "COVID-19 and excess mortality in the United States: A county-level analysis", *PLOS Medicine*, Vol. 18/5, p. e1003571, https://doi.org/10.1371/journal.pmed.1003571. [7]

Tanaka, T. and S. Okamoto (2021), "Increase in suicide following an initial decline during the COVID-19 pandemic in Japan", *Nature Human Behaviour*, Vol. 5/2, pp. 229-238, https://doi.org/10.1038/s41562-020-01042-z. [59]

Tan, C. et al. (2021), "Pan-Sarbecovirus Neutralizing Antibodies in BNT162b2-Immunized SARS-CoV-1 Survivors", *New England Journal of Medicine*, https://doi.org/10.1056/nejmoa2108453. [118]

Tarke, A. et al. (2021), "Impact of SARS-CoV-2 variants on the total CD4+ and CD8+ T cell reactivity in infected or vaccinated individuals", *Cell Reports Medicine*, Vol. 2/7, p. 100355, https://doi.org/10.1016/j.xcrm.2021.100355. [120]

Tauchi, K. (2021), *Traffic deaths hit lowest level ever in 2020 as people stayed at home*. [80]

The Canadian Press (2021), *Ontario Provincial Police say traffic collisions down, but fatalities up in 2020*. [82]

The Economist (2022), *The pandemic's true death toll*, The Economist Group Limited, https://econ.st/3yE7flu. [1]

The Economist (2021), "Last year, more people in San Francisco died of overdoses than of covid-19", *The Economist*, https://www.economist.com/united-states/2021/05/15/last-year-more-people-in-san-francisco-died-of-overdoses-than-of-covid-19. [50]

the European Influenza Surveillance Network (2021), "Very little influenza in the WHO European Region during the 2020/21 season, weeks 40 2020 to 8 2021", *Eurosurveillance*, Vol. 26/11, https://doi.org/10.2807/1560-7917.es.2021.26.11.2100221. [85]

The Sex, Gender, and COVID-19 Project (2021), *The COVID-19 Sex-Disaggregated Data Tracker*, https://globalhealth5050.org/the-sex-gender-and-covid-19-project/the-data-tracker/ (accessed on 2021). [10]

U. S. Surgeon General (2021), *Protecting Youth Mental Health*, https://www.hhs.gov/sites/default/files/surgeon-general-youth-mental-health-advisory.pdf. [63]

UN Women (2020), *COVID-19 and Ending Violence Against Women and Girls*, https://www.unwomen.org/en/digital-library/publications/2020/04/issue-brief-covid-19-and-ending-violence-against-women-and-girls#view. [64]

UNDP (2020), *Attitudes towards politics in Latin America: A review of regional perception data*. [129]

UNODC (2021), *World Drug Report 2021*, United Nations. [55]

Vahratian, A. et al. (2021), *Symptoms of Anxiety or Depressive Disorder and Use of Mental Health Care Among Adults During the COVID-19 Pandemic — United States, August 2020–February 2021*, https://www.cdc.gov/mmwr/volumes/70/wr/mm7013e2.htm?s_cid=mm7013e2_e&ACSTrackingID=USCDC_921-DM53115&ACSTrackingLabel=MMWR%20Early%20Release%20-%20Vol.%2070%2C%20March%2026%2C%202021&deliveryName=USCDC_921-DM53115. [48]

Vince, R. (2021), "The Intersection of Societal Inequalities and Health Care", *JAMA Oncology*, https://doi.org/10.1001/jamaoncol.2021.2750. [43]

Vogt, T. (2013), "How Many Years of Life Did the Fall of the Berlin Wall Add? A Projection of East German Life Expectancy", *Gerontology*, Vol. 59/3, pp. 276-282, https://doi.org/10.1159/000346355. [126]

Warah, R. (2021), *The invisible pandemic: COVID-19's toll on African women and girls*, ONE Campaign, https://www.one.org/africa/blog/invisible-pandemic-gender-based-violence/. [65]

WHO (2021), *Immunization services begin slow recovery from COVID-19 disruptions, though millions of children remain at risk from deadly diseases*, https://www.who.int/news/item/26-04-2021-immunization-services-begin-slow-recovery-from-covid-19-disruptions-though-millions-of-children-remain-at-risk-from-deadly-diseases-who-unicef-gavi (accessed on September 2021). [44]

Wiemers, E. et al. (2020), *Disparities in Vulnerability to Severe Complications from COVID-19 in the United States*, Cold Spring Harbor Laboratory, https://doi.org/10.1101/2020.05.28.20115899. [27]

Williamson, E. et al. (2020), "Factors associated with COVID-19-related death using OpenSAFELY", *Nature*, Vol. 584/7821, pp. 430-436, https://doi.org/10.1038/s41586-020-2521-4. [28]

Woo, G. (2019), "Age-dependence of the 1918 pandemic", *British Actuarial Journal*, Vol. 24, https://doi.org/10.1017/s1357321719000023. [117]

Woolf, S. et al. (2021), "Excess Deaths From COVID-19 and Other Causes in the US, March 1, 2020, to January 2, 2021", *JAMA*, Vol. 325/17, p. 1786, https://doi.org/10.1001/jama.2021.5199. [36]

Woolf, S., R. Masters and L. Aron (2021), "Effect of the covid-19 pandemic in 2020 on life expectancy across populations in the USA and other high income countries: simulations of provisional mortality data", *BMJ*, p. n1343, https://doi.org/10.1136/bmj.n1343. [31]

World Health Organisation (2020), *The top 10 causes of death*, https://www.who.int/news-room/fact-sheets/detail/the-top-10-causes-of-death. [137]

World Health Organization (2021), *Second round of the national pulse survey on continuity of essential health services during the COVID-19 pandemic*, https://www.who.int/publications/i/item/WHO-2019-nCoV-EHS-continuity-survey-2021.1. [34]

Zhang, P. et al. (2018), "Long-term consequences in lung and bone associated with hospital-acquired severe acute respiratory syndrome: a 15-year follow-up from a prospective cohort study", *The Lancet*, Vol. 392, p. S11, https://doi.org/10.1016/s0140-6736(18)32640-0. [113]

Notes

[1] As of January 14, 2022.

[2] This compares to 8.9 million deaths from ischaemic heart disease in 2019, the world's biggest cause of death (World Health Organisation, 2020[137]).

[3] As of January 14, 2022.

[4] Simple average across countries and weeks.

[5] Calculations based on male mortality with improvements from the AG2020 mortality table, assuming excess mortality of 8.7% in 2020, 10.4% in 2021 (the actual average weekly excess mortality observed each year in the Netherlands), and 5% in 2022.

[6] Based on the 2019 general population life tables from the Human Mortality Database.

[7] Note by Türkiye: The information in this document with reference to "Cyprus" relates to the southern part of the Island. There is no single authority representing both Turkish and Greek Cypriot people on the Island. Türkiye recognizes the Turkish Republic of Northern Cyprus (TRNC). Until a lasting and equitable solution is found within the context of the United Nations, Türkiye shall preserve its position concerning the "Cyprus" issue

[8] The potential magnitude of this difference is shown in Figure 4.2.

5 How assets earmarked for retirement can support economies and benefit members

This chapter discusses the conditions under which assets earmarked for retirement can support the economy during and in the aftermath of the COVID-19 crisis. It considers how pension providers may invest the retirement savings of their members in distressed companies or in long-term recovery projects, while upholding their fiduciary duty to invest in the best interest of members. It also discusses the investment vehicles that pension providers may use to invest and meet financing needs in the economy.

COVID-19 containment measures have weighed heavily on economic activity around the world. To limit the spread of the virus, most countries have enforced lockdowns of varying degrees and lengths during 2020 and 2021, causing business disruptions and large reductions in activity levels. As a result, most economies have experienced unprecedented contractions in real gross domestic product (GDP). In the OECD area, real GDP fell by 10.5% in the second quarter of 2020 and 4.9% for 2020 as a whole. The Q2 2020 fall is the largest drop ever recorded for the OECD area, significantly larger than the 2.3% fall recorded in the first quarter of 2009, at the height of the financial crisis (OECD, 2021[1]).

To bring economies back on their feet, countries will need private capital to support businesses and finance recovery projects. To cushion the blow of the COVID-19 crisis, governments implemented quick, large and innovative support measures, subsidising workers and firms. As a result, government budget deficits are elevated and public debt is set to rise to exceptionally high levels in many countries (OECD, 2021[2]). However, the path to recovery requires more spending to support the transition of capital and workers from impaired sectors and businesses towards expanding ones. Furthermore, investment in infrastructure, such as hospitals, housing, schools, renewable energy and digital networks could create jobs and deliver tangible assets that will fuel long-term economic growth. Moreover, investing in environmental, social and governance (ESG) long-term sustainable projects would also support economies in the long term. Given budget constraints, there is likely to be calls on private institutional investors such as pension funds to play a bigger role in financing the economic recovery.

This chapter discusses the conditions under which assets earmarked for retirement can support the economy during and in the aftermath of the COVID-19 crisis. It considers how pension providers may invest the retirement savings of their members in distressed companies or in long-term recovery projects, while upholding their fiduciary duty to invest in the best interest of members. It also discusses the investment vehicles that pension providers may use to invest and meet financing needs in the economy. These discussions apply to all types of pension providers, i.e. pension funds, as well as insurance companies, banks and investment managers operating in asset-backed pension systems.[1] Although the focus is on the post-COVID-19 recovery, the analysis is also relevant for future crises, and also to sustainable, and ESG investment opportunities.

Pension providers can play a role in supporting the economy. They already have experience in investing in the economy, as they purchase a range of assets to diversify their exposures, and their scale and long-term investment horizon allow them to consider long term, including illiquid, investments. Many pension providers are also seeking out investment opportunities that can deliver higher returns in a low interest rate environment.[2]

However, challenges exist. A paucity of opportunities, regulatory barriers and lack of capability can impede pension providers' involvement in supporting the economy. The current crisis also brings new risks that pension providers need to consider before investing amid pressures to financially support domestic businesses and projects. Strong governance, appropriate investment and risk management strategies, and suitable investment opportunities are essential to ensure that pension providers invest in the best interest of members in a way that supports businesses and stimulates an economic recovery. In addition, pension providers can use various investment vehicles to gain exposure to investments that support the economy, such as COVID-19 bonds, instruments that provide immediate financing to businesses and governments, and instruments that can help finance a recovery. Indeed, there is already significant use of instruments such as these. For example, governments, companies and multinational organisations raised billions of US dollars globally from selling COVID-19 bonds, or debt whose proceeds are broadly earmarked for work linked to the pandemic.[3]

The chapter is structured as follows. Section 5.1 explains why pension providers can play a role in supporting the economy. Section 5.2 describes the obstacles and risks that pension providers face when considering investments in businesses and recovery projects. Section 5.3 then presents solutions to overcome these challenges, by reviewing the elements of the governance and investment frameworks that safeguard people's retirement savings when pension providers consider new investment opportunities. It then describes the steps that policy makers could take to ensure that suitable investment opportunities are available to pension providers. Section 5.4 discusses the different investment vehicles that could allow pension providers to support businesses and gain exposure to investments that contribute to the economic recovery. Finally, Section 5.5 concludes with policy implications for pension providers and policy makers to foster greater investment to support the economy, while ensuring that these investments are in the best interest of members.

5.1. Pension providers can play a role in supporting the economy

Investing in the economy is part of the business of pension providers. Pension providers collect and invest contributions with the sole objective of financing the retirement benefits of the plan members and beneficiaries. Pension providers may invest indirectly in the economy through government bonds. However, proceeds from these government bonds may not only help to finance public expenditure, they may also help to balance the general government budget. Pension providers also invest in the economy directly, through equities (listed and unlisted) and corporate bonds. In 2019, equity investment represented 30% or more of total investment in 15 OECD countries, with a maximum of 82% in Poland.[4] Direct corporate bond holdings represented 15% or more of total investment in 9 OECD countries, with up to 32% in the Slovak Republic.[5] Overall, when also including investments in land and buildings, loans, hedge funds, private equity funds and structured products, total direct investment in the economy represented more than half of total investment in Australia, Austria, Chile, Colombia, Finland, Iceland, Lithuania, the Netherlands, New Zealand, Norway, Poland and Switzerland (Figure 5.1).

The COVID-19 crisis may offer good and novel investment opportunities for pension providers. Some pension providers may be looking for other asset classes than government bonds to generate returns. New opportunities may arise to invest in the economy. The crisis has prompted a number of companies to issue new shares or new debt to raise money amid a financial crunch.[6] As long as pension providers expect that purchasing these shares and bonds is in line with their investment strategy and fiduciary duty, they can invest in such securities to help mitigate the impact of the COVID-19 crisis on businesses, while delivering good returns to their members.

Beyond equity and bond investing, alternative investments are likely to play an important role in financing the post-COVID-19 economic recovery. Investment in new infrastructure, such as hospitals, schools, renewable energy and digital networks, could provide good returns, while also creating jobs and delivering tangible assets that will fuel long-term economic growth. Real estate may also be a promising asset class for pension providers in some countries. Rescue packages amounting to trillions of dollars have been announced around the world to help individuals and businesses weather the COVID-19 storm and have squeezed governments' budgets. As governments face a reduced capacity to finance alternative investment projects, there may be a greater role of pension providers in this area. Equally, by making such investments, pension providers can manage risk through greater diversification of investments.

Figure 5.1. Pension providers' direct investment in the economy in selected OECD countries, 2019

As a percentage of total investment

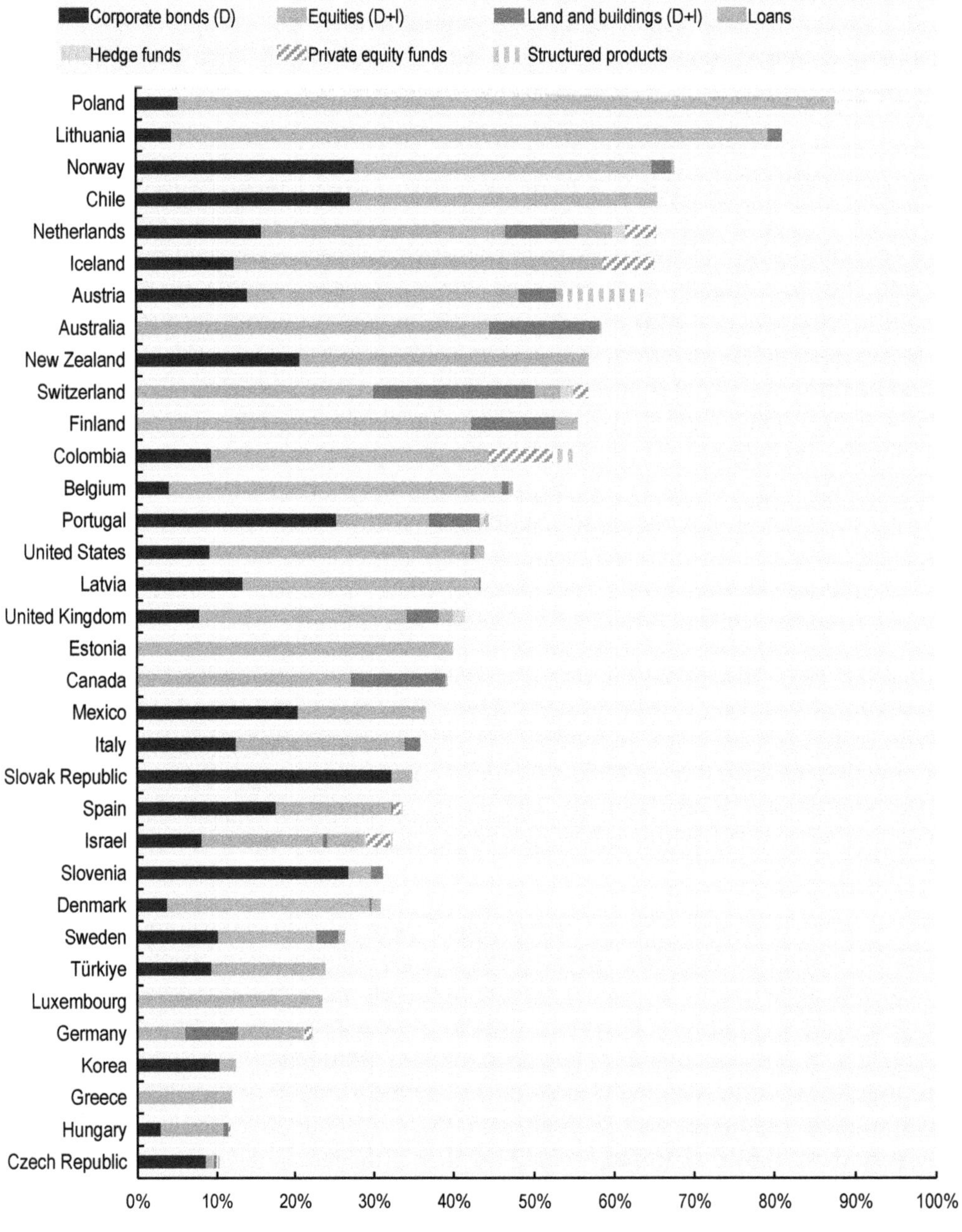

Notes: Data include both domestic and foreign investments. Data refer to pension plans through pension funds, pension insurance contracts or other financing vehicles, depending on the structure of each asset-backed pension system and data availability for each country. "D" means direct investment; "D+I" means direct investment plus indirect investment through collective investment schemes (CIS). For some countries, the look-though of CIS investment and/or the split between corporate and public bonds are not available; investment in some underlying asset classes is therefore under-estimated for these countries.
Source: OECD Global Pension Statistics.

Pension providers are natural investors in less liquid, long-term assets such as infrastructure. Infrastructure investment can provide stable and regular cash flows over the long term, thereby providing an alternative to fixed-income instruments to match pension providers' cash requirements. In addition, cash flows can be inflation linked, making them a natural inflation hedge for pension providers that need to manage inflation risk. Pension providers can also take advantage of an illiquidity premium rewarding them for exposure to less liquid, long-term assets such as infrastructure. Moreover, infrastructure investment can help pension providers to diversify their portfolio across asset types and geographies. Finally, holding investments over the long term can reduce turnover within portfolios and thereby lower transaction costs.

However, data show that current levels of investment in infrastructure projects from pension providers are still low, suggesting there is room to increase allocations. In 2019 for example, direct equity investments in infrastructure projects (e.g. transport, utilities and energy, communications, social infrastructure) and unlisted infrastructure equity funds only represented 2% of pension funds' total investment in Israel and the Netherlands, and 1% in Austria and Portugal (OECD, 2020[3]). Among large pension funds around the world, direct infrastructure investment in the form of unlisted equity and debt represented 1.3% of total assets under management in 2017. Among those investing in infrastructure, allocations ranged from 0.1% to 10.1%, and were usually below the targets established by the funds (OECD, 2019[4]). Given the overall low levels observed, increasing interest from pension providers in infrastructure, and potential to meet target allocations, there is scope for pension providers to increase their allocations to infrastructure investment to finance the economic recovery.

Pension providers could also support the economy by investing in small and medium sized enterprises (SMEs). SMEs play a major role in the global economy and are being severely affected by the COVID-19 pandemic given their higher levels of vulnerability and lower resilience due to their size. Surveys on the COVID-19 impact on SMEs show that more than half of SMEs faced severe losses in revenues, while one-third feared they would be out of business without further support within one month, and up to 50% within three months (OECD, 2020[5]). Pension providers could complement banks to help SMEs cope with urgent liquidity needs. However, pension providers' engagement in SME financing remains, so far, limited (OECD, 2015[6]) and some shortcomings still need be addressed to allow pension providers to invest in these businesses. In particular, as this chapter discusses, given the heightened risks of investing in SMEs, there is a potential role for policy makers to help ensure pension providers make any such investments prudently and in the best interests of members.

Finally, the COVID-19 crisis may accelerate the integration of environmental, social and governance (ESG) factors into the investment policies of pension providers. Many countries target recovery projects that are in line with sustainability goals, building on an existing global trend that has seen a strengthening of ESG considerations for investment decisions. For example, the funds of the EUR 750 billion EU recovery plan will be used to reach the EU's objectives of climate neutrality and digital transformation, as well as to offer social and employment support. The OECD recommends that recovery plans should be designed to "build back better", meaning that they should lead to investment and behavioural changes that will reduce the likelihood of future shocks and increase societies' resilience to them (OECD, 2020[7]). If the ESG characteristics of the projects financed by such recovery plans are made clear, this could facilitate the integration of ESG factors into investment policies.

5.2. But challenges to further support the economy exist

5.2.1. General obstacles to investing in businesses and recovery projects

Several obstacles may impede pension providers to be more involved in supporting the economy. These include the existence of regulatory barriers or the absence of regulation where it is needed, limited investor capability to handle complex investments, and a lack of investment opportunities and clarity of government policy.

Regulatory barriers

Investment regulation may impede pension providers from investing in securities and instruments that may help with the economic recovery. Some countries do not impose any quantitative investment limits and require pension providers to invest according to the prudent person rule, which ensures that investments are carried out in a prudent manner considering the best interest of members and beneficiaries. This is the case in Australia, Austria, Belgium, Canada, the Netherlands, New Zealand, Norway, the United Kingdom, and the United States. Other OECD countries set investment ceilings or caps, sometimes in addition to the prudent person rule, limiting the share of the portfolio that can be invested in particular securities or instruments.

Among OECD countries with investment restrictions, most set limits for equities, corporate bonds, real estate, loans and private investment funds (Annex Table 5.A.1 in Annex 5.A). Caps may vary according to the fund, in particular when plan members can select their investment strategy. Therefore, funds that are more conservative have lower caps in riskier asset classes, and vice-versa. In some countries, the regulation completely forbids pension providers to invest in some asset classes, such as loans (Colombia, Greece, Italy, Korea, Latvia, Lithuania, Mexico and the Slovak Republic) or real estate (Lithuania and Poland).

Most countries have stricter limits for investments not traded in regulated markets. Investment limits are more stringent for unlisted securities than for listed ones in many countries. For example, in Finland, there is a limit of 10% for investments in unlisted equities but a 50% limit for listed equities for voluntary company and industry-wide pension funds. Lower caps for unlisted equities compared to listed equities also exist in France, Germany (for *Pensionskassen*), Hungary, Korea, Slovenia, Spain and Sweden. Unlisted bonds are also capped in Estonia, Latvia and Sweden. Finally, most countries put ceilings on investments in private investment funds. When investment in private investment funds is not forbidden, the ceiling may be as low as 5%, such as in Chile, Colombia, the Czech Republic, Greece and Hungary.

Some of these limits may represent a barrier to SME financing or infrastructure investment. For example, private credit (loans by pension funds), unlisted bonds (private placements of debt) and private equity represent important market-based instruments for SME financing and tend to be tightly curtailed for pension providers. Similarly, low limits for unlisted equities and unlisted infrastructure funds affect the capacity of pension providers to invest in infrastructure projects. In particular, some of the largest pension funds around the world have reported regulatory challenges to increasing their infrastructure allocation. For example in Hong Kong (China), pension funds can only invest in listed markets, while funds in Chile and Romania mention regulatory constraints as barriers to infrastructure investment (OECD, 2019[4]). It is noteworthy that in Denmark, a country without quantitative investment limits, allocation to unlisted investments for pension and insurance companies represented 27% of total investment by June 2020 (Danmarks Nationalbank, 2020[8]).

Accounting standards as well as funding and solvency regulations may reduce allocations to listed equities. Mark-to-market valuations and risk-based solvency and funding regulations may affect investment strategies in two main ways. First, using market interest rates to discount liabilities creates a higher sensitivity of liabilities, and hence of solvency or funding levels, to market conditions. In order to reduce the volatility of solvency and funding levels, pension providers may have an incentive to hold more fixed-income securities. Second, under risk-based solvency and funding regulations, asset classes with a higher volatility, such as equities, are subject to a higher capital charge or reserving. This may lead pension providers to reduce exposure to such asset classes. Severinson and Yermo (2012[9]) show that the introduction of fair valuation principles and risk-based funding regulations led pension providers in Denmark, the Netherlands and the United Kingdom to move away from listed equities towards fixed-income securities and alternative investments, in particular private equity, hedge funds, real estate and unlisted infrastructure equity.

Finally, the absence of regulatory barriers can also deter institutional investment. A strong rule of law and a robust and transparent regulatory environment are key drivers in investors' decisions regarding which jurisdictions to invest in (OECD, 2014[10]). Weak institutions create uncertainties about the quality of regulations and therefore increase country risk (Hammami, Ruhashyankiko and Yehoue, 2006[11]). Another key deterrent to investors' willingness to engage in long-term investments is any perceived risk of political instability or political pressures on regulatory schemes (OECD, 2014[10]).[7] Potential investors may also perceive a risk that political considerations might encourage governments to engage in riskier projects than is in the public interest (Hammami, Ruhashyankiko and Yehoue, 2006[11]).

Additionally, too few limits on individual savers to switch investments may also reduce pension providers' appetite for illiquid investments, particularly those without a readily ascertainable market value, such as infrastructure. Members of defined contribution asset-backed pension arrangements generally can switch providers. They can also usually choose from a range of investment options with varying risk profiles, and transfer between the different options available within certain limits. However, this means that pension providers may be exposed to significant outflows, reducing the expected duration and investment horizon of their investment strategy. Pedraza Morales et al. (2017[12]) find a correlation of over 0.5 between fund flows across providers and holdings of short-term and more liquid assets in Chile, Colombia and Mexico. The correlation with respect to the volume of transfers across investment options within a provider was lower in all countries, except for Chile. This suggests that pension providers may hold more liquid and short-term assets in order to accommodate for unexpected outflows, reducing the part they can invest in long-term assets.

Limited investor capability

Some investments may require specific skills and expertise that some pension providers may lack. A number of risks are typically more relevant for alternative investments (e.g. hedge funds, private equity, real estate, commodities, structured products and infrastructure), such as liquidity risk, integrity risk, operational risk, limited transparency, valuation weaknesses, control issues, counterparty risk and conflicts of interest (Stańko and Ásgrímsson, 2017[13]). Analysing these risks often requires sophisticated methods of risk management and analysis, as well as scale and dedicated resources. Small and medium-sized pension funds, or more generally funds that do not have well-developed in-house investment and risk management teams, may lack the capability of investing on their own in alternative investments.[8]

Lack of objective information and quality data may further complicate the task. In particular, historical data on infrastructure deals are scarce and often proprietary. Without a suitable benchmark panel data, pension providers may not be in a position to assess the different degrees of risk of a certain project or its different phases (OECD, 2014[10]). Similarly, a shortage of data on creditworthiness, financial performance and financing track record of SMEs is one of the most significant impediments to market-based SME financing, especially through debt instruments. Moreover, lack of standardised reporting by SMEs impedes comparability and does not allow investors to perform comprehensive and well-informed analysis on the underlying exposures (OECD, 2015[6]). Innovative techniques using artificial intelligence and machine learning models could reduce such information asymmetries by using big data to assess the creditworthiness of 'thin file' clients and provide credit ratings to 'unscored' clients with limited credit history or lack of tangible collateral. It should be noted, however, that such techniques and the use of inadequate data in lending can raise risks of disparate impact in credit outcomes and the potential for biased, discriminatory or unfair lending. What is more, tail events, such as the COVID-19 crisis, give rise to discontinuity in the datasets that are used by machine learning models and are practically difficult to overcome at this stage (OECD, 2021[14]).

Non-traditional assets also tend to be more expensive to manage. Arrangements to invest in alternative assets can be complex, calling for greater scrutiny, analysis and monitoring compared to other financial products. As such, high fees have been a deterrent to these kinds of investments for some time. This is particularly the case for SME financing, as investors need to build capacity to deal with the huge amount of heterogeneity among businesses. Moreover, pension providers lacking the scale or capability to invest directly in infrastructure projects can use unlisted infrastructure funds. However, these funds tend to charge high fees to investors for providing access to diversified pools of infrastructure assets (Belt and Nimmo, 2013[15]).

Lack of investment opportunities and clarity of government policy

Lack of clarity of government policy, in particular in the infrastructure sector and on ESG, as well as the lack of investment opportunities, are impediments for pension providers to invest in recovery projects. Where governments do not make political commitments over the long term, or where they are fragmented across different levels of government, investors can be deterred from including infrastructure in their long-term investment strategy. Further, lack of clarity on investment opportunities can make it harder for pension providers to make long-term decisions (Della Croce, 2011[16]). Pension providers need a clearer understanding of the government's infrastructure plans beyond the political cycle. For example, the Australian Institute of Superannuation Trustees mentions regulatory uncertainty, especially in sectors such as renewable energy, as a barrier to invest in new infrastructure projects (AIST, 2020[17]). Similarly, a survey of retirement schemes in the United Kingdom revealed that many had misgivings about the availability of appropriate domestic opportunities. They stated they would invest elsewhere if the right opportunities that meet their investment strategy and risk/return profile were not available.[9]

Lack of awareness from entrepreneurs about market-based financing possibilities for SMEs and issuance costs also limit the number of investment opportunities in this area for pension providers. SMEs are often not aware of alternative means of finance available through the markets, beyond bank lending. In addition, they often lack the skills to face the process of bond or equity issuance, for which costs can be disproportionately high. This drives down the number of issuances (OECD, 2015[6]).

5.2.2. Risks in the current context

The primary objective of pension providers is to invest assets earmarked for retirement in the best interest of plan members. Not fulfilling this objective creates a long-term risk to societies, as people may not have enough to live on in retirement and may need to rely on public safety nets. The COVID-19 crisis may bring additional risks, beyond the general obstacles described earlier, that pension providers need to consider when investing in businesses and recovery projects, especially when they may weaken the requirement to act in the best interest of members. There may be calls on pension providers to invest in instruments to support the economic recovery, but at the cost of potentially generating lower returns relative to other investment opportunities with the same risk profile or increasing concentration. In addition, pension providers may deviate from their strategic asset allocation to seize investment opportunities. Finally, measures taken by governments to grant contribution holidays and help members access their savings during the crisis may reduce room for investment in illiquid assets.

Risk of prioritising the economic recovery at the detriment of the best interest of members

There have been calls on pension providers to use savings earmarked for retirement to address the impact posed by COVID-19 on the economy, investing in recovery and ESG projects. Pension providers could play a more active role in the current economic situation as long as the risk-return profile of the corresponding investments is acceptable. Some sectors have been hit hard by the lockdown and ensuing social distancing measures, such as civil aviation, tourism, and cultural and leisure sectors. Suggestions that pension providers could support companies in these sectors to help cushion the blow from the COVID-19 crisis abound. However, these investments may yield poor returns, as the outlook for some companies may be negative. Indeed, consumers may have changed some of their habits, reducing permanently the demand for certain goods and services. For example, air travel may not go back to pre-pandemic levels, as enhanced video conferencing capabilities may permanently reduce the need for physical meetings at work. There is a risk that investing in such sectors may deliver poor value for members, or worse than they otherwise would have gotten from other investments. In turn, this could reduce trust in asset-backed pension arrangements.

A fast and strong economic recovery is in the best interest of members, but bailing out ailing companies is not the role of pension providers. The pressure may be particularly strong for industry or sector-wide pension funds to invest in their own industry or sector, as their members can only continue to save for retirement if they remain employed. In addition, a faster economic recovery should lead to a faster recovery of financial markets and therefore of asset values. However, there should be a clear delineation of roles between the government and pension providers. The role of the government is to help businesses keep workers when it is expected that demand for their goods and services will eventually recover, or to help workers retrain so they can take new jobs that are more needed in the post-crisis economy. The role of pension providers is to select investment opportunities that will deliver good risk-adjusted returns to their members to finance their retirement income. The fact that pension providers may face a shrinkage of their membership base because the sector needs to downsize following the crisis should not interfere in their investment decisions.[10]

Pressures to invest in local businesses or infrastructure projects may also be strong for public pension funds, public pension reserve funds, as well as mandatory pension funds. Governments, as well as the population, may believe that pension providers that are financed at least partly with public money, or collecting mandatory contributions from employers and workers, should take a more active role to help with the economic recovery. To maintain good relations with their stakeholders, pension providers might give in to government and public (soft) pressure to support national initiatives to help meet financing gaps for long-term projects, such as infrastructure investments, aimed at stimulating the economy. Infrastructure projects can come with significant benefits, such as diversification, low volatility, and cash yields in the future. However, infrastructure projects can be complex and pension providers need to make sure that they understand all of the implications of the investments. Moreover, infrastructure may be overvalued due to increased demand or because future returns are overestimated. Pension providers should not blindly trust public investment projects, and should exercise their due diligence to assess expected returns.

Concentration risk

Channelling more funds into the domestic economy might reduce geographical diversification of the portfolios of pension providers. There have been signs of pressure for pension funds to invest domestically. For example, in March 2020, the Icelandic Pension Funds Association urged pension funds to limit their purchases of foreign investments over the following three months. In consultation with the Central Bank of Iceland, pension funds stopped purchasing foreign currency from 17 March 2020. This was partly to reduce instability over the Icelandic krona as the country's export revenues were projected to decline temporarily.[11] This issue is particularly relevant for small economies. However, geographical diversification can be an important feature to consider to bring down investment risk, as more waves of the virus are affecting various regions of the world differently and at different times, allowing lower returns in some regions to be potentially compensated by higher returns in others. To the contrary, geographical concentration in one economy may imply greater investment losses in the event of a new lockdown in that economy.

Systemic concentration risk may also arise if many pension providers invest in the same sectors or projects due to government/public pressure or herding behaviour. If all or several pension providers of a country invest in the same projects and these projects perform badly, then they will all suffer investment losses at the same time, potentially reducing trust in the pensions industry.

Liquidity risk

Measures to provide employees and employers with short-term relief may create liquidity constraints and reduce pension providers' capacity to invest in illiquid assets. Pension providers need to hold cash and liquid assets in their portfolios to address liquidity demands from regular benefit payments and exceptional withdrawals. They also count on contribution inflows to manage liquidity needs. However, certain countries have allowed employers and/or employees to defer or even stop contributions to asset-backed pension arrangements to provide them with short-term financial relief. In addition, members who lost their jobs or experienced a reduction in working hours can more easily access their savings early to weather financial hardship in a number of countries (see Chapter 2). Not only may this force pension providers to act pro-cyclically by selling assets in falling markets and materialise losses, it also increases liquidity demands. These measures jeopardise the capacity of pension providers to invest in long-term, illiquid assets, such as infrastructure, as they need to keep a larger share of the portfolio in liquid assets. These measures may also create a precedent for future withdrawals, so that pension providers might not trust that assets will be locked away for the long-term going forward, further reducing their appetite for long-term investment.

Deviation from the strategic asset allocation

Finally, the current crisis offers new investment opportunities but may spur pension providers to deviate from their strategic asset allocation. In order to seize opportunities that could potentially fetch higher returns, for example to participate in new infrastructure projects, pension providers may increase the overall risk profile of their portfolio. The investment strategy may no longer be in line with the investment objective of the pension provider, increasing the risk that it will not deliver on its promises. Moreover, pension providers should not pursue complex investments, e.g. private equity, if they do not have the expertise to conduct the same risk assessment as for any other type of investment.

5.3. Overcoming challenges to investing requires strong governance, appropriate investment strategies and suitable investment opportunities

Strong governance and appropriate investment strategies will help ensure pension providers act in the best interest of members when they invest in projects supporting the economy. The *OECD Core Principles of Private Pension Regulation* provide governments, regulators and supervisors with high-level guidance on the design and operation of asset-backed pension systems (OECD, 2016[18]). They aim to strengthen the regulatory framework around asset-backed pensions in order to promote the sound and reliable operation of asset-backed pension plans. Core Principle 3 on "Governance" and Core Principle 4 on "Investment and Risk Management" are particularly relevant to address some of the issues identified earlier, as they set out the characteristics and behaviours that regulators should encourage in the governance frameworks and investment policies of pension providers, respectively. In particular, ensuring the accountability and suitability of the governing body of pension providers, defining an appropriate investment policy, designing a sound risk management strategy and having appropriate investment regulations can all contribute to safeguarding members' assets while supporting the economy at the same time.

5.3.1. Accountability and suitability of the governing body

A governing body should be accountable to members and beneficiaries, and should guarantee that investment decisions are at arm's length from governments. Core Principle 3 recommends that every pension provider establishes a governing body to administer the pension fund. The governing body should ultimately be responsible for the protection of the best interest of members. Its fiduciary duty towards members includes prudent and efficient investment of the assets, as well as exercising due diligence in the investment process. Mechanisms for achieving accountability and transparency include robust public reporting and a publicly available code of conduct governing the actions of employees, officers, and board members of pension providers. The accountability of the governing body may be reinforced through the legal liability of any actions that are inconsistent with its fiduciary duty. The governing body should therefore not bend to government or public pressure to make a particular investment if this is not in the best interest of the members of the pension provider.

Independence also guarantees that decisions taken by the board are based solely on the mission of the pension provider. Core Principle 3 recommends that adequate internal controls are in place to promote the independence and impartiality of the decisions taken by the governing body. In selected Canadian public pension funds for example, independence from government is enshrined in legislation and is enabled by a strong board member appointment process and the protection of fund managers to allow them the appropriate autonomy (The World Bank, 2017[19]).

Good governance should also ensure that the members of the governing body have the appropriate skills and experience to understand the different products that they may invest in. According to Core Principle 3, members of the governing body should be subject to minimum fit and proper standards in order to ensure a high level of integrity, competence, experience and professionalism in the governance of the pension provider. In addition, they should collectively have the necessary skills and knowledge to oversee all the functions performed by the pension provider, including investment management. In the event that they lack sufficient expertise to assess particularly complex investments such as infrastructure, derivatives, private equity and others, they should either seek expert advice or reject the investment. In case they seek advice, the governing body should be able to understand the advice, and in any case the governing body keeps ultimate responsibility for the decision of whether or not to invest in the product. These requirements regarding suitability and expert advice should ensure that the governing body only pursues investments that it fully understands.

5.3.2. Well-defined investment policy

Having a well-defined investment policy should avoid a situation whereby the pension provider would engage in unsuitable investments. According to Core Principle 4, the governing body of a pension provider has to define an investment policy in a written statement. That investment policy should establish clear investment objectives for the pension provider consistent with its retirement income objective and specific attributes (e.g. liabilities, risk appetite of members and the plan sponsor). Among other things, the investment policy should identify the asset allocation strategy for the pension provider. Deviations from the asset allocation strategy may be tolerated, but the investment policy should clearly identify when and to what extent such deviations may happen. The investment policy should therefore establish limits to the extent to which a pension provider may deviate from its strategic asset allocation by seizing opportunities for new investments.

In addition, the investment policy should provide a clear framework regarding investments in non-traditional or less transparent asset classes such as infrastructure, as well as investments in non-regulated markets, such as unlisted securities (Core Principle 4). The investment policy should detail the circumstances under which the pension provider might pursue such investments (e.g. the rationale, investment limits, and vehicles to use). This should be in line with the investment regulations in place as well as the level of expertise of the governing body in the area of alternative investments.

The investment policy should also be regularly reviewed and potentially updated to reflect changes in the investment environment. Core Principle 4 recommends the governing body to periodically review the investment strategy to determine whether there is a need to change the policy. If new opportunities arise and can adequately fit in the strategic asset allocation to pursue the investment objective, it would be legitimate to revise the investment policy by including new instruments in the available asset mix, if permitted. For example, the investment policy may not allow infrastructure investment because at the time of setting up the fund, such investments were not available or suitable for the pension provider.

5.3.3. Sound risk management strategy

Existing risk management strategies should already allow pension providers to identify all material investment risks. Core Principle 4 states that the governing body of a pension provider should establish an investment risk management process to support the achievement of the investment objectives. The OECD/IOPS Good Practices for Pension Funds' Risk Management Systems[12] note that "an effective risk management system is comprised of strategies, processes and reporting procedures necessary to identify, measure, monitor, assess, control and report, on a continuous and an ad hoc basis, all material risks, at an individual and an aggregated level, to which the pension fund or plan is or could be exposed, and their interdependencies". Material investment risks include risks related to movements in interest rates or other market prices, credit risk and liquidity risk. A sound investment risk management strategy should ensure that all the risks related to a particular investment product are considered and assessed before investing in such a product, and that a mechanism is put in place afterwards to control and monitor those risks on an ongoing basis.

5.3.4. Appropriate investment regulations

Investment regulations could guide the definition of the investment policies of pension providers, in particular with respect to investments in alternative assets. When legal provisions stipulate maximum levels of investment by category, Core Principle 4 recommends that these provisions address the use of more complex and less transparent asset classes, taking into account their utility and the risks of their inappropriate use. Annex Table 5.A.1 shows that many countries indeed establish specific limits for non-traditional investments. Such limits sometimes apply in addition to the prudent person rule. This is not the case, however, in countries only requiring pension providers to invest according the prudent person rule. In addition, Stańko and Ásgrímsson (2017[13]) find no significant differences in the supervision of pension funds' investments in respect to traditional or non-traditional investments (including no specific guidelines for non-traditional investments). This may be because in some jurisdictions, direct investment in non-traditional investments is not allowed or because non-traditional investments are still insignificant.

Investment regulations should also evolve over time to allow pension providers to adapt their investment strategies to new challenges and new products available. In particular, Core Principle 4 warns that quantitative portfolio limits should not inhibit adequate diversification, nor the ability of pension providers to implement optimum investment strategies. They should therefore be regularly assessed and amended as necessary. In particular, investment in alternative asset classes may be gradually relaxed as pension providers improve the skills of their investment teams. Table 5.1 provides the example of Mexico, where the investment regime for pension funds gradually introduced new asset classes. This gradual shift was accompanied by an increased sophistication of investment teams in pension funds. For example, pension funds incorporated new domestic certifications for staff members performing the analysis of alternative instruments and increased the number of staff members with certifications from international bodies (FIAP, 2018[20]).

Some countries have recently increased regulatory limits to allow pension providers to invest more in alternative asset classes and to support the economy during the COVID-19 crisis. For example, in Chile, the Productivity Law promulgated on 25 October 2016 allows pension funds to invest directly in alternative assets.[13] Alternative assets include instruments, operations and contracts related to real estate, private equity, private debt, infrastructure and other assets established by the investment regime. The maximum limits were established between 5% and 15% of assets depending on the type of fund. In April 2020, the Central Bank of Chile increased the caps for alternative assets to help diversify investments and improve risk-return prospects.[14] As of October 2020, Swiss pension funds have been able to invest up to 10% of their assets in infrastructure. The investment category for infrastructure was initially grouped together with hedge funds, private equity, insurance linked securities and commodities, jointly capped at 15% of total investments. Infrastructure is now separated and has its own 10% limit to allow pension funds to expand their exposure to infrastructure. To support financing for start-ups and innovative companies during the COVID-19 crisis, Icelandic pension funds are temporarily allowed to own up to 35% of the units or shares of venture capital funds (instead of 20%), as long as these investments do not exceed 1% of pension fund assets. This authorisation is valid until 1 January 2025. Israel has amended some investment regulations applying to institutional investors in response to the COVID-19 outbreak. Institutional investors can now hold up to 49% of a single corporate bond series (instead of 25%), and up to 7.5% of the means of control of other investors (instead of 5%). This change intends to support capital markets and the economy. Lifting these investment restrictions should, however, go hand in hand with strong governance, clear and well-described investment policies and risk-management strategies, to ensure that investments are made in the best interest of members. Finally, Colombia loosened a limit on investment in private debt. This would help channel money to SMEs, which were particularly hit by the crisis.

Table 5.1. Evolution of the investment regime for Mexican pension funds since 1997

Year	Allowed asset classes and instruments
1997	Federal Government securities; Cash
2001	Derivatives; Securities lending (bonds)
2005	Foreign securities; Equities
2007	Development capital certificates (CKDs); Mexican real estate investment trusts (FIBRAs); Structured assets
2010	Initial public offerings (IPOs); Subordinated debt
2011	Commodities
2013	Real estate investment trusts (REITs); Swaption operations
2016	Investment project certificates (CERPIs); FIBRA-E (energy infrastructure)
2019	Repurchase agreements (Repos); Securities lending (equities); Private placements

Source: CONSAR.

Risk-based requirements present an alternative approach to quantitative investment limits. They do not impose hard restrictions on investment, but instead impose a higher risk charge for investments with a higher level of risk, providing an incentive to better manage risks. Investment regulations for pension providers tend to focus on qualitative requirements with respect to risk management processes, in particular the prudent person principle and fiduciary duties. However, few jurisdictions have fully implemented risk-based capital requirements for pension funds (OECD, 2015[21]). Some jurisdictions also continue to apply quantitative investment limits alongside risk-based requirements.[15]

Investment regulation may also include self-investment limits to reduce conflicts of interest and pressures to invest in a particular company or sector. Table 5.2 shows that most countries impose investment limits on securities issued by employers sponsoring occupational pension plans. A 5% limit is common when there is a single employer sponsoring the plan, while many countries set a 10% limit when the sponsoring employer belongs to a group. These limits are in line with the recommendations in Core Principle 4. Only Germany, Italy and Slovenia address the case of several employers sponsoring the same plan. Italy has different limits in the case of multi-employer funds and industry-wide funds. This helps to address issues related to potential pressures arising from governments or the public to invest in the sector or industry in which the members of the pension fund work.

Table 5.2. Investment limits in securities issued by employers sponsoring occupational pension plans, selected OECD countries, 2019

As a percentage of total investment

	Securities issued by the sponsoring employer (single-employer plan)	Securities issued by entities belonging to the same group as the sponsoring employer (single-employer plan)	Securities issued by several sponsoring employers (multi-employer plan)
Australia	5%		
Austria	5%		
Belgium	5%	10%	
Finland	5%		
Germany – *Pensionsfonds*	5%	10%	
Germany – *Pensionskassen*	5%	5%	15%
Greece	5%	10%	
Ireland	5%	10%	
Italy	5%	10%	Multi-employer funds: 20% Industry-wide funds: 30%
Korea		DB plans: 5% DC plans: 10%	
Luxembourg	5%	10%	
Netherlands	5%		
New Zealand	5%		
Norway	4%		
Portugal	5%	10%	
Slovenia	5%		10%
Spain		5%	
Sweden	5%	10%	
Switzerland	5%		
United Kingdom	5%		
United States	10%		

Notes: DB means defined benefit; DC means defined contribution.
Source: OECD Annual Survey of Investment Regulation of Pension Funds and Other Providers.

In addition to ensuring the adequate regulations are in place, policy makers can facilitate the mobilisation of private capital towards long-term investment. In particular, they can set up public-private partnerships (PPPs), provide financial incentives and promote special vehicles for investment in alternative assets. Doing so can help make projects available that would suit the investment parameters of pension providers.

5.3.5. Availability of suitable investment opportunities

Policy makers across OECD countries have taken steps to ensure that suitable investment opportunities are available to pension providers, particularly for alternative asset investments. The steps to ensure suitable investment opportunities involve making the right projects and partnerships available, providing financial support for investments, and helping set up investment vehicles or platforms.

Policy makers could encourage greater institutional investment in public projects simply by making regular investment opportunities available, and through transparency and clarity about their long-term strategic policy frameworks. This is in line with Principle 1 of the *G20/OECD High Level Principles of Long-Term Investment Financing by Institutional Investors* (OECD/G20, 2013[22]). A limited pipeline of opportunities can be a hindrance to investment in infrastructure. Furthermore, pension providers need clarity on the government's long-term infrastructure plans to inform their investment strategies. Having national infrastructure plans is one way governments can clarify to investors their political commitment to infrastructure over the long term (Della Croce, 2011[16]).

One key way to attract investors such as pension providers to invest in long-term assets is by setting up public-private partnerships (PPPs) that balance the benefits of such investments with potential moral hazard problems.[16] PPPs are contractual arrangements where the private sector provides public services based on a pre-agreed risk and profit sharing with the public sector, and where the public sector retains planning and control functions (OECD, 2014[10]). Depending on how self-sustainable the projects are, different projects will need different arrangements for the government's financial contributions. Generally, the greater the government's financial contributions to PPPs, the greater the propensity for the private sector to invest.[17] While in the past PPPs have shown good results in terms of cost efficiency, recent data and academic research have demonstrated that excessive risk taking by the public sector discourages the private sector from carrying out careful risk analysis and risk management, leading to moral hazard and ultimately to lower value for money for the public sector (OECD, 2014[10]). This can place significant burden on taxpayers. As such, there is a case for public authorities to better weigh the competing considerations and rebuild trust in PPPs, for example by balancing these moral hazard problems with the benefits of such investments.

Public authorities could also take steps to make investments more financially appealing to pension providers, while bearing in mind the trade-offs in doing so. There are many examples of OECD countries providing financial support to attract private investors, although in drawing on those examples, governments should conduct their own due diligence regarding those expenditures and consider the opportunity costs. Examples of financial support initiatives include:

- The public sector subsidising projects through contributions or grants, whose purpose is either to reduce the private commitment or to increase the return of an otherwise unprofitable project (OECD, 2014[10]). Grants during the construction phase can decrease the initial contribution that lenders provide to the project, leading to higher returns for the private sector. Contributions during the construction phase can also include the provision of public assets (asset recycling) and/or the possibility to use public land for free during the period of the concession (OECD, 2014[10]). Subsidies during the project's operational phase are also a means to stabilise or increase revenues to the private party. Examples are feed-in tariffs in the renewable energy sector (i.e. forms of subsidy paid to the producer of renewable energy to incentivise them to move away from conventional fossil fuels), the provision of a floor protection against drop in traffic volumes in the transportation sector, and a minimum rental payment in students' accommodation/social housing projects. Another example is the public sector contributing to debt service, where the public entity pays a portion of the interest payment or margin that the project bears during the amortisation period of the loans. Alternatively, it can provide tax relief during that period (OECD, 2014[10]). Grants, loans, and tax relief directed towards clean energy projects are particularly relevant in the current context, where many OECD countries have directly linked such support to a green recovery.
- The public sector offering guarantees or back-up liquidity facilities to infrastructure creditors to overcome structural problems incurred during its development or to guarantee cases of refinancing risk (OECD, 2014[10]). Examples include the liquidity back-up facility of the 2020 Project Bond Initiative started by the European Union and the European Investment Bank (EIB), the unconditional UK Guarantee Scheme, and the Singapore Government guarantee on debt via the Infrastructure Guarantee Fund (IGF) (OECD, 2014[10]). However, while government backing and guarantees are useful to secure financing from private investors, they may also have a high fiscal cost over the medium to long term in case they are exercised that needs careful assessment.
- Providing indirect investment to encourage private financing. This can include co-investment with the private sector. The objective of such an agreement is to get a level of return proportional to the

risk taken in the project. The co-investment can take the form of equity, subordinated debt, a debt contribution, or indirectly via investment vehicles for infrastructure (OECD, 2014[10]).

- Making debt financing for infrastructure projects more attractive. Examples include through tax incentives for infrastructure bonds (such as the Build America Bonds) or for governments to change the risk profile of investments by providing subordinated debt, thereby boosting a project or portfolio's credit rating (2011[16]).[18]

Public authorities could directly intervene in the market by promoting or providing the seed capital to set up suitable investment instruments or platforms. Governments can provide the seed capital to set up investment funds that make it possible for pension providers to gain exposure to investments. The Pan African Infrastructure Development Fund, the Philippine Investment Alliance for Infrastructure fund, and the Marguerite fund in Europe are all examples of institutions that pool institutional capital, set up through seed money from governments (OECD, 2014[23]).

Alternatively, policy makers can also promote greater pooling and collaboration between institutional investors in order to create institutions with sufficient scale. Governments themselves can help set up an investment platform for pension providers to pool their investments. The greater scale this brings can help investors build the expertise they need to implement a broader investment strategy and undertake better due diligence and risk management. Pension providers can also benefit from collaboration through lower fees, a spreading of risk, and access to investments with longer time horizons. Over time, such investment can in turn also boost demand for alternative investments and encourage better alignment between pension providers and the industry.

5.4. There are a number of investment vehicles pension providers can use to support the economy

Pension providers can play a role in meeting the financing needs created by the COVID-19 crisis to address the accompanying shocks to the economy, as well as those created by environmental, social and governance (ESG) objectives. However, pension providers can only invest in a way that supports businesses and promotes economic growth, and do so in the best interest of their members, if appropriate market structures exist for these investments to happen.

This section examines the types of financing instruments that can allow pension providers to gain exposure to investments that support the economy. This section explores two broad areas where financing from pension providers can help mitigate the effects of the crisis. The first involves investing in instruments that aim to meet the immediate needs of businesses and governments in direct response to the crisis situation. In this context, the COVID-19 crisis has seen some investment vehicles, such as COVID-19 bonds, emerging precisely to channel funds towards expenditure programmes that address the pandemic's effects. Traditional instruments that provide financing to governments and businesses, such as government bonds, corporate bonds and equities, have also seen increased issuances in response to the crisis. Pension providers continue to invest in such vehicles, which are often a core part of their investment strategy. However, the current context has also led to greater interest in other investment vehicles that provide support to SMEs, which do not have the same access to financing as larger companies.

The second broad area of interest for pension providers is in providing financing for investment in long-term assets such as infrastructure or real estate, which could play a particularly important role in promoting economic growth to aid in the recovery. These instruments would also help pension providers to get involved in ESG and sustainable investment opportunities. Pension funds in some jurisdictions already invest in large-scale long-term assets that can serve this purpose, although the choice of investment vehicle can vary significantly. In other cases, there may be a case for pension providers to newly explore such investment opportunities, spurred on by a greater appetite to participate in a recovery and the economic case for investing in projects with good return prospects.

This section explores the different options that are available to institutional investors like pension funds to provide financing under the two broad areas mentioned above. It provides examples of the investment vehicles available, other than government bonds, to outline the different avenues for supporting the economy during and as the world emerges from the crisis. Notwithstanding, this distinction is not a firm one, and some instruments, such as investment in listed equities can apply to both phases.

5.4.1. Financing instruments to meet direct needs arising from the crisis

As the experience of the 2020 crisis has shown, shocks trigger a need for urgent financing to support governments, businesses and individuals. Financing needs arise to address the first priorities of crises, such as the need for medical care and rapid economic rescue packages. Businesses also can face cash shortages and may need urgent support. Pension providers can help meet these financing needs via different investment vehicles. In particular, 2020 saw the emergence of COVID-19 bonds to support programmes aimed at addressing the essential priorities of the crisis. Other financing instruments can act as more direct financing vehicles. Corporate bonds and listed equities typically expose investors to debt and equity financing for larger businesses. Other instruments, such as private equity, securitised SME loans and SME covered bonds also make it possible for investors such as pension providers to provide financing to smaller businesses.

COVID-19 bonds to support programmes addressing the effects of the pandemic

COVID-19 bonds have quickly emerged as a leading means of providing financial support to stakeholders in need of immediate financing. COVID-19 bonds can carry a bond label – such as a social, green or sustainability-linked bond label – or can be a non-labelled thematic bond. The year 2020 saw a particularly notable boom in social bond issuances because of the large number of COVID-19 bonds that are labelled as social bonds.[19,20] Much of the proceeds from COVID-19 bonds have been to help finance the wide-reaching public sector spending programmes to address the impacts of the pandemic. Governments have spent a great deal on surges in their health care system capacity, labour market and business support programmes, restructuring public facilities and cities for pandemic safety, improving supply chains and trade through digitisation, and so on. COVID-19 bonds have also emerged as a way to deliver assistance to businesses that have seen pressures to their existing functions, such as due to business downturns, and to businesses that may need loans or cash injections to continue to operate. Other businesses also need to make investments to transform their operations so that they are able to function under the new environment and meet consumer demands for safer spaces (e.g. restaurants refitting for social distancing, offices needing to set up remote working operations, hiring staff to enforce social distancing rules). Finally, some businesses have seen added demand for services, such as businesses producing medical equipment or doing research. The COVID-19 bonds that have been issued to date aim to meet one or many of these financing needs.

All types of issuers in debt capital markets can issue a COVID-19 bond, including supranational entities, governments, the financial sector, and businesses. For example, with respect to issues of Social Bonds related to COVID-19, the International Capital Market Association states that any entity can issue the bond as long as all the four core components of the Social Bond Principles are addressed.[21] It also requires that the use of proceeds of the bond goes exclusively towards addressing or mitigating social issues wholly or partially emanating from the coronavirus outbreak.[22]

The majority of COVID-19 bond issuances have come from supranational entities such as development banks. Many have issued multi-billion dollar programmes to help governments' efforts to respond to and contain the spread of the coronavirus. Many supranational entities such as development banks have high credit ratings and have preferred creditor status, making their bonds attractive investment opportunities.

As such, they would fit into pension providers' investment policies. Examples include the bonds issued by the World Bank's International Bank for Reconstruction and Development, the International Finance Corporation, the Development Bank of Latin America, and the Nordic Investment Bank. The bonds have common themes, in that they all broadly aim to provide financial support to health care systems, domestic labour market solutions, or loans to businesses.[23] Some pension funds stated that they purchased COVID-19 bonds. The Nordic pension funds PKA and Folksam have invested EUR 1 billion in development bonds from the World Bank.[24] The Swedish pension funds Skandia and Länsförsäkringar have also invested SEK 450 million and SEK 380 million respectively in the Sustainability Awareness Bond issued by the EIB.[25]

Governments around the world have also issued COVID-19 bonds. While most governments have raised capital for their spending programmes through issuing sovereign debt via traditional standard bond issuances, others have issued bonds whose proceeds are specifically tied to addressing the impacts of the pandemic.[26] For example, the European Commission has issued social bonds to cover the costs directly related to the financing of national short-time work schemes, and other similar measures they have put in place as a response to the pandemic. The bonds were purchased by pension providers, including PGGM and APG in the Netherlands and Sampension in Denmark.[27] Guatemala issued a social bond to finance social investments that included its response to COVID-19. The expenditure programmes included providing medical insurance to students, promoting preventive health and medical practices, supporting health recovery in hospitals, and other COVID-19 related investments approved under the law (Republic of Guatemala, 2020[24]).The Latvian Government has established a fund with a target size of at least EUR 100 million to provide liquidity and capital support to large enterprises in Latvia affected by the pandemic, through debt and equity instruments. The state will provide an investment of EUR 50 million in the fund and the commercially managed Latvian pension investment funds will contribute the same amount. The fund also aims to attract private investors (European Commission, 2020[25]).

Different private sector entities in the finance sector have also issued COVID-19 bonds since the crisis began. The *Cassa depositi e prestiti* (CDP), an Italian investment bank, issued a EUR 1 billion 3- and 7-year dual-tranche COVID-19 Social Response Bond. Its aims were easing access to credit – both directly and indirectly through the banking system – for Italian SMEs intensely affected by the pandemic, and supporting public administrations and local authorities to implement health care support measures (Cassa depositi e prestiti, 2020[26]). Bpifrance issued a COVID-19 Response corporate bond to alleviate the impact of the pandemic on French companies. Its purpose was to assist companies in France with ongoing cash flow difficulties to finance their operations and costs related to their employees (Bpifrance, 2020[27]). The Dutch pension fund, ABP, announced that it invested in this bond.[28] Japan's biggest lender, Mitsubishi UFJ Financial Group, has announced its intention to issue sustainability bonds worth USD 1.42 billion, aimed at raising funds from individual investors to help smaller companies and hospitals tackle the pandemic.[29] The Korean bank Kookmin Bank issued a COVID-19 bond, stating that it intended to use 90% of the proceeds to extend loans to SMEs affected by the virus, small offices, and home businesses.[30] Bank of America sold a USD 1 billion four-year COVID-19 bond to help finance the health care industry as it tackles the pandemic. It will pay investors a yield above benchmark Treasuries, which is broadly in line with the bank's existing non-COVID-19 bonds.[31]

Some large businesses have also raised financing by issuing bonds to finance efforts to combat the pandemic or develop new lines of business. Such issuances differ from standard corporate bonds in the sense that the proceeds are specifically linked to pandemic relief. The drug maker Pfizer issued the first biopharmaceutical COVID-19 bond, issuing USD 1.25 billion in 10-year bonds. One purpose of the bond is to make capital investments in manufacturing and development for medicines and vaccines (Pfizer Inc., 2020[28]). Similarly, Getinge, a Swedish medical technology company, developed a COVID-19 financing framework in line with the International Capital Market Association's Social Bond Principles. The company stated that the proceeds will be allocated to financing the production of medical supplies such as ventilators, extracorporeal life support (ECLS) equipment, and intensive care equipment.[32]

Corporate bonds

Corporate bonds are standardised securities that finance the balance sheets of corporations (OECD, 2015[29]). Like direct investment in listed equities that are issued by private companies, corporate bonds are a way for companies to access cash during crunch times. Purchasing such bonds is one way pension providers can support businesses, as long as such investments are likely to yield returns and are in line with their investment strategy. Most have inflation-linked payments. Instead of bearing the risks of an individual project, corporate bonds' investors bear the risk of the issuing corporate entity. Thus credit-worthiness is determined by an issuer's general ability to service the debt, making them less risky than project bonds (discussed below) (OECD, 2015[29]). Corporate bonds have broad appeal to institutional investors. They tend to have long-term tenors, allowing borrowers to gain access to long-term financing. As such, they are core holdings in most investment portfolios and provide an alternative to lower-yielding government bonds.

Pension providers can also access bonds issued by SMEs, especially through private placements and bond funds. Public corporate bond markets are not well suited for smaller SMEs. This is because the costs related to reporting requirements associated with bond issuance together with the cost of obtaining a credit rating are disproportionately high for SMEs when compared to the overall size of the average deal. Thus, this market is suited mostly to the upper segment of the SME size spectrum (OECD, 2015[6]). Private placements offer an alternative to public corporate bond issuance, as they do not require a formal credit rating or reporting requirements. Privately placed bonds are negotiated and placed with a small number of mostly institutional investors in countries where a framework for such instruments exists (e.g. France, Germany and the United States). In theory, privately placed bonds can cater to the needs of small issuers, as there is no minimum size limit. In practice, however, the instrument still serves the upper end of the SME size spectrum, according to market observers (OECD, 2015[6]). Finally, SME bond funds are collective investment schemes that pool together bonds issued by SMEs (public or private placement). Such funds address the scale problem that constrains institutional investors' appetite for SME bonds and allow further diversification by pooling the bonds together (WBG, IMF and OECD, 2015[30]).

Listed equities

Pension providers could help mitigate the impact of the COVID-19 pandemic on businesses by investing in listed equities such as those of companies particularly affected by the downturn. The crisis has prompted many companies to issue new stock to raise money amid a cash crunch. If purchasing shares in such companies is in line with pension providers' investment strategy, and if they expect returns on the investment, investing in such securities is one way pension providers can support businesses. In recent years, new investment vehicles such as index funds have been created for those not able or willing to make their own investment.

Although listed equities are mostly issued by large companies, pension providers can also invest in equities issued by some SMEs. Public equity markets are better suited to high-growth, innovative SMEs, where unpredictable cash flows and lack of track record renders bank lending difficult. Some countries have also developed specialised SME equity platforms, or growth markets, targeting smaller issuers as an alternative to main exchange listings. Such exchanges seek to alleviate the burden and cost of regulatory compliance that may deter SMEs from listing. The lighter requirements apply to performance, disclosure and governance to cater to SMEs' inherent characteristics (OECD, 2015[6]).

Private equity investment

Pension providers could use private equity to purchase the illiquid equity securities of operating companies, always bearing in mind the requirements for strong governance, well-defined investment policies and sound risk-management strategies. Such instruments are particularly relevant for SME financing, especially for start-ups, technology-based companies and those with exceptionally high growth prospects. The equity is not publicly traded. In exchange for their capital, private equity investors take ownership stakes in the companies. Private equity investors typically hold these securities for a period of three to seven years with the expectation of generating attractive risk-adjusted financial returns upon exiting the investment. Private equity investment encompasses various stages of investment, such as venture capital in early-stage companies (e.g. start-ups), growth equity in more established companies looking for expansion capital, or buyouts in the latter stages of a company's growth. However, a key deterrent to investing in such securities is the lack of transparency around these arrangements, which can make it difficult for pension providers to conduct a thorough analytical process to inform investment decisions.

SME loan securitisation

SME loan securitisation offers pension providers the possibility to indirectly finance SMEs. It consists of the transformation of SME loans, which are illiquid in nature, into tradable securities that institutional investors can buy.[33] Through securitisation, a bank or SME lender bundles a package of SME loans into a pool ("portfolio") and sells the portfolio to capital market investors through the issuance of securities by a special purpose vehicle (SPV). The securities are backed by the loan portfolio (The World Bank Group, 2020[31]).

There are several benefits of using SME loan securitisation, for both SMEs and pension providers (OECD, 2015[6]). SME loan securitisation allows banks to partially transfer credit risk to the market while achieving capital relief. As a result, capital is freed up and can potentially generate additional loans to SMEs. Pension providers can diversify their investment portfolios and get exposure to the SME asset class, while still achieving potentially attractive returns, in line with their investment objective. Indeed, investors can select in which tranche of the loan to invest depending on their risk profile.[34]

SME covered bonds

Similarly to loan securitisation, covered bonds provide pension providers with an indirect tool to finance SMEs. Covered bonds are debt securities issued by a credit institution that are backed by a dynamic cover pool of high quality assets (WBG, IMF and OECD, 2015[30]). Investors have double recourse to the issuer and to the cover pool. So, unlike with loan securitisation, covered bonds remain on the balance sheet of the bank. This feature creates asset encumbrance and limits the issuance of covered bonds as compared to loan securitisation. However, one advantage of the covered bond system is the high quality of the "cover pool", which is based on strict standards imposed by regulations. In particular, such standards include precise definitions of eligible collateral. This helps to ensure the homogeneity of the cover pool and the quality of the underlying loans. This allows pension providers to invest in the asset without the need for extensive due diligence on the underlying assets.

Insurance linked securities

Insurance-linked securities, such as catastrophe bonds, are debt instruments issued to fund a special-purpose entity that assumes insurance risk. Under such instruments, the proceeds from a bond sale are placed in the special purpose entity to back the assumed risk and generate a market and risk return. The occurrence of catastrophe events that exceed a pre-defined trigger leads to a pay-out of some or all of the proceeds from the bond to the issuer.[35] Pension funds are important investors in insurance-linked securities which usually provide exposure to a risk that is not correlated with financial market performance. According to one estimate, pension funds from around the world have invested more than USD 22 billion in insurance-linked securities since 2006.[36] Insurance-linked securities provide an important source of capital for the insurance sector (as reinsurance and retrocession capacity) which supports the ability of the insurance sector to assume risk from policyholders.

The COVID-19 crisis has accelerated the shift to a "hard market cycle" for insurance and reinsurance coverage – that is, higher prices and lower coverage limits for policyholders. It has also brought to light a significant gap in insurance coverage for the revenue losses faced by businesses forced to close or otherwise curtail their activities as a result of the public health measures implemented to slow the spread of the virus. The insurance-linked securities market has contributed to reducing insurance and reinsurance market cycles in the past (OECD, 2018[32]). And it could potentially play a similar role in the aftermath of the crisis. Additional investment in this market by pension funds could therefore support the economic recovery by contributing to lower insurance costs and contributing greater insurance availability, including for losses not currently covered in insurance markets.

5.4.2. Instruments to finance investments that promote economic growth

Pension providers can be key investors in asset classes aiming to promote economic growth and thus stimulate crisis-hit economies. Such investments are different to those that aim to address the immediate priorities in a crisis, as discussed above. Rather, there is already much discussion about sustainable and ESG investments, in real assets, projects, companies or funds and how they can help to create jobs or generate lasting productivity improvements to reinvigorate post-COVID-19 economies. Some pension fund investors have already indicated a willingness to participate in such efforts. For example, the Australian Institute of Superannuation Trustees (AIST) declared that it stands ready to invest in affordable housing in Australia, given the shortage of affordable housing in the country and the competitive returns that this asset class tends to deliver when properly structured (AIST, 2020[17]).

In this context, many countries have also discussed how alternative investments, particularly green infrastructure investments, will be a core part of the recovery. These views are in line with the OECD's calls for a sustainable, resilient recovery from the crisis with investments and projects that aim to "build back better". The significance of long-term sustainable investments in building resilience against future crises is also recognised (OECD, 2021[33]). The UK Government, for example, has pledged to invest in an infrastructure revolution including green projects as a way of lifting the economy out of the crisis.[37] Similarly, the French Government has announced a "big green recovery plan", with a post-COVID-19 economic stimulus package focussing on an "ecological transition" and "greening the economy". There is already significant discussion on the role that private capital will play in such efforts to mobilise investment in similar areas. And indeed, some pension funds have already indicated a willingness to participate in a greener recovery. For example, the London Pension Fund Authority has agreed to divest from fossil fuels and increase its green investments, in line with the city of London's pledge to finance green energy, buildings, transport and other investments to help it recover from the pandemic and tackle climate change.[38]

This section describes the vehicles that investors typically use to finance long-term investments that can have the effect of promoting economic growth. The investment vehicles include different forms of direct unlisted equity investment, listed equities, unlisted infrastructure funds, government, municipal and sub-sovereign bonds, project bonds, debt funds, and green bonds.

Direct unlisted equity investment

Direct unlisted equity investments are those which are made directly in stand-alone assets, bypassing fund managers (OECD, 2015[29]). Direct investment can give pension providers ownership and control over alternative asset classes such as infrastructure, real estate, and private equity. Only the largest investors can invest directly in such large-scale projects, making some pension providers good candidates to undertake these investments.

Canadian and Australian pension funds have pioneered direct investment in infrastructure in OECD countries, although direct investment is also growing in Europe. The OECD Annual Survey of Large Pension Funds and Public Pension Reserve Funds showed that Canada had two of the largest investors in infrastructure by investment size. The Canada Pension Plan Investment Board, for example, invested over USD 20 billion (7.5% of total investments) in unlisted infrastructure equity in 2017, and 99.8% was through direct investment or co-investment (OECD, 2019[4]). Australian pension funds have also been pioneers in the field since the early 1990s, and their financial industry coined the term "infrastructure as an asset class" (Inderst and Della Croce, 2013[34]). Unlike in Canada, the majority of unlisted infrastructure investment in Australia happens through unlisted infrastructure funds, but direct investment is growing. In 2017, three of the largest Australian superannuation funds, AustralianSuper, Hostplus, and CBUS, reported having invested 48.3%, 22.6%, and 10.6%, respectively, of their unlisted infrastructure investments as direct investment (OECD, 2019[4]). Some European pension funds have also started investing directly in infrastructure. The Dutch pension fund PGGM exemplifies this trend. It stated that it would increase its direct investment to reduce cost, to take control of decision making at the asset level, and to have assets that matched its liabilities in a way that seven-to-ten year unlisted infrastructure funds could not deliver (van de Brake, 2017[35]).

Despite its growth in some regions, direct investment poses challenges for many pension providers. Direct investment requires scale, good governance to oversee complex investment programmes, the organisational structure and compensation model to attract a talented in-house investment team, and long-term patient capital (The World Bank, 2017[19]). Some projects also require pension providers to engage in a competitive tender process, and it can be expensive, time-consuming and laborious to submit individual bids (Belt and Nimmo, 2013[15]).

Canadian pension funds are a good example of those who have these characteristics, making them the leading example of direct investing in alternative asset classes. Key characteristics include operating at arm's length from the government, and having large amounts of assets under management and therefore the scale to make direct investments. Other important characteristics are having highly diversified investment portfolios, and having an ability to attract and remunerate the talent they need (The World Bank, 2017[19]).[39] However, these Canadian pension funds tend to have good in-house investment teams given their scale, which can have a relatively high fixed cost that is often excessive to small and medium sized pension funds.

Direct unlisted equity investment through collaboration

Since direct unlisted equity investments can be quite large, in particular for infrastructure projects, it is becoming more common for institutions such as pension providers to pair up with other investors or even fund managers to collaborate for investment. Some pension providers collaborate to benefit from a better alignment of interest with other pension providers having common investment horizons, lower fees, get better control of the characteristics of the investment, pool local knowledge, and share risk (OECD, 2015[29]).

Collaboration can take many forms. It can involve co-investing on an ad-hoc basis, such as alongside a general partner, with the pension provider being the limited partner. Alternatively, pension providers can form a joint owned fund manager or an investment instrument.

Some pension providers enter into co-investments with partner investors on an ad-hoc basis. That is, they enter into the agreements without entering into a formalised permanent collaboration vehicle. The California Public Employees' Retirement System (CalPERS) is an example of a pension fund with extensive experience with the use of co-investments. It has historically teamed up with a number of different investment manager general partners for its private equity investments.

Other models of collaboration include institutional investors jointly owning a fund manager. The UK's Pensions Infrastructure Platform (PIP) was set up by the UK's National Association of Pension Funds (now the Pensions and Lifetime Savings Association) to channel investment by UK pension funds into UK infrastructure. It is open to all UK pension schemes. Similarly, the Global Strategic Investment Alliance (GSIA), a global co-investment alliance platform, was launched in 2012 by the Ontario Municipal

Employees Retirement System (OMERS), one of Canada's largest pension funds. The GSIA was designed to gather like-minded investors (mainly pension funds) to directly invest in infrastructure assets. An example from Australia is IFM Investors, which is owned by 27 pension funds and other investors and has an independent investment board. The initiative has been broadly successful and has amassed a significant portfolio of assets worth AUD 140.4 billion in June 2019. Its success also comes from its ability to pool a common risk appetite and invest in a variety of deals, allowing for diversification and more stable long-term returns. IFM was also able to overcome the costs of the competitive bidding process, since the cost of each unsuccessful bid was spread over a large number of participants (Belt and Nimmo, 2013[15]).

Another interesting model of pension funds' collaboration is the syndicated model developed by the Canada Pension Plan Investment Board (CPPIB) and the Ontario Teachers' Pension Plan (OTPP). The model involves a large institutional investor taking the lead by investing directly in a project. Then, the lead investor creates an option for others to opt in by structuring a vehicle and setting a minimum investment requirement for additional investors. This allows larger investors, who tend to have greater capacity to lead an investment process in larger, and therefore less competitive projects, to do so without necessarily investing on their own (Belt and Nimmo, 2013[15]). Subsequent investors then share the lead investor's costs proportionately. The approach is a good way for smaller investors to access direct investments while circumventing infrastructure funds. However, each investor still needs to do their own due diligence, which some smaller investors may not be capable of.

More recently there have been examples of pension funds owning companies themselves, such as infrastructure companies. Polhem Infra is a Swedish company founded in 2019 and is jointly owned by the AP Funds, which manage funded capital in the income-based pension system in Sweden. Polhem Infra's focus is direct investment in unlisted Swedish or Nordic infrastructure companies in the private and public sectors. As another example, Globalvia, a transportation infrastructure developer, is 40.8% owned by the Netherlands' PGGM, 40.3% owned by Canada's OPTrust, and 18.9% owned by Britain's USS. It oversees a portfolio of highway and railway projects across Europe and the Americas.

Hybrid forms of direct unlisted equity investment through regulated structures

Some other countries use hybrid forms of domestic unlisted equity investment through regulated structures. In Namibia, the supervisory authority NAMFISA, recently devised Regulation 29, requiring all pension funds to invest in unlisted Namibian companies through regulated vehicles (The World Bank Group, 2020[36]). The supervisor also introduced a high level of regulatory oversight for investment managers and investment vehicles (special purpose vehicles, SPV). Regulation 29 established a compulsory allocation to unlisted assets with a minimum of 1.75% and a maximum of 3.5% of assets under management. Pension funds have to invest directly through SPVs, rather than directly investing via asset managers. While requiring investments in certain asset classes is not in line with the *OECD Core Principles of Private Pension Regulation*, the World Bank notes that the small percentage of required direct investments made it possible for them to be accommodated within existing investment strategies (The World Bank Group, 2020[36]).

Another example of investment through regulated structures is how the Mexican system allows investment in alternative assets. Mexican pension funds can currently invest in alternative assets through Development Capital Certificates (CKD), Investment Project Certificates (CERPI), Real Estate Investment Trusts (*Fideicomiso de Infraestructura en Bienes Raíces*, FIBRA) and Infrastructure Investment Trusts (FIBRA-E). CKDs are investment trusts that issue securities for obtaining resources destined for financing one or more projects, or for the acquisition of one or more companies. The securities grant their holders the right to participate in the revenues the asset generates and give the holders equity rights. A seat is provided in the technical or investment committees of the CKD for every 10% held. The CERPIs emerged in 2016 to complement CKDs. The difference between the two is that the CERPIs do not require the approval of the Technical Committee or the Certificate Holders' Meeting to make investments. This gives the general partner greater flexibility. In 2018, 8% of pension administrators' portfolios were held in CKDs and CERPIs. Over the years, these structures' availability has led to an increase in infrastructure investment and a reduction in exposure to government debt (FIAP, 2018[20]). FIBRAs are owners of diversified real estate portfolios that they rent and manage. The products are distributed among the investors as dividend pay-outs. Investors buy a certificate acquiring part of the equity of the FIBRA, which comes with administrative rights (votes) and economic benefits such as dividends (Poó Rubio, Rocha Chíu and Lara Poó, 2020[37]). FIBRA-Es are investment vehicles similar to FIBRAs, except they allow sponsors to securitise energy or infrastructure projects.

Unlisted infrastructure funds

Unlisted infrastructure funds are structures like private equity funds, which invest by constructing a portfolio of investments and charging fees to investors. Most unlisted infrastructure funds are traditional closed-end private equity type fund structures, managed by the general partner of the fund (GP), often an investment bank or investment management firm. Institutional investors like pension providers participate in unlisted infrastructure funds as limited partners (LPs). The GP invests capital commitments to the fund in various infrastructure assets on behalf of the LPs, selecting assets and managing the day to day operations of the fund.

A key shortcoming of infrastructure funds is that the lifespan of the vehicle they offer is often too short term (often 5-10 years), which some pension providers may view as a misalignment of interests. Pension providers have also criticised them for charging high fees. This has motivated some larger pension providers to invest directly. However, the vehicle remains relevant for smaller pension providers and those lacking the scale or capability to engage in investments directly. Its primary benefit remains that it allows pension providers to access diversified pools of infrastructure assets without having to build in-house investment expertise or make large capital commitments (Belt and Nimmo, 2013[15]).

Notwithstanding the shortcomings, unlisted infrastructure funds remain the preferred mode of investment in infrastructure in many parts of the world, like in Europe. Investments in unlisted infrastructure funds accounted for 61.8% of total investments in infrastructure assets of the pension funds surveyed by the OECD.[40] In addition, funds based in Europe, particularly those based in Spain, Ireland, Germany, and the Netherlands tended to use funds rather than direct investment (OECD, 2019[4]). Australian superannuation funds, on the other hand, tended to use a mix of investment funds and direct/co-direct investments, with a slight tilt toward investment funds. Examples of large unlisted infrastructure funds are those offered by Macquarie Infrastructure and Real Assets, which partners with more than 650 pension funds, sovereign wealth funds, and insurance companies to manage their long-term savings (Macquarie, 2020[38]). Its largest funds include the Macquarie European Infrastructure Fund II, Macquarie Infrastructure Partners, and Macquarie European Infrastructure Fund IV.

Listed equities

Investing in listed securities is also one of the simplest ways pension providers can get exposure to long-term asset classes. Investors can buy a stake in publicly listed companies that operate in particular sectors such as infrastructure or real estate or buy shares in publicly listed funds investing in those asset classes. Alternatively, pension providers can invest in listed funds traded on a stock exchange. Listed funds are similar to unlisted funds in that an external manager invests on behalf of investors in various assets. While the fund is publically listed, the assets invested in by the fund may or may not be listed (OECD, 2014[23]). The model makes it possible for both retail and institutional investors to gain exposure to these assets. However, these financial products lost some favour after the global financial crisis, due to revelations of high levels of debt and investors having to pay inflated fees (OECD, 2014[23]).

Listed indexed funds are another way pension providers can gain exposure to long-term assets. Such funds track the performance of listed companies in the asset classes that are available in established stock-market indices. They allow for passive asset management. Examples include the S&P Global Infrastructure Index and the MSCI Core Real Estate Index. However, a shortcoming of such indices is that it is not always clear how a particular asset class is defined and whether the index reflects the true exposure that investors seek (OECD, 2014[23]).

Investments in shares in listed companies and funds have pros and cons. They deliver greater liquidity than other investment vehicles and can make it possible to diversify across geographical regions and sectors. However, a key disadvantage of these approaches to investment is that doing so might lack the benefits that are most desirable for pension providers' infrastructure investments. Namely, publically listed companies may have a higher correlation with pension providers' existing equity investments, making the portfolio less diversified (Belt and Nimmo, 2013[15]).

Government, municipal, and other sub-sovereign bonds

Government, municipal, and other sub-sovereign bonds are bonds issued by public entities in capital markets in order to finance the construction and operation of an infrastructure asset. Issues are sponsored by federal governments, local governments and sub-sovereign entities such as government agencies and multi-lateral development banks that bear an implicit backing of the sovereign entity (OECD, 2015[29]).

There are two main types of government and municipal bonds: revenue bonds, which are payable from specific project-related revenues, and general obligation bonds, which are paid from general appropriations. Since general obligation bonds are linked to the creditworthiness of the borrower, rather than the infrastructure asset, they may not be considered infrastructure finance (OECD, 2015[29]). On the other hand, payments from revenue bonds are directly linked to an infrastructure project, so they are treated as a market-based instrument to finance infrastructure and do not contribute to public deficits (OECD, 2015[29]). Municipal bonds typically have lower interest rates than comparable corporate bonds (Chan et al., 2009[39]).

Revenue bonds are sold directly to investors through fixed income markets, have long maturities, and are rated by major rating agencies. Their long-dated maturities and high credit quality make them good instruments to assist in pension providers' liability driven investments and duration hedging. This type of borrowing is common in North America, where revenue bonds are one of the main sources of debt financing of public infrastructure (Chan et al., 2009[39]). In the United States, they are mainly issued by quasi-government authorities, cities, towns, districts, and local authorities. The favourable tax treatment of municipal debt instruments in the United States has contributed significantly to their growth.[41]

Project bonds

Project bonds are standardised securities that finance individual stand-alone infrastructure projects. They can be issued in public markets, or placed privately. Project bonds are a growing area of project finance and provide a potential solution to finance brownfield projects with long-term debt. Project bonds can be more risky than corporate bonds, because the risk of loss can be higher for a specific project compared with a diversified portfolio of projects (OECD, 2015[29]).

Project bonds are set up by a project company's special purpose vehicle (SPV). The SPV is a distinct legal entity which is formed as part of the project finance procurement process. Project bonds most commonly cover the operational phase of the project, which is when the project starts to generate a cash flow (rather than the construction phase). The project bond can be a straight bond, whose creditworthiness is linked directly to the cash flow performance of the SPV, or it can carry credit-enhancement mechanisms. Until the global financial crisis when the model collapsed, the most common credit-enhancement mechanism was mono-line insurance.[42]

There are a number of examples of pension funds investing in project bonds, especially in Latin American countries such as Chile, Colombia and Peru. Many of the project bonds used to be wrapped by mono-line insurance. However, there have also been newer cases of project bonds with guarantees. For example, Chile has issued government-guaranteed revenue floors for transportation infrastructure with revenues relying on use through tolls. They offered either a total guaranteed revenue (where the present value of revenue was guaranteed) or a minimum guaranteed revenue (where, if revenue is below a pre-agreed fixed threshold, the government makes up for the shortfall) (Credit Agricole, 2018[40]). To illustrate, the rehabilitation of the Ruta 5 highway project involved a pre-agreed revenue stream paid directly by the Chilean Government in the event that revenues from toll collections are below a pre-agreed minimum (Credit Agricole, 2018[40]).

Debt funds

Pension providers can provide financing to real asset and ESG investment projects through debt funds, which are now an alternative to traditional debt from banks. Project finance is a long-term loan structure where the project's cash flows repay a loan. In recent years, banks have reduced their lending appetite due to increased capital constraints and regulatory restrictions (Rothschild&Co, 2020[41]). Debt funds are investment vehicles created as mutual funds or non-banking financial companies that give investors exposure to debt markets for investments in asset classes such as infrastructure or real estate. They are a way of investing in assets that are relatively safe but generally offer higher yields than corporate bonds. They are also an opportunity to invest in senior debt over equity (OECD, 2014[23]). Debt funds pool lenders, lowering each investor's risk compared with direct lending. Although the market for debt funds is still small compared with private debt in some places (like Europe), recent years have seen significant growth.[43]

Debt funds are increasingly trying to attract assets from pension providers. Schroders recently announced that it would launch a UK-dedicated infrastructure debt fund, with a focus on UK pension funds and insurance companies. The fund aims to target junior loans in the transport, energy, environmental, social infrastructure and telecoms sectors to find higher yielding opportunities (Schroders, 2020[42]). Similarly, Macquarie's infrastructure debt platform recently raised EUR 2.95 billion predominantly from UK corporate pension funds, local pension schemes and insurance companies.[44] The fund stated that it attracted maturing defined benefit schemes and insurance companies who aimed to increase their exposure to inflation-linked infrastructure debt to better match their liabilities. Investors had also been attracted to the prospect of higher returns and the lower risk profile of the asset class when compared to corporate debt. UBS Asset Management has also launched its second infrastructure debt fund with EUR 448.4 million of seed commitments from insurance companies and pension funds from nine investors spread across five European countries and Japan.[45] Brunswick Real Estate secured investments from Norway's largest pension company, KLP, in its real estate debt fund focussing on sustainable property development. Similarly, real estate debt funds managed by entities such as ICG-Longbow and Allianz Real Estate have increasingly reached out to pension funds to join their investment vehicles.[46]

Green bonds

Green bonds are a subset of corporate bonds, project bonds, and sub-sovereign bonds that finance investment in green assets such as clean energy. Green bonds can be originated through development banks, governments, municipalities, corporations, banks (as covered bonds) or by SPVs as project finance and asset backed instruments (OECD, 2015[29]). In general, proceeds can go toward new or existing projects that are meant to have positive environmental or climate impacts. From a financial markets perspective, green bonds are not different from other project bonds or debt instruments. However, green bonds are sometimes treated differently due to their growing appeal and potential role in financing clean energy and climate change initiatives.

The OECD Annual Survey of Large Pension Funds and Public Pension Reserve Funds showed a growing number reported allocations to green investments. Funds based in Europe, namely Belgium and Sweden, reported the largest allocations to green bonds (OECD, 2019[4]). Green bonds are becoming increasingly relevant as some governments around the world have committed to the idea of building back better or even building back greener.

5.5. Policy implications for pension providers and policy makers

As economies around the world grapple to emerge from the recent economic and health crisis, there are growing calls for greater private investment to help fuel a recovery. Pension providers, i.e. pension funds, as well as insurance companies, banks and investment managers operating in asset-backed pension systems, are potential candidates to invest funds earmarked for retirement in such a way that helps the economy.

Pension providers can play a role to further support the economy given that they already invest significantly in businesses. Investments in equities and corporate bonds directly finance companies and represent the main vehicles through which pension providers invest in the economy. In addition, pension providers can invest directly or indirectly in instruments to finance SMEs. Finally, investment in long-term assets and ESG investment opportunities is likely to play an important role in financing the post-COVID-19 economic recovery, and pension providers are natural investors in illiquid assets due to their long-term investment horizon.

However, several obstacles and new risks may impede greater involvement by pension providers in supporting the economy. Lack of investment opportunities, regulatory barriers and limited investor capability to handle complex investments are general obstacles to investing in businesses and recovery projects, in particular infrastructure. New risks and uncertainties have also emerged with the COVID-19 crisis. There may be calls on pension providers to invest in companies or projects that may generate poor returns. Pension providers may also deviate from their strategic asset allocation to seize investment opportunities. Finally, measures taken by governments to provide relief to plan members during the crisis increase the need for liquidity and may reduce room for investment in illiquid assets.

Strong governance and appropriate investment strategies are essential to ensure that pension providers invest in the best interest of members. Pension providers should invest in projects to support the economy as long as they do not generate lower returns relative to other investment opportunities with the same risk profile, and they do not unduly increase the overall risk in the portfolio. Ensuring the accountability and suitability of the governing body of pension providers, defining an appropriate investment policy, designing a sound risk management strategy and having appropriate investment regulations can all contribute to safeguarding members' assets while investing them in businesses and recovery projects.

Moreover, policy makers can take steps to ensure that suitable investment opportunities are available to pension providers. Public authorities can facilitate the mobilisation of private capital towards long-term investment by setting up PPPs, providing financial incentives and promoting special vehicles for investment in alternative assets.

Finally, pension providers can only invest in a way that supports businesses, promotes economic growth, stimulating a recovery, and supporting ESG objectives if appropriate market structures are in place. Pension providers can direct financing to support entities and initiatives that address immediate financing needs, but they can also be involved in investments aimed at stimulating an economic recovery as countries emerge from the crisis. To do so they can use different channels, financial structures and instruments. They can invest in COVID-19 bonds that channel funds towards key expenditure programmes. They can also provide direct support to businesses affected by the pandemic through corporate bonds, listed equities, private equity, SME loan securitisation and SME covered bonds. But pension providers can also play a role in investing in a way that generates long-term economic growth after the crisis, including ESG opportunities. The vehicles that investors typically use to finance long-term investments include direct unlisted equity (whether alone, through collaborative arrangements, or other hybrid forms); listed equities; unlisted infrastructure funds; government, municipal or sub-sovereign bonds; project bonds; debt funds; and green bonds.

A number of policy implications can be derived from the analysis, for both pension providers and policy makers, to make sure that pension providers can play an active role in supporting the economy during and in the aftermath of the COVID-19 crisis. At the same time, these investments should ensure the protection of members and their interests, compliance with investment rules, and the stability of pension providers. These considerations apply to any situation where pension providers can play a role in investing and supporting the economy like in sustainable investment and environmentally friendly programmes.

5.5.1. Implications for pension providers

Do not engage in investments that are beyond available assessment capabilities

Pension providers lacking the skills and expertise to appropriately assess the risks and potential rewards of new investment opportunities should not engage in those investments. There can be a temptation for pension providers to seize opportunities for new investments, particularly one-off private equity ventures, during the recovery. While such opportunities may offer promising returns, pension providers should scrutinise them with reference to the same risk assessment standard as any other investment. If the pension provider does not have the expertise to conduct such assessment for complex investments, then it should not pursue them.

Carefully assess new investment opportunities

Pension providers should take care when investing in distressed companies. They should only do so if they genuinely expect a return to normal for that company and have a fair degree of confidence in the future value for the investment. For instance, there can be legitimate cases for investment in firms that were investment grade prior to the crisis but were in sectors particularly affected by the downturn. Indeed, perceptions of short-term risk might skew investments' merits when in fact focus should be on long-term investment horizons. However, any such investments should be founded on a firm expectation that the company is capable of weathering the storm and generating long-term returns on investments.

Pension providers should also check that recovery projects are in line with their investment objective and fiduciary duty. Governments can have many different motivations for engaging in large-scale investments. They can have social, political, environmental or development reasons. Not all those motivations coincide with a value for money approach. In addition, infrastructure investments may be overvalued due to increased demand or because future returns are overestimated. As such, pension providers should take care to only engage in projects that are consistent with genuine returns to members.

Act in accordance with investment and risk-management strategies

Pension providers should stay the course of their investment strategy. All pension providers should have an investment policy establishing clear investment objectives consistent with their retirement income objective and liabilities. It is important that pension providers adhere to these investment objectives to be able to deliver on their promises. In particular, pension providers should maintain diversified investments, both domestically and globally. The uncertainty that comes with a pandemic brings new risks to consider when it comes to which jurisdictions or sectors to invest in, but also adds to the case for geographical diversification. Domestic investment should also be diversified across sectors. Pension providers should, however, remain agile in their asset allocation. As such, the investment policy may need to be reviewed to check whether adjustments are necessary given the new investment environment.

Pension providers should also stay the course of their investment risk management strategies, but potentially consider any additional risks stemming from the current crisis. Rules for analysing and selecting potential investments should not be changed on an ad-hoc basis. Pension providers should apply the existing investment analysis rules and due diligence standards. Investments should remain in line with investment objectives, the fund's desired risk-return profile, a pre-determined asset allocation strategy, liquidity needs, as well as risk management procedures. Sound risk management strategies allow pension providers to identify, measure and monitor all material risks related to investment. However, given the circumstances, pension providers may need to take extra care to consider added risks such as heightened credit and currency risk where relevant.

Explore opportunities for partnerships with issuers of investment instruments

The recent crisis has highlighted the benefits of greater collaboration between pension providers and issuers of investment instruments. Pension providers can establish longstanding partnerships with organisations such as development banks, which seek to attract financing from impact investors. Such partnerships can help better align the interests of organisations that aim to deliver financing solutions quickly (such as with the recent issuance of COVID-19 bonds) with pension providers' investment strategies. As an example, the Japan Government's Pension Investment Fund has entered into partnerships with the European Bank for Reconstruction and Development and the World Bank to strengthen their capital market co-operation and to better integrate ESG considerations in their investment strategy.[47]

5.5.2. Implications for policy makers

Ensure the independence of pension providers in their investment decisions

Governments should take any opportunity to reinforce the independence of entities managing people's retirement savings. By doing so, policy makers will avoid any perceptions of interference, including soft pressure, in what should be independent decisions by pension providers. If governments nudge pension providers into investments that eventually deliver poor returns, the population could blame both governments and pension providers for misusing their retirement savings in times of crisis. This could erode confidence in asset-backed pension systems, push members out of asset-backed pension arrangements and hurt retirement income adequacy.

Promote suitable investment vehicles

Policy makers could consider structural solutions to develop the market for investment vehicles, with a view to encouraging investments that help stimulate a post-COVID-19 economy. They could, for example, provide direct financial assistance to create investment funds aimed at investing in infrastructure assets. They could also promote greater pooling and collaboration between institutional investors in order to create institutions with sufficient scale to better analyse the available data and potentially explore new investments such as in infrastructure and SME financing markets.[48] Both solutions would help smaller pension providers to have access to a range of new asset classes.

Enhance the quality of data to assess investments

Policy makers could help pension providers gain access to better quality data to assess investments. Pension providers often view a lack of reliable data as a barrier to investing. While data challenges have tended to be a greater issue for more opaque investment classes like alternative assets, they can also be an impediment for pension providers to invest in newer instruments such as COVID-19 bonds. Government departments and research bodies can play a key role in collecting and disseminating data to help in this respect. Institutional investors could be encouraged to report their recent allocation to and performance of different assets following standardised classifications and methods.[49] Governments can also mandate requirements to provide information and data on key activities (Della Croce, 2011[16]). Alternatively, a third party, such as an independent private sector operator, could be responsible for collecting information, standardising how performance is measured and reported, and distributing it to potential investors (Inderst, 2009[43]).

Similarly, policy makers could set up and maintain central depositories of high quality, easily accessible and standardised information around SME creditworthiness. Information around the creditworthiness of SMEs is particularly important given the high heterogeneity of the SME sector. However, SME entrepreneurs may be less prone, willing or able to share sensitive risk information. In addition, sourcing and monitoring SME financing entails a significant fixed cost for market participants. Central credit registers and Data Warehouses, owned and operated by central banks or financial supervisors for example, could address this issue (OECD, 2015[6]).

Adjust investment regulations

Governments could relax investment restrictions that limit investment in less liquid assets. In line with the development of skills and experience in the investment team of pension providers, policy makers could gradually increase investment ceilings for private equity or alternative asset classes such as real estate and infrastructure. Risk-based regulation presents an alternative approach to quantitative investment limits. It does not impose hard restrictions on investment, but instead imposes a higher risk charge for investments with a higher level of risk, providing an incentive to better manage risks.

Regulations could also better account for the nature of different investments in solvency calculations for defined benefit plans.[50] There is sometimes a perception that infrastructure investment regulations do not fully account for the particular business model of infrastructure investment and their lower default and higher recovery rates as compared to more traditional investments in corporate loans and bonds (OECD, 2014[10]). Moreover, regulations that require market valuations for solvency calculations may discourage investment in infrastructure, which do not typically trade in a secondary market. As such, there can be a case for governments to adapt regulatory structures to account for the long-term nature of some asset classes, so that investments can better align with the purpose and objectives of a pension plan.

Enhance pension providers' capabilities to invest in different asset classes

Policy makers could improve the skills of members of the governing board of pension providers through targeted educational initiatives. In some cases, board members simply do not have the technical skills to assess complex investment decisions, and may not have any experience with some asset classes. As such, they may be reluctant to invest in something new, such as a COVID-19 bond or an SME covered bond. And indeed, it would not be appropriate for boards to make decisions on investments they do not fully understand. Specific training and education programmes for board members could boost their understanding of investments, so they could later on feel comfortable to engage with new instruments and asset classes.

Governing body members may alternatively choose to outsource investment decisions to external bodies, particularly if the board itself lacks the skills and knowledge to take certain new investment decisions. However, doing so should not absolve a governing body of responsibility for those decisions. Rather, they should again ensure they are capable of understanding advice from external parties and undertake due diligence processes in outsourcing arrangements. Again, training and education programs can help prepare governing bodies to oversee and approve any outsourced tasks, and undertake appropriate due diligence processes.

Promote a favourable environment for long-term investment

Governments should provide regulatory certainty to investors. Investors look at fundamental conditions when deciding where and how to invest. Their investments will likely outlive political cycles, and they require a high degree of certainty about government policy to feel safe in their investments. As such, clear and stable regulation, efficient procurement procedures, and practical support for projects such as certainty of timing are all important factors for investors that governments can help secure. Governments seeking to build investors' confidence in long-term investment could also provide clear evidence of independence in terms of their choice of projects for investment as well as any financial support they provide. A robust system of checks and balances by the legislature can also bolster trust in governments, building investors' confidence to invest in a jurisdiction.

Governments should also promote transparency when designing long-term projects. Some governments will invest in nation-building projects in an attempt to revive economies. Many of these projects will rely on PPPs. Where they do, governments should be transparent about the rationale for the project, the potential benefits to investors, risks, and uncertainties. Co-ordination between different financial regulators, central banks and ministries of finance can also further financial stability and better investment governance. Policy makers should provide as much information as possible for pension providers to make decisions about whether investments are in the best interests of members. This can include providing confidence intervals or probability curves for expectations around future returns, results of stress tests, etc. Notwithstanding, the timing and value of returns from large-scale sustainable investments are often very uncertain.

Ensure appropriate alternative investments are available and financially attractive

Governments could seek to better understand and account for institutional investors' desired risk and return profiles when selecting projects for which they seek private capital. Mismatches between the risk and return profiles that investors look for and the projects that are available have at times been a deterrent to investment by pension providers. The key way governments can influence the risk and return profile of investments is through the design of PPPs, which dictate how risks and profits are shared between the private and public sectors.[51] Governments should better account for the desired risk and return profiles of pension providers to ensure enough projects are available to encourage their participation. They could consult potential investors early in a project's life to facilitate private investment in long-term investments such as infrastructure. Large-scale investments can be optimised if representatives from the pensions industry act as partners when governments deliberate on the scope and financing of the investments. The Australian Institute of Superannuation Trustees believes that such early-stage consultation between governments and pension funds could overcome some of the barriers that currently limit the deployment of institutional capital for infrastructure projects (AIST, 2020[17]). However, they should also carefully assess how to balance the share of returns between the public and private sectors in PPP operations to avoid excessive risk taking by the public sector and moral hazard from the private sector.

Governments could also encourage direct private financing for alternative investments through effective subsidies, bearing in mind the trade-offs of doing so.[52] This can take the form of grants, contributions, guarantees, back-up liquidity facilities or tax relief. While government subsidies are useful to secure financing from private investors, including pension providers, they may also have a high fiscal cost over the medium to long term and should therefore be carefully assessed. Notwithstanding, financial public support is not the most relevant factor investors look at when deciding to allocate resources to infrastructure in a given country. Empirical evidence has shown that more important factors are a clear institutional framework, transparent bidding and awarding procedures, a robust rule of law, and the absence of political interference (OECD, 2014[10]).

Limit early access to retirement savings to promote long-term investing

Finally, policy makers should carefully consider the effect that policies granting early access to retirement savings accounts have on investment policies. Not only do such policies pose adequacy concerns, they also limit pension providers' capacities to invest in long-term, illiquid assets (OECD, 2020[44]; OECD,

2020[45]). Pension providers need to hold more cash and liquid assets to face potential withdrawal requests. This leaves less room for other illiquid investments that could support businesses and boost the economy.

Annex 5.A. Quantitative investment limits for pension funds

Annex Table 5.A.1. Quantitative investment limits in equities, corporate bonds, real estate, loans and private investment funds, selected OECD countries, 2019

As a percentage of total investment

	Equities	Corporate bonds	Real estate	Loans	Private investment funds
Chile	5% to 80% depending on the fund	3% to 30% depending on the fund	Alternative assets: 5% to 10% depending on the fund (e.g. syndicated loans, private equity, private debt, co-investment)	Alternative assets: 5% to 10% depending on the fund (e.g. syndicated loans, private equity, private debt, co-investment)	- Alternative assets: 5% to 10% depending on the fund (e.g. syndicated loans, private equity, private debt, co-investment) - Risky assets: 0% to 20% depending on the fund (not investment grade, illiquid and high-risk instruments)
Colombia	20% to 70% depending on the fund	- Securities issued by entities supervised by the FSC: 30% - Securities issued by entities not supervised by the FSC: 60%	0% to 25% depending on the fund	0%	- National private equity funds that invest 2/3 of the fund's value in infrastructure: 0% to 7% depending on the fund - National and foreign private equity funds not including infrastructure and real estate private equity funds: 0% to 15% depending on the fund Programmed Retirement Fund: - Alternative investments (local and foreign private equity funds, collective investment schemes that invest in real estate and REITs): 10% - Local and foreign private equity funds: 5% - Private equity funds that invest in infrastructure: 2%
Czech Republic	Transformed funds: - Equities traded on OECD regulated markets: 70% - Non-OECD equities: 5% Participating funds:	Transformed funds: - Bonds traded on OECD market: 70% - Bonds non-traded on OECD market: 5% Conservative	0% to 10% depending on the fund	0% to 5% depending on the fund	Transformed funds: - Private investment funds traded on OECD markets: 70% - Other private investment funds: 5% Participating funds

	Equities	Corporate bonds	Real estate	Loans	Private investment funds
	- Equities not traded on regulated market or multilateral trading facility verified by the CNB: 0%	participating funds: - Bonds with a rating among the best 5 rating categories: 30%			(excl. conservative): - Specialised investment funds:20% or 10% in securities that do not replicate the composition of a financial index, which may be the underlying of a derivative
Estonia	Conservative funds: 10%	Unlisted bonds: 50%	40% to 70% depending on the fund	10%	
Finland	Mandatory schemes - Equities and private investment funds: 65% Voluntary schemes - Listed equities: 50% - Unlisted equities: 10%	Voluntary schemes: - Bonds issued by companies on regulated OECD markets: 50% - Bonds issued by other companies: 10%		Voluntary schemes: - Mortgage loans (including investment in real estates and buildings): 70% - Subordinated loans: 10%	Mandatory schemes - Equities and private investment funds: 65% Voluntary schemes: - Non-listed private investment funds: 10%
France (pension funds)	Investments not traded in regulated markets: 30%	Bonds issued by special purpose vehicles: 5%	5% by real estate project or share on a real estate instrument	10%	
Germany (*Pensionskassen*)	- Listed equities: 35% - Unlisted equities: 15%	All bills and bonds issued by public and private sectors: 50%	25%	- Mortgage loans: 50% - Other loans: 50% - ABS/CLN and other securitisations: 7.5% - Loans to other undertakings domiciled in EEA or OECD countries if these loans are sufficiently secured by a property lien or under the law of obligations: 5%	- Alternative investment funds: 7.5% (e.g. hedge funds and commodity related risks) - Closed-end private equity funds: 15%
Greece	70%	70%	20%	0%	Private equity and financial derivatives: 5%
Hungary	Unlisted equities: 5%	10%	Real estate and real estate investment funds: 10%	0% to 5% depending on the fund	- Derivative fund: 5% - Risk capital: 5%
Iceland	60%	80%	60%		60%
Israel			15%	Commercial loans rated less than BBB- or non-rated: 5%	
Italy			Real estate funds: 20%	0%	Real estate funds, private investment funds and securities not traded in regulated markets: 30%
Korea	DB plans: - Listed equities: 70% - Unlisted equities: 0% DC plans:	- Bonds rated as investment grade BBB- or higher: 70% - Bonds rated below BBB-: 0%	DB plans: - REITs listed on regulated market: 70% DC plans: Real estate: 0%	0%	0% to 70% depending on the fund

	Equities	Corporate bonds	Real estate	Loans	Private investment funds
	- Equity investment through retail investment funds: 80%				
Latvia	Mandatory scheme: 75%	Unlisted bonds: 0%	0% to 15% depending on the fund	0%	Mandatory scheme: 15% (non-UCITS funds)
Lithuania	Pension asset preservation fund: 20%	Pension asset preservation fund: 30%	0%	0%	0% to 30% depending on the fund
Mexico	0% to 50% depending on the fund		0% to 10% indirect exposure depending on the fund	0%	Private equity funds: 0% to 20% according to the fund (CKDs and CERPIs)
Poland		OFE and PPE: 40%	0%	OFE and PPE: 1.5% PPK: 30%	0% to 10% depending on the fund
Slovak Republic	0% to 80% depending on the fund		Mandatory plans: - Mortgage bonds: 50% Voluntary plans: - Shares/units of special real-estate funds: 10%	0%	0%
Slovenia	Unlisted equities: 5%		20%		Venture capital funds: 1%
Spain	Securities not admitted to be traded on a regulated market: 30%	Securities not admitted to be traded on a regulated market: 30%	Real estate, mortgage loans and shares in real estate investment institutions: 30%	Real estate, mortgage loans and shares in real estate investment institutions: 30%	30%
Sweden	- Listed equities: 25% - Unlisted equities: 10%	Unlisted bonds: 10%		Unlisted loans: 10%	
Switzerland	50%		30%	Mortgage loans: 50%	Alternative investments: 15% (infrastructure, hedge funds, private equity, insurance linked securities and commodities)
Türkiye			Real estate funds, ETFs and private equity funds: 20%	Debt instruments and reverse repo: 10%	Real estate funds, ETFs and private equity funds: 20%

Notes: DB means defined benefit; DC means defined contribution.
Source: OECD Annual Survey of Investment Regulation of Pension Funds.

References

AIST (2020), *Profit-to-member funds' statement of intent to government about investing in Australia's economic recovery*, https://www.aist.asn.au/AIST/media/General/Media%20Releases/2020/PROFIT-TO-MEMBER-FUNDS-STATEMENT-OF-INTENT-TO-GOVERNMENT-ABOUT-INVESTING-IN-AUSTRALIA-S-ECONOMIC-RECOVERY.pdf. [17]

Belt, B. and J. Nimmo (2013), *Catalyzing Pension Fund Investment in the Nation's Infrastructure A Roundtable Discussion*, Milken Institute, https://assets1b.milkeninstitute.org/assets/Publication/ResearchReport/PDF/Pension-Funds-and-Infrastructure.pdf. [15]

Bpifrance (2020), *Bpifrance Financement: Covid-19 Response Bond Framework-Background and rationale for issuing Covid-19 Response Bonds*, https://www.bpifrance.fr/content/download/105407/935627/version/1/file/Bpifrance%20-%20Covid-19%20Response%20Bond%20Framework.pdf. [27]

CAF (2020), *CAF's Social Bond Framework*, https://www.caf.com/media/2678628/caf-s-social-bond-framework.pdf. [50]

Cassa depositi e prestiti (2020), *Press Release: CDP successfully launches a 1 billion euro dual-tranche "Covid-19 Social Response Bond"*, https://www.cdp.it/sitointernet/page/en/cdp_successfully_launches_a_1_billion_euro_dualtranche_covid19_social_response_bond?contentId=CSA27859 (accessed on 30 September 2020). [26]

Chan, C. et al. (2009), "Public Infrastructure Financing: An International Perspective", *Productivity Commission Staff Working Paper* March 2009, https://core.ac.uk/download/pdf/30685486.pdf. [39]

Credit Agricole (2018), *Project Bonds in Latin America*, https://www.ca-cib.com/sites/default/files/2018-11/Project%20Bond%20Focus%202018%20-%20Latin%20America%20_%20FINAL.PDF. [40]

Danmarks Nationalbank (2020), *More pension savings in unlisted assets*, https://www.nationalbanken.dk/en/statistics/find_statistics/Pages/2020/Insurance-and-pension-20200903.aspx (accessed on 8 September 2020). [8]

Della Croce, R. (2011), "Pension funds investment in infrastructure: Policy actions", *OECD Working Papers on Finance, Insurance and Private Pensions* 13, https://doi.org/10.1787/5kg272f9bnmx-en. [16]

European Commission (2020), *State aid: Commission approves Latvian fund to enable €100 million of liquidity and capital support to large enterprises affected by the coronavirus outbreak*, https://ec.europa.eu/commission/presscorner/detail/en/ip_20_1272. [25]

FIAP (2018), "Pension Fund Investment in alternative assets: Chile and Mexico", *Pension notes* 32, https://www.fiapinternacional.org/wp-content/uploads/2016/01/Pension-Note-No-32_Pension-Fund-Investment-in-alternative-assets_Dec.-2018.pdf. [20]

Hall, D. (2009), *Infrastructure, the crisis, and pension funds*, Public Services International Research Unit, https://core.ac.uk/download/pdf/67297.pdf. [47]

Hammami, M., J. Ruhashyankiko and E. Yehoue (2006), "Determinants of Public-Private Partnerships in Infrastructure", *IMF Working Paper* 06/99, https://www.imf.org/en/Publications/WP/Issues/2016/12/31/Determinants-of-Public-Private-Partnerships-in-Infrastructure-19086. [11]

Inderst, G. (2009), "Pension Fund Investment in Infrastructure", *OECD Working Papers on Insurance and Private Pensions* 32, https://doi.org/10.1787/227416754242. [43]

Inderst, G. and R. Della Croce (2013), "Pension Fund Investment in Infrastructure: A Comparison between Australia and Canada", *OECD Working Papers on Finance, Insurance and Private Pensions* 32, https://doi.org/10.1787/5k43f5dv3mhf-en. [34]

Jain, S. (2011), "Investing in Distressed Debt", *UBS Alternative Investments*, https://ssrn.com/abstract=1865378. [46]

Macquarie (2020), *Putting the world's long-term savings to work*, https://www.mirafunds.com/au/en/our-approach/our-funds.html. [38]

Nordic Investment Bank (2020), *NIB issues inaugural Response Bond*, https://www.nib.int/who_we_are/news_and_media/news_press_releases/3476/nib_issues_inaugural_response_bond. [51]

OECD (2022), *OECD Economic Outlook, Volume 2022 Issue 1*, OECD Publishing, Paris, https://doi.org/10.1787/62d0ca31-en. [53]

OECD (2021), *Artificial Intelligence, Machine Learning and Big Data in Finance*, https://www.oecd.org/finance/artificial-intelligence-machine-learning-big-data-in-finance.htm. [14]

OECD (2021), "COVID-19 and a new resilient infrastructure landscape", *OECD Policy Responses to Coronavirus (COVID-19)*, https://doi.org/10.1787/d40a19e3-en. [33]

OECD (2021), *News Release: OECD GDP growth Quarterly National Accounts*, https://www.oecd.org/sdd/na/GDP-Growth-Q420.pdf. [1]

OECD (2021), *OECD Economic Outlook, Volume 2021 Issue 2*, OECD Publishing, Paris, https://doi.org/10.1787/66c5ac2c-en. [2]

OECD (2020), "Building back better: A sustainable, resilient recovery after COVID-19", *OECD Policy Responses to Coronavirus (COVID-19)*, https://doi.org/10.1787/52b869f5-en. [7]

OECD (2020), "Coronavirus (COVID-19): SME policy responses", *OECD Policy Responses to Coronavirus (COVID-19)*, https://doi.org/10.1787/04440101-en. [5]

OECD (2020), *OECD Global Pension Statistics*, https://www.oecd.org/finance/private-pensions/globalpensionstatistics.htm. [3]

OECD (2020), "Retirement savings and old-age pensions in the time of COVID-19", in *OECD Pensions Outlook 2020*, OECD Publishing, Paris, https://doi.org/10.1787/67ede41b-en. [44]

OECD (2020), "Retirement savings in the time of COVID-19", *OECD Policy Responses to Coronavirus (COVID-19)*, https://doi.org/10.1787/b9740518-en. [45]

OECD (2019), *Annual Survey of Large Pension Funds and Public Pension Reserve Funds*, http://www.oecd.org/daf/fin/private-pensions/Survey-of-Large-Pension-Funds-2019.pdf. [4]

OECD (2018), *The Contribution of Reinsurance Markets to Managing Catastrophe Risk*, https://www.oecd.org/daf/fin/insurance/the-contribution-of-reinsurance-markets-to-managing-catastrophe-risk.htm (accessed on 9 December 2021). [32]

OECD (2016), *OECD Core Principles of Private Pension Regulation*, https://www.oecd.org/daf/fin/private-pensions/Core-Principles-Private-Pension-Regulation.pdf. [18]

OECD (2015), *Infrastructure Financing Instruments and Incentives*, http://www.oecd.org/finance/private-pensions/Infrastructure-Financing-Instruments-and-Incentives.pdf. [29]

OECD (2015), *Opportunities and constraints of market-based financing for SMEs, OECD report to G20 Finance Ministers and Central Bank Governors, September 2015*, https://www.oecd.org/finance/financial-markets/Opportunities-and-Constraints-of-Market-based-Financing-for-SMEs.pdf. [6]

OECD (2015), *Regulation of Insurance Company and Pension Fund Investment: OECD Report to the G20 Finance Ministers and Central Bank Governors*, https://www.oecd.org/g20/summits/antalya/Regulation-of-Insurance-Company-and-Pension-Fund-Investment.pdf. [21]

OECD (2014), *Pooling of Institutional Investors Capital - Selected Case Studies in Unlisted Equity Infrastructure*, https://www.oecd.org/finance/OECD-Pooling-Institutional-Investors-Capital-Unlisted-Equity-Infrastructure.pdf. [23]

OECD (2014), *Private financing and support to promote long-term investments in infrastructure*, https://www.oecd.org/daf/fin/private-pensions/Private-financing-and-government-support-to-promote-LTI-in-infrastructure.pdf. [10]

OECD/G20 (2013), *G20/OECD High Level Principles of Long-Term Investment Financing by Institutional Investors*, http://www.oecd.org/daf/fin/private-pensions/G20-OECD-High-Level-Principles-Long-Term-Investment-Financing-By-Institutional-Investors.pdf. [22]

Pedraza Morales, A. et al. (2017), "Pension funds and the impact of switching regulation on long-term investment", *IOPS Working Papers on Effective Pensions Supervision* 28, http://www.iopsweb.org/WP_28-Pension-Funds-Impact-Switching-Regulation-LTI.pdf. [12]

Peeters, S., M. Schmitt and A. Volk (2020), *Social Bonds Can Help Mitigate the Economic and Social Effects of the COVID-19 Crisis*, https://www.ifc.org/wps/wcm/connect/ec548185-5e62-4f34-86db-b4d92872cd8e/EMCompass-Note-89-Social-Bonds-COVID-19.pdf?MOD=AJPERES&CVID=ngSZy60 (accessed on 5 October 2020). [48]

Pfizer Inc. (2020), *Pfizer Completes $1.25 Billion Sustainability Bond for Social and Environmental Impact*, https://investors.pfizer.com/investor-news/press-release-details/2020/Pfizer-Completes-125-Billion-Sustainability-Bond-for-Social-and-Environmental-Impact/default.aspx. [28]

Poó Rubio, A., L. Rocha Chíu and V. Lara Poó (2020), *Real Estate Real Investment Trust in México*, https://doi.org/10.2139/ssrn.3558742. [37]

Prequin (2016), *The UK Infrastructure Market*, https://docs.preqin.com/reports/Preqin-UK-Infrastructure-Market-May-2016.pdf. [52]

Republic of Guatemala (2020), *Offering memorandum: US$700,000,000 6.125% Notes due 2050; US$500,000,000 5.375% Notes due 2032*, https://dcp-web.minfin.gob.gt/Sie_Abrir_Archivo.aspx?file=C:%5C%5CPublicaciones%5C%5CSistemas%5C%5CDCP-WEB%5C%5CDocumentos%5C%5COffering%5C%5COffering%20Circular%202020.pdf (accessed on 30 September 2020). [24]

Rothschild&Co (2020), *Wealth Management: Instant Insights – Syndicated and direct lending strategies*, https://www.rothschildandco.com/en/newsroom/insights/2020/02/syndicated-and-direct-lending-strategies/. [41]

Schroders (2020), *Schroders launches its first UK infrastructure debt fund*, http://State aid: Commission approves Latvian fund to enable €100 million of liquidity and capital support to large enterprises affected by the coronavirus outbreak. [42]

Severinson, C. and J. Yermo (2012), "The effect of solvency regulations and accounting standards on long-term investing: Implications for insurers and pension funds", *OECD Working Papers on Finance, Insurance and Private Pensions* 30, https://doi.org/10.1787/5k8xd1nm3d9n-en. [9]

Stańko, D. and B. Ásgrímsson (2017), "Supervision of pension investment management including non-traditional investment", *IOPS Working Papers on Effective Pensions Supervision* 29, http://www.iopsweb.org/WP_29_Supervision-Pension-Investment-Management.pdf. [13]

The World Bank (2020), *World Bank Raises Record-breaking USD8 Billion from Global Investors to Support its Member Countries*, https://www.worldbank.org/en/news/press-release/2020/04/15/world-bank-raises-record-breaking-usd8-billion-from-global-investors-to-support-its-member-countries. [49]

The World Bank (2017), *The Evolution of the Canadian Pension Model: Practical Lessons for Building World-class Pension Organizations*, http://documents1.worldbank.org/curated/en/780721510639698502/pdf/121375-The-Evolution-of-the-Canadian-Pension-Model-All-Pages-Final-Low-Res-9-10-2018.pdf. [19]

The World Bank Group (2020), *Capital markets and SMEs in emerging markets and developing economies: Can they go the distance?*, http://documents1.worldbank.org/curated/en/270221582271669731/pdf/Capital-Markets-and-SMEs-in-Emerging-Markets-and-Developing-Economies-Can-They-Go-the-Distance.pdf. [31]

The World Bank Group (2020), *Leveraging Pension Fund Investment for Domestic Development: Namibia's Regulation 29 Approach*, http://documents1.worldbank.org/curated/en/125241594367606090/pdf/Leveraging-Pension-Fund-Investment-for-Domestic-Development-Namibia-s-Regulation-29-Approach.pdf. [36]

van de Brake, E. (2017), *How PGGM's direct approach has helped shape the market*, https://www.pggm.nl/en/blogs/how-pggm-s-direct-approach-has-helped-shape-the-market/. [35]

WBG, IMF and OECD (2015), *Capital market instruments to mobilize institutional investors to infrastructure and SME financing in Emerging Market Economies, Report for the G20*, https://www.oecd.org/g20/topics/financing-for-investment/WB-IMF-OECD-report-Capital-Markets-Instruments-for-Infrastructure-and-SME-Financing.pdf. [30]

Notes

[1] Reserve funds may also invest their assets to support the economy, but their mandate is different from the one of pension providers, in particular because they do not have members. Although some of the discussion in this chapter is also relevant for reserve funds, they are mostly outside the scope of the analysis.

[2] However, many countries have been raising interest rates since the end of 2021 to contain inflation (OECD, 2022[53]).

[3] https://www.wsj.com/articles/investors-channel-over-150-billion-into-coronavirus-bonds-11591178004

[4] The look-through of collective investment schemes (CIS) is not available for all countries. Total equity investment may therefore exceed the 30% threshold for some other countries when counting the part of their CIS investment in equities.

[5] This does not include corporate bond investment through collective investment schemes.

[6] During the 2008 crisis, several pension funds invested in distressed debt, which are below investment grade obligations of issuers in weak financial conditions (see for example https://www.newyorkfed.org/education/talf101.html and (Jain, 2011[46])). However, there is no data to check whether those investments have paid off.

[7] Lack of certainty is one reason why investors have criticised private finance initiative (PFI) projects in the United Kingdom – investors have grown to mistrust PFIs at times, due to constant pressure to renegotiate or terminate contracts (Hall, 2009[47]).

[8] Section 5.4 presents arrangements that could make it easier and cheaper for such entities to assess and manage their risks.

[9] https://www.ft.com/content/d2f9d976-a730-4f9b-9c45-2da69f117142

[10] However, they may have to adjust their investment strategy to reflect new levels of cash flows.

[11] This measure was initially supposed to last for three months, but was further extended for another three months until 17 September 2020.

[12] See http://www.oecd.org/pensions/private-pensions/46864889.pdf

[13] Subsequently, in October 2017, the Pensions Commission issued regulations that finally allowed pension funds to invest in these kinds of instruments.

[14] The least conservative fund (fund A) may now invest 13% in alternatives, up from the previous limit of 10%, set in 2017. Fund B's alternatives exposure was increased from 8% to 11%; fund C from 6% to 9%; and fund D from 5% to 6%. The investment limit for fund E, the most conservative fund, was maintained at 5%.

[15] Some jurisdictions may also not have (fully) implemented risk-based capital requirements for pension funds because of existing security mechanisms, such as sponsor support and pension protection schemes.

[16] Although some infrastructure projects are purely private transactions (particularly in the energy sector), PPPs are still the dominant type of infrastructure project.

[17] However, there is some evidence showing that in some cases higher public sector involvement has led private investors to perceive a risk of political interference in the project (OECD, 2014[10]).

[18] Build America Bonds were taxable municipal bonds that featured federal tax credits or subsidies for bondholders or state and local government bond issuers. Build America Bonds were introduced in 2009 as part of the American Recovery and Reinvestment Act with the goal of creating jobs and stimulating the economy. The Build America Bonds programme expired in 2010.

[19] Peeters, Schmitt and Volk (2020[48]) and https://www.ai-cio.com/news/pandemic-spurs-investor-interest-social-bonds/

[20] https://esgclarity.com/COVID-19-fuels-social-bond-issuance-will-they-overtake-green-bonds-in-2020/

[21] The four core Social Bond Principles are: use of proceeds; process for project evaluation and selection; management of proceeds; and reporting.

[22] https://www.icmagroup.org/assets/documents/Regulatory/Green-Bonds/Social-Bonds-Covid-QA310320.pdf.

[23] The World Bank issued a USD 8 billion 5-year global benchmark bond aimed at financing sustainable development projects and programmes, including member countries' efforts to prevent, detect, and respond to the rapid spread of COVID-19 (The World Bank, 2020[49]). The International Finance Corporation has issued a USD 1 billion 3-year social bond that aims to support the private sector and jobs in developing countries affected by COVID-19 outbreak. The European Investment Bank has issued a EUR 1 billion Sustainability Awareness Bond which aimed to alleviate the social consequences of COVID-19 by financing health care systems and labour market solutions. The Development Bank of Latin America (*Corporación Andina de Fomento*, CAF), issued a EUR 700 million 5-year COVID-19 Response social bond to support its member countries' COVID-19-related relief and recovery costs. The proceeds will be allocated to health care systems and emergency economic support to tackle the COVID-19 crisis (CAF, 2020[50]). The Nordic Investment Bank (NIB) has issued a EUR 1 billion Response Bond. It aims to use the proceeds of the bond to finance projects that alleviate the social and economic consequences of the COVID-19 pandemic in NIB's member countries. It is mainly focussed on promoting the efficient operation of health care systems and provides financial support and labour market solutions to alleviate supply chain frictions (Nordic Investment Bank, 2020[51]). The African Development Bank has issued a USD 3 billion social bond called the Fight COVID-19 Social bond. It was aimed at lessening the severe economic and social impact on countries and companies in Africa's group members. This includes the financing of access to health and essential goods, services and infrastructure. The *Caisse Française de Financement Local* (CAFFIL), a French public development bank, issued a 5-year covered bond aiming to directly or indirectly fund sectors affected by the pandemic.

[24]https://www.ipe.com/news/nordic-duo-invests-in-world-banks-1bn-COVID-19-linked-bond-issue/10045104.article

[25]https://www.europeanpensions.net/ep/Skandia-invests-SEK-450m-to-fight-against-COVID-19.php

[26] It should be noted that there are still no market practices to guide issuers and investors on COVID-19 bonds, unlike the frameworks that exist for bonds like social bonds and green bonds. While some COVID-19 bonds might fall within the ambit of social bonds, this is not necessarily the case. As such,

potential purchasers may not be able to accept the label at face value and instead analyse bond issuances on a case-by-case basis.

27 https://www.ipe.com/news/pension-funds-and-the-eus-inaugural-sure-bonds/10048538.article?utm_campaign=159245_22.10.20%20ipe%20daily%20news&utm_medium=email&utm_source=IPE&dm_i=5KVE,3EVH,C5K8L,DP39,1

28 https://www.europeanpensions.net/ep/ABP-increases-investments-in-corona-bonds-to-470m.php

29 https://www.japantimes.co.jp/news/2020/08/25/business/financial-markets/mufg-COVID-19-bonds/

30 https://www.nasdaq.com/articles/kookmin-bank-prints-koreas-first-COVID-19-bond-2020-04-24

31 https://www.ft.com/content/03dbe400-1bea-4475-bda7-2fbc1d9ce062

32 https://news.getinge.com/us/getinge-issues-sek-1-billion-COVID-19-commercial-paper

33 Pension funds in some jurisdictions can also provide loans directly to companies, including SMEs. Minimum credit ratings may be required, such as in Israel (Annex Table 5.A.1 in the Annex).

34 Pension providers may get a credit rating agency to provide some risk analysis, thereby avoiding the need for direct communication with the SME. Alternatively, if they do not want to rely on credit rating agencies, they need to run all the data analysis of the underlying loans in-house, provided that data are available.

35 A trigger could be an indemnity trigger based on the cedant's losses or a non-indemnity trigger based on a loss index, modelled loss estimate or the parameters of the event

36 https://www.artemis.bm/pension-funds-investing-in-insurance-linked-securities-ils/

37 https://www.gov.uk/government/speeches/pm-economy-speech-30-june-2020

38 https://uk.reuters.com/article/global-cities-investment-climatechange/cities-promise-to-divest-from-fossil-fuels-to-boost-green-recovery-idUSL5N2GJ2TM

39 The World Bank study looks at four Canadian pension funds and finds that exceeding USD 15 billion allows them to make direct investments.

40 See also Prequin (2016[52]).

41 Income from investing in municipal bonds is generally exempt from Federal and state taxes for residents of the issuing state. While the interest income is tax-exempt, any capital gains distributed are taxable to the investor.

42 Mono-line insurance is a credit-enhancement mechanism that was common prior to the onset of the global financial crisis. A wrapped bond bears the credit rating of the mono-line insurer. For instance, an insurer with a AAA rating would confer a AAA rating on a wrapped bond.

43 https://realassets.ipe.com/infrastructure/infrastructure-debt-funds-come-of-age/10043408.article

44 https://realassets.ipe.com/news/macquarie-pulls-27bn-for-uk-infrastructure-debt-strategy/10046404.article

[45]https://realassets.ipe.com/news/pension-funds-insurers-back-ubs-ams-new-infrastructure-debt-fund/10023733.article

[46]https://realassets.ipe.com/news/icg-longbow-raises-500m-for-uk-senior-real-estate-debt-fund/10043149.article

https://realassets.ipe.com/news/bvk-becomes-first-third-party-investor-in-allianz-real-estate-debt-fund/10045832.article

[47] https://www.eib.org/en/press/news/eib-engages-for-more-clarity-within-g20-framework-on-sustainable-finance-in-co-operation-with-gpif

https://www.worldbank.org/en/news/press-release/2019/04/08/world-bank-group-and-gpif-deepen-partnership-on-building-sustainable-capital-markets

[48] In line with Principle 2 of the G20/OECD High Level Principles of Long-Term Investment Financing by Institutional Investors

[49] In line with Principle 7 of G20/OECD High Level Principles of Long-Term Investment Financing by Institutional Investors.

[50] In line with Principle 4 of G20/OECD High Level Principles of Long-Term Investment Financing by Institutional Investors.

[51] See the discussion on risk and return profiles in OECD (2014[10]).

[52] In line with Principle 5 of the G20/OECD High Level Principles of Long-Term Investment Financing by Institutional Investors.

6 Main policy guidelines to strengthen asset-backed pension systems in a post-COVID-19 world

This chapter summarises the main policy guidelines learnt during the COVID-19 pandemic and its aftermath with a view to providing guidance to policy makers to move forward and to be able to face and address similar crises in the future.

This publication has examined the impact of COVID-19 on asset-backed pension arrangements. It has also looked at the different policies implemented and has examined their success and alignment with the main OECD policy messages. The analysis has also looked at the impact of the pandemic on mortality and the potential implication for future mortality improvements, as well as on how assets earmarked for retirement can support economies and benefit members in a post-COVID-19 world.

This final chapter presents the main policy guidelines learnt during the COVID-19 pandemic and its aftermath with a view to providing guidance to policy makers to move forward and to be able to face similar crises in the future.

Main policy guidelines

Policy makers should make sure that people saving for retirement and pension providers stay the course

- Maintain investments in retirement portfolios to avoid selling and materialising value losses when markets are low. Saving for retirement is for the long term.
- Continue contributing to retirement plans. Governments may subsidise the income of people, as part of the many programmes to assist the populations facing the economic fallout from any widespread economic shock like COVID-19 and its associated economic downturn.
- Act in accordance with investment objectives. Pension providers should adhere to their investment objectives and carefully assess new investment opportunities. Their investment decisions should be at arms-length from governments.

Policy makers, regulators, and supervisors[1] should:

- Allow in time of crisis for regulatory flexibility in recovery plans to address funding problems stemming from retirement promises (e.g. defined benefit pension arrangements, and lifetime income products). Measures providing flexibility should be removed once the emergency is over.
- Make sure that funding and solvency rules for defined benefit plans are counter-cyclical. Introducing flexibility in meeting funding requirements avoids 'pro-cyclical policies' and allows pension funds to act as long-term investors and potentially stabilising forces within the global financial system.
- Provide proportionate, flexible, pragmatic and risk-based supervisory oversight coupled with adequate communication to reduce frauds and facilitate efficient operations. Supervisory oversight should concentrate on prudential and market conduct regulation, including ensuring protection of members and beneficiaries against COVID-19 related scams, especially for the most vulnerable individuals. During times of crises, supervisors should communicate to market participants and individuals on their prudential expectations and recommendations as well as actions taken to facilitate pension funds' operations and to ease administrative burden.
- Allow access to retirement savings only as a measure of last resort and based on individual specific exceptional circumstances. Retirement pots are intended to finance retirement. Accessing retirement savings could lead to materialising temporary asset values losses, liquidity, and investment management problems to pension funds, and, more importantly to retirement income adequacy shortfalls.

- Legislate and include in their regulatory framework early access, as well as the conditions of exceptional circumstances under which it would be allowed, to avoid legislative changes in the middle of a crisis that can have long-lasting negative impacts on retirement income adequacy. Those regulatory frameworks should only be expanded further on a temporary and targeted manner, where needed, to address genuine financial hardship.
- Consider mechanism for individuals to build emergency savings. However, the savings in emergency accounts may need to come from new savings to avoid lower retirement savings that may affect retirement income adequacy.
- Maintain projections on future improvements in mortality and life expectancy, disregarding the mortality experience during exceptional shocks like COVID-19, and step-up monitoring. Shocks like pandemics can significantly increase mortality, but mortality levels and improvements are likely to return to their previous trajectory following the shock. Therefore, any calibration of models used to establish mortality assumptions should exclude, or at least just adjust, the exceptional mortality experience in the years the shock occurred (e.g. 2020-22). Nevertheless, significant uncertainty remains regarding the long-term impacts of shocks like COVID-19 on health and mortality, which will require close monitoring to inform assumptions going forward.
- Promote the use of assets earmarked for retirement to support the economy. Policy makers can enhance the quality of data to assess investments as well as pension providers' capabilities to invest in different asset classes; adjust investment regulations; promote a favourable environment for long-term investment and suitable investment vehicles; and ensure appropriate alternative investments are available (like public-private partnerships or special vehicles for alternative assets) and financially attractive.
- Make sure that safeguards are in place so that pension providers continue acting in the best interest of members when using assets earmarked for retirement to support the economy. Ensuring the accountability and suitability of the governing body of pension providers, defining an appropriate investment policy, designing a sound risk management strategy and having appropriate investment regulations can all contribute to safeguarding members' assets while supporting the economy at the same time.
- Develop close co-operation with stakeholders, regulators, and supervisors at the national and international levels, to share solutions and effective ways to deal with crises.

1. This is in line with the IOPS statement on pension supervisory actions to mitigate the consequences of the COVID-19 crisis: http://www.iopsweb.org/IOPS-statement-on-pension-supervisory-actions-COVID-19-crisis.pdf

www.ingramcontent.com/pod-product-compliance
Ingram Content Group UK Ltd.
Pitfield, Milton Keynes, MK11 3LW, UK
UKHW051501290926
15471UKWH00008B/1351

9 789264 773691